D0974416

VOICES FROM THE STORM

VOICE OF WITNESS

McSWEENEY'S BOOKS
SAN FRANCISCO

For more information about McSweeney's, see mcsweeneys.net
For more information about Voice of Witness, see voiceofwitness.org

Copyright © 2008 McSweeney's

Cover photo by Aric Mayer
www.aricmayerstudios.com

All rights reserved, including right of
reproduction in whole or part in any form.

McSweeney's and colophon are registered
trademarks of McSweeney's Publishing.

Second Edition

ISBN-13: 978-1-934781-24-1

VOICES FROM THE STORM
THE PEOPLE OF NEW ORLEANS ON
HURRICANE KATRINA AND ITS AFTERMATH

EDITED BY
LOLA VOLLEN AND CHRIS YING

INTERVIEWS BY
STACY PARKER AAB · MARY BETH BLACK
COLIN DABKOWSKI · BILLY SOTHERN
ANDY YOUNG

With additional material from
DANA LEVENTHAL · CLAIRE SMITH
MARY ANN PENDINO · SHARON FERRANTI

VOICE OF WITNESS

VOICE OF WITNESS

The Voice of Witness series allows those most affected by contemporary social injustice to speak for themselves. Using oral history as a foundation, the series illustrates human rights crises through the stories of the men and women who experience them. These books are designed for readers of all levels—from high school and college students to policymakers—interested in a reality-based understanding of ongoing injustices in the United States and around the world. Visit voiceofwitness.org for more information.

VOICE OF WITNESS BOARD OF ADVISORS

ROGER COHN
Former Editor-in-Chief,
Mother Jones

MARTHA MINOW
Professor of Law,
Harvard Law School

ORVILLE SCHELL
Director, Center on U.S.-China
Relations, Asia Society

MARK DANNER
Author, professor, UC Berkeley
Graduate School of Journalism

SAMANTHA POWER
Professor, Kennedy School of
Government, Harvard University

STUDS TERKEL
Author, oral historian

HARRY KREISLER
Executive Director,
Institute of International
Studies, UC Berkeley

JOHN PRENDERGAST
Senior Advisor,
International Crisis Group

WILLIAM T. VOLLMANN
Author

The editors would like to thank the men and women of New Orleans who participated in this project. In the wake of tragedy, they donated valuable time and energy to tell us their stories. The editors would also like to thank Stacy Parker Aab, Colin Dabkowski, Kalamu Ya Salaam, and Billy Sothern for their assistance in producing this book.

GENERAL ASSISTANCE: Noa Bar, Momo Chang, Miles Clark, Earl Downing, Kelly Dunleavy, Eric Falcao, Jim Fingal, Susan Fridy, Courtney Jones, Amanda Hurtado, Rachel Khong, Patrick Knowles, Steven Leckart, Julie Limbaugh, Matt Mengarelli, Julia Meuse, Jared Moore, Angela Petrella, Bernice Santiago, Brian Short, Tavia Stewart, John Thayer, Rebecca Turnbull, Todd von Ammon, Michael Patrick Welch, Andy Werner, Jami Witek. COPY EDITOR: Darren Reidy. OTHER: Brian McMullen, Eli Horowitz, Andrew Leland, Jordan Bass. RESEARCH: Dave Levin, Sam Weiss, Dan Sanders. MANAGING EDITOR: Chris Ying. SERIES EDITORS: Dave Eggers, Lola Vollen.

CONTENTS

INTRODUCTION

by Lola Vollen and Chris Ying

Voices from the Storm tells the story of thirteen New Orleans residents whose lives were forever changed by the American government's disastrous response to Hurricane Katrina. These stories were compiled and edited from interviews gathered throughout the country in the weeks and months following the storm. This book is a rich tapestry of oral histories—created in close cooperation with the participants—that details the narrators' day-to-day experiences during what began as the worst natural disaster in American history and ended as a monument to governmental indifference and incompetence.

These accounts chronicle the racial discrimination and outright neglect many endured in the aftermath of Hurricane Katrina. They depict the ways in which the U.S. government, entrusted with the protection and safety of its citizenry, failed the poor and minority residents of New Orleans. In the midst of a terrifying natural disaster, the government responded with lethal apathy, leaving storm victims to fend for themselves, depriving them of the most basic necessities, and exposing them to dehumanizing conditions.

Dan Bright was abandoned in a locked prison cell as floodwaters swallowed the building; the guards had abandoned the prisoners. Outside the Morial Convention Center, soldiers clad in black uniforms fixed laser-guided automatic rifles on Patricia Thompson's granddaughter Baili. The six-year-old held her hands in the air and asked, "Mama, am I doing it right?" as Thompson looked on in horror. Abdulrahman Zeitoun—who emigrated from Syria decades earlier—traveled around the city for days rescuing neighbors until he was arrested under suspicion of terrorism. He and another Arab-American were imprisoned and held for weeks without charges.

Before the storm, the Federal Emergency Management Agency listed a major hurricane hitting New Orleans as one of the country's three most dire threats—along with terrorist attacks and an earthquake in California. Of course, hurricanes were nothing new for New Orleans. Katrina was the fiftieth recorded hurricane to have passed through Louisiana, and as Katrina gathered strength over the Atlantic Ocean, New Orleanians watched the storm with only mild interest, expecting that the city would direct them if they were in any real danger. On August 25, Katrina made landfall on Florida's southern coast, heading northwest toward the city. The following day, the National Hurricane Center issued a warning, and the state of Louisiana and the city of New Orleans initiated the emergency-response and recovery programs that were designed to protect those in the hurricane-prone region. The primary strategy for ensuring the safety of New Orleans residents was to evacuate them by car from the low-lying city to Texas or inland Louisiana.

When Hurricane Katrina hit New Orleans, 67 percent of the population was African-American and 22 percent was living below the poverty line. At a time when the national unemployment rate was 7 percent, New Orleans's rate was 13 percent. Many of those that did have jobs worked as housekeepers, porters, drivers, and cooks, serving the city's high volume of tourists. They were part of America's working poor, getting by on one paycheck to the next. If they had cars—and 24 percent of New Orleans did not—many still could not afford to buy a full tank of gas in advance of the hurricane; their pay was not due to arrive until after the storm.

Some New Orleanians, like Kalamu Ya Salaam, made it out of town the day before the storm and watched on television as his city was engulfed. Meanwhile, in the city, the police knocked on Sonya Hernandez's door to tell her to evacuate. With borrowed money, she bought diapers, water, candles, and some other survival necessities, and went to the Superdome—the city's only available shelter—where she huddled together with four of her children and two grandchildren. Conditions there quickly became abhorrent.

New Orleans's flood-prevention system had failed. Anthony Letcher stood with his aunt on her porch surveying the scene. As they watched the waters roll in, his aunt cried out, "Oh Lord Jesus! Look at those two babies down in that water, Lord!" Moments later, Anthony dove into the water. Letcher made his home where many other African-Americans lived—a low-lying area known as the Ninth Ward. It was where literary activist Salaam grew up. It was where Hernandez—a Cuban transplant who cleaned houses for a living—raised her five children. When the first levees succumbed to the hurricane, the lower Ninth Ward suffered the brunt of the resulting floodwaters.

In the wake of the destruction of the World Trade Center, the Bush administration put disaster prevention and response at the top of its agenda. It merged twenty-two separate agencies, including FEMA and the Coast Guard, under the banner of the newly-formed Department of Homeland Security. Katrina was the first test of the DHS and the country's post-9/11 disaster-response program.

The U.S. government had been warned for years that the New Orleans levee system would not withstand a major hurricane. Days before the storm, National Hurricane Center Director Max Mayfield reiterated this concern in a conference call with President Bush and Secretary of Homeland Security Michael Chertoff. They thanked him for his input, and proceeded according to the national response plan outlined by the Department of Homeland Security.

Optimism quickly faded as bureaucratic red tape paralyzed the agency. The world watched as conditions quickly deteriorated in New Orleans, where between August 29 and September 2, an estimated 100,000 men, women, and children were trapped. Residents were stranded for days on rooftops and in nursing homes and hospitals. They waded through filthy, chest-high waters in search of high ground, and suffered at the Superdome and the Convention Center. Government agencies at the city, state, and federal level could not manage to pull together a rescue operation for their desperate citizens. It took a full five days for adequate food and water to arrive and for a somewhat orderly evacuation process to begin.

In addition to exposing monumental shortcomings in the nation's Department of Homeland Security, the storm's aftermath also exposed America's profound racial and class divide. It was the poor who were stranded in New Orleans. The fact that most of them were African-American serves as a reminder of the enduring economic disparities that exist between Americans.

Voices from the Storm joins a growing body of literature on Hurricane Katrina. Many of these books provide insight on the meaning of the disaster in a larger political and social context. The stories chronicled here are meant to convey the day-to-day experience of those who lived through the storm. Through their stories, *Voices from the Storm* raises questions about the success of the civil-rights movement and the legacy of racism in American society. Moreover, it empowers the victims of this tragedy to finally speak for themselves. They do so with incredible honesty, insight, and warmth—even though it's clear that in most cases, so much that they loved and trusted was lost during the storm. Still, their interwoven stories provide an invaluable addition to our understanding of Hurricane Katrina, helping to illuminate an astonishing human-rights crisis that unfolded on our own soil.

LIFE BEFORE THE STORM

PATRICIA THOMPSON

I was born August 18, 1956. I was born out of wedlock. My dad was addicted to alcohol and my mom was addicted to him. I've seen the hungry days, I've seen the days with no lights and water in the house, I've seen the days I couldn't find my mom or dad. I wouldn't wish my childhood on a dog. I really would not.

Mama died August 31, 1960, and her mother raised us. It was six siblings—there's only three left. Life was hard with my grandmother because my grandmother was born August 12, 1900, and she tried to raise us like she was raised. She was a Choctaw Indian. She was a plain woman. She never wore curls in her hair, never wore a piece of jewelry. But she was a woman who could do almost anything. She baked from scratch; she did things like make her own mayonnaise; she made her own hair grease. This woman was amazing. Some of the things that this woman did I truly didn't understand. I mean, this lady, she would file her fingernails on the sidewalk.

She was a very, very strict woman, so needless to say I got in a lot of trouble. But believe it or not, everything came full circle, because had it not been for that woman and her teachings, I don't know if we'd've made it. The older we get, the more we see ourselves turn into this lady.

When I moved out of my grandmother's house, I moved into a development called the St. Thomas Housing Project. And I lived in the St. Thomas Housing Project I think from age seventeen to thirty-four. There I had a chance to see that racism is alive and well.

Anything bad that you can imagine that might happen to a poor community my kids and I have seen. I see these kids where we were from cut up and die young. I've been to the graveyard with my friends so many times, burying their babies, that my saying is, "They go from the womb to the tomb." I didn't want that. I wasn't gonna lose my children.

Some years ago, while I was living in the St. Thomas Housing Project, we really got tired of the abuse. Through this organization called the People's Institute for Survival and Beyond, we started doing "Undo Racism" workshops. From what I understand, they're pretty much all over the United States. We could see that all white folk wasn't bad, and white folk saw all of us wasn't bad. It was definitely a big learning experience because what I found out with a lot of white people was that they had been taught racism in the home. They had been taught that Negroes were lazy, and listless, and didn't want to do anything, which is not true.

At the time, I had three daughters that were already grown and on their own, but I had three kids still at home—two girls and a boy. These kids were still pretty much in elementary school. The Institute for Survival became my main support system. As this happened for me, it also started happening for my kids. See, these kids had to do "Undo Racism" workshops, too. We had a chance, my kids and I, to take a trip back in our past. We've been to slave quarters, the Civil Rights Museum, the Civil Rights Institute. We've been to Martin Luther King, Jr.'s gravesite, and to the house where he grew up. We were able to step back in our past and see some of the things that caused us to live as we do. The problems that we had in New Orleans did not start with the hurricane.

The community formed a consortium. We had clinics, we had doctors, we had a place called Agenda for Children that dealt with children's issues. There was St. Thomas Legal Services. So many different programs and organizations in that area came to sit on the St. Thomas Consortium Board. We stepped off onto these different jobs.

The job I was on at that time was called Plain Talk, and that's just what it was, plain talk. The Annie E. Casey Foundation had funded five different sites around the country where teenage pregnancy and STDs were on the rise, and our community just happened to be one of them. I started talking to different people, seeing different things outside Louisiana.

But what happened with St. Thomas was we started coming up. We started making a name for ourselves. And, of course, you have whites and blacks, for whatever reason, that don't want this stuff to happen. They attacked our community. They came with all this good stuff about, "We are going to tear the community down, build it back up, make it a better place." You know, all of this good stuff, which of course came to be anything but the truth.

St. Thomas was fifteen hundred and some units. Lo and behold they tore it down, and people from St. Thomas were supposed to get the first option to go back once the houses were rebuilt. It was going to be called the New St. Thomas. Of course, it came back something else; it's called River Garden. They took the name, everything. The promise that was made to St. Thomas was swept under the rug. People were fighting. I wound up in the Melphomene Housing Development, which is now called the William J. Guste Development.

I started a job locating housing for the relocated residents. After these people had been lied to, and they had played politics with these people's lives, so many people were homeless. People were living under the bridge. People were living in homeless shelters. It was just a sad situation. Since I had been blessed to kind of understand the race card that was being played, I felt compelled to help do the work.

I never got off. It's been as late as twelve, one o'clock at night, somebody's callin' my house and they're like, "Pat, they're trying to put me out. I don't know what to do. They gave me ten days to move."

I did that until this young woman I worked with forced me to leave the job. I really believe she went to bed thinking, "How can I make her day miserable tomorrow?" I dealt with it as long as I could, but what she did was she just stopped calling me to come to work.

Keep in your mind, I'm living in a public-housing development. My rent is supposed to be based on the amount of money that I'm making. It got so bad for me, the only thing I could find to do was a part-time job that only paid $200 a month. Housing authority raised my rent to $191, and I'm asking, "I'm supposed to survive on nine dollars a month?"

RENEE MARTIN

My name is Renee Martin. I was born in Honolulu, Hawaii, in 1958 in September. My mom was a native Hawaiian, and half Japanese. My dad was in the military station in Hawaii—Pearl Harbor base. He's half Spanish and half black-American.

I lived in Hawaii from birth up until I was six years old. I can remember running around on the base with other kids. We were considered military brats. I didn't understand what it was at that time, but it was fun.

We moved to Santa Monica, California. My dad was stationed there. Then he was stationed in San Diego, California, and we were there with him, and then I remember going to New Orleans.

I remember we were living in the heart of New Orleans. It was my older sister and my older brother and myself, and we were all going to this elementary school called Telmelaphona Elementary.

Back then, it was an all-black school, and I didn't feel too comfortable. We got teased a lot; we didn't talk. Me and my sister got our hair pulled a lot. But the teachers were really nice. There was this one teacher, her name was Mrs. Mead. She was my older sister's teacher first, and the next year she was my teacher, and then the next two years she was my brother's. We would go over to her house on the weekends, and she would take us to places—the zoo, and parties, and trick or treating. That was right in the beginning, when we first moved to New Orleans, around 1964.

Then when I was six, I was raped over and over by someone who was close to me. It was painful, but I was afraid to tell anyone.

But one day when I went to school and the bell rang at two o'clock, I stayed there. Everybody was leaving, and I just stayed there. Mrs. Mead, she said, "What's wrong Renee? Why you not getting up and going home?" I said I didn't want to, and I wouldn't tell her why. And she said, "Well, it's time to go home."

I said, "Please don't make me go home. Take me home to your house."

And she kept on asking what's wrong. Finally, I came around. I told her and she brought me home with her, and she fed me, and she let me take a bath. Then she was on the phone, and she was discussing it with one of the other teachers, trying to figure out what to do. Back then, they didn't have Child Protection, where they would move the child out of the home and stuff like that. So she didn't have many choices. The police came to her house, and I had to recall all over again and tell them what had happened. And then they called my mom. My mom had to come over to the house, and they talked to my mom about it.

They told her that she could take me home. And I remember I said, "Can I please stay here?" My teacher wanted me to figure it out between my mom and me. When we got outside, my mom was really angry.

That was a part of my life that affected me a whole lot. I was six years old and she didn't believe me, and I was her child. It wasn't my fault. That was his choice; he was a grown man. I was a child.

Then we had Hurricane Betsy. I was six, seven years old. Well, it flooded real bad. I was a little girl, but I can remember when they would talk about when Betsy came, the gates, the canal gates, were shut. They opened 'em up and allowed all that water to come in the Ninth Ward where it flooded the whole area.[1] They had coffins floating in the water. They had bodies floating in the water. They had so many bodies. They were trying to pull all of those coffins out of the water.

It was hard on a lot of people, even us. We didn't even have food. I was used to Mom having something for us to eat, and I didn't understand why we didn't have the proper amount of food, or no electricity, why we went to the bathroom in a bucket. Stuff like that I can remember.

I remember it rained a lot and I can remember the looting, too. We were walking in the downtown area and the water was real high, and there was debris everywhere. Canal Street had broken windows,

---

[1] The Ninth Ward is located on the eastern edge of New Orleans. It is bordered by the Mississippi River to the south and the Industrial Canal to the west. The Lower Ninth Ward comprises mostly working-class African-Americans, and is among the city's poorest neighborhoods. See page 42 for a map.

people comin' in getting things. I was a little girl then, but I guess I looted, too, because I got a baby doll. It was something I wanted for Christmas and it was called a Thumbelina Doll. It actually looked like a real baby, and you pressed its stomach and it moved, it waggled his head, and you fed it, and it cried. It was in the window. You know how they have toys in the showcase? Well, my mom was walking with us, and I said, "Mom, can I have that baby?" And she said, "Well, it's right there." So I had a baby doll. I had it for a long time, too. So Betsy affected me in a good way; I got a baby doll.

My dad was still in the military and he was away, stationed in Korea, and we couldn't go. We were living in this area that they would call the Tremé area.[2] It was what they would consider a target area. Like low-income families, you know, stuff like that. It was rough.

I made the best of things, and as years passed, I got older, and I found myself getting depressed. I just remember lying there being depressed about being in New Orleans, just the situation of living, the situation of the environment. Just a lot of things.

My mom was always gone. She had ten of us and I was the second to the oldest, and my older sister didn't like being home and missing the parties and after-school football games and all of that, but I did. I loved caring for people, babies and everybody. I had one sister and six brothers still at home. I missed a lot of dances, football games, parties. I missed all of that, and I missed school a lot, too.

When I was in high school, I was definitely trying to accomplish. I was a majorette; I was in the choir; I played tennis. I did a lot in school, but a lot of the times I'd get up, get dressed, couldn't wait to get to school, but my mama wasn't home and I had a choice: I could leave my sisters and run away from home and say, "These are

---

[2] Tremé is one of the oldest neighborhoods in New Orleans. Located adjacent to the Sixth Ward and the French Quarter, it is a predominately African-American area.

not my kids," leave my sisters and brothers at home to go to school by theirself. I couldn't let 'em.

So I missed a lot of my teenage years. I know my sisters and brothers didn't go to school much either, but I was too young to know that they're supposed to be goin' to school every day, doing their homework, you know, getting them ready, all that kind of stuff. I didn't know nothing about all that kinda stuff. The easiest thing for me to do for them was keep them home.

We had a grocery store the next block from our house, and it was two old ladies running the store, and I used to go down there and I used to lie and tell them, "My mom said let me get this and this and put it on her bill, and when she gets home she's gon' come pay y'all." We had to get food somehow. Then I would ask them, "How do you cook red beans and rice?" I wrote it down. I go home and try to cook it—you put so much water in the pot and put an onion and your green pepper, and garlic and this stuff—but it didn't come out right. The beans were hard, but we ate it.

I had to make the best of a bad situation because I had my little brothers and my little sister—I had to do what I could do. Some of them would say, "This don't taste good," but they ate it. I didn't know how to cook; I was only fourteen. And it went on like that for years.

I left home when I was about seventeen. I got deliberately pregnant because I was getting tired of being home. So I got pregnant, I had my baby at eighteen, and I stayed with my older sister for a while. I had a job working at a Wal-Mart. I was a cashier and from there I got my own apartment, furnished and everything. Got it by myself. One piece at a time, but I got it. First thing I got was a baby.

In the nineties, I was a student. I got my GED through this program called the Toyota University Program. I was one of the best students. I made the superintendent's award, the award of courage, and the community profile award. I was determined. That's what it was. And I got my GED within two months, and the next year, they came back and hired me to tutor other students, and I did. This was in 1991.

After that, I went to school to be a clinical nursing assistant. I wanted to go for nursing, but I also wanted to do work in a medical facility. So I went for six months, got my license, and I have been doing that up until today.

JACKIE HARRIS

I'm a native New Orleanian. My mother met my father just before World War II and they got married, and I was born one or two years after they were married. The first house that I can remember that we had was in the Calliope project. The Calliope project was like the new frontier for African-Americans at that time because the projects were actually like a new development and they were the houses that were especially young, and even older African-Americans were looking to move into them because the living conditions were far better in those new developments than in the other houses.

I was always fascinated with the music and entertainment industry. When I got older, I met a friend who had a production company, and they produced concerts, and maybe about two or three times, I worked with them to produce some shows. They were all rhythm-and-blues shows. And then the New Orleans Jazz and Heritage Festival was looking for some people to work there, so I applied for a stagehand job. They told me all the stagehand positions were full but I could get an administration job. So I became the assistant to the site coordinator, and I was actually supposed to keep his books. After that one year, I was in charge of security, the cleanup operation, and site development.[3]

There was an organization within the festival, Koindu, that had been identified to attract the black community so they could prosper from the festival experience. But there was kind of a split between different factions within that group, and they needed an African-American to mediate. Since I happened to be on the festival staff, I was the person that worked with the two groups. And then the following year, the New Orleans Jazz and Heritage Foundation decided that there was not enough African-American participation at the management level of the festival, and I was hired as assistant to the fair manager. I was in charge of operations, and my job was to actually build the festival grounds. I became night concerts producer, and I did that until 1994, at which time I moved to become the executive director of the music and entertainment commission of Mayor Morial's administration.

Of course, we know New Orleans is the birthplace of jazz, but I felt that there was a lot lacking in jazz education for young people. And I felt that if we are the birthplace of jazz, we should certainly be attracting young people from all over the United States and all over the world to travel to New Orleans in a somewhat structured environment.

Many artists come to New Orleans and they want to be in the environment and they want to drink the water and they want to eat the food. They want to see what comes up out of the concrete and the pavement and what makes New Orleans what it is, and what is

---

[3] The New Orleans Jazz and Heritage Festival, or Jazz Fest, has been held annually since 1970.

that spirit, what does it take to perpetuate and create this tradition that we have. And a lot of that for the most part has been learned on the streets and in the nightclubs, but I also felt that there was a great need to teach that in a structured format. I felt that I really needed to do something, so I created the Louis Armstrong Summer Jazz Camp.

What started off as a one-week program with thirty-five students has now evolved into a twelve-year program that serves anywhere from eighty-five to a hundred young music students annually. It's always been presented in a public-school environment. It's not sponsored by New Orleans public schools, but we always felt that since New Orleans schools are so depleted of arts education, that it was important to keep this program in a New Orleans public school. We had invitations to move it, but we kept it there. Now, the program provides three weeks of intense music education. The classes start at nine o'clock in the morning and go till three o'clock in the evening. It's school. It's music school.

We have a culminating concert each year, and we also, for the last twelve years, have had a national artist in residence to spend the last week of camp there: Wynton Marsalis, Donald Byrd, Reggie Workman, Rufus Reed, Jon Faddis, Cecil Taylor, Barry Harris, Clark Terry, Donald Harrison Jr. Just artists from all spectrums of jazz.

Some of our young people will become jazz artists, and at the same time some of the young people are interested in other areas of the music industries. And so we created these other workshops for our kids to get a look at other ways to learn and earn extra money as they work their way through college. They learn music engineering and production. They learn how to make a CD and they are recorded as well.

Art is essential to the development of a young individual. Arts are the things that feed entertainment. If you are careless or non-supportive of the arts in your city, well, your entertainment is not going to really grow, and it's not going to be as successful as it can be. New Orleans has hosted more Super Bowls than any city in the United States, but people do not return to the same location over and over just to go to an attraction. The Jazz Festival, the French Quarter Festival, the Essence Music Festival, all these festivals have proven that people will return year after year after year for a celebration of your culture and your art. I'm a little biased because I worked in the Morial administration, and I have to say that particular group got it. They understood that, first off, art really defines and determines and raises the quality of life for people living in the city.

If you don't educate young people and you don't have a future, well, you're not going to sustain yourself. That's been my mantra. So you gotta educate youngsters. You gotta support your musicians, your visual artists, the opera, the symphony, all of these institutions that are there. You must support that in order to maintain your future and your culture.

RHONDA SYLVESTER

Well, I was born in Louisiana—born and raised in the Desire Housing Project. My mother was a single parent; she raised seven kids. In 1979, she passed away, so my sister, who was seventeen or eighteen, was left to raise six of us, plus herself.

I had a rough life. Early on, I had a fast life. I had a street life. But after I had got in trouble with the law, I began to rehabilitate myself.

When the storm hit, I was living with my niece. I had just come out of prison in 2004—Louisiana Correctional Institution for Women in Saint Gabriel, Louisiana. I had been out only about a year and a couple of months before the hurricane hit. I was restabling my life, doing positive things. I had a job, I was getting my life in order, I was going to school. It wasn't easy for me when I first came home out of prison. I had to strive for everything I had. But everything was starting to fall right in place.

I didn't have trouble getting a job in New Orleans. I used to work one job Monday through Thursday from six in the morning till 4:30 in the evening at Blue Plate Mayonnaise Company. I was working full-time, but I was working through a temporary service called Task Force. We do seasonal work, but I had been working there over a year. They never gave benefits because we do temp work. You were assured four days a week, ten hours a day. We made like $5.85 an hour to start out, and I earned $206 a week. Then on weekends I used to work at the zoo, the Audubon Zoo.

I work hard. I was going to adult GED education on St. Claude Street. Monday, Wednesday, and Friday, I went to school between the hours of five-thirty and eight-thirty at night at Louisiana Adult Education. I was gonna get my GED, so I probably could get a grant or something and go on to college and major in something. I was right at the edge of getting my GED before the storm hit.

So that was my life. I was getting my life back, and I felt good about getting my life back.

DAN BRIGHT

I'm Dan Bright. I grew up in the Florida Housing Project. It's not there no more. They tore it down and they modernized it so the project I grew up in, that's not the projects no more. Right now it's like townhouses. I grew up, I'm sad to say, in the real projects. You'd see three, four guys get killed in a day. I had a brother that got killed in the projects.

I have two twin daughters, a son, and my oldest daughter. My oldest daughter is sixteen. My twins are eleven, and my son is ten. Now my twins and my oldest daughter stay with my mother because my twins' mother died. She died of a blood disease called lupus. My oldest daughter's mama is on drugs and my son is with his mother Gloria. I'm kind of like, "I'm screwed all around," but I'm happy to be out and I'm enjoying my freedom and I'm going to look at the bright side of everything. So that's where I stand at.

I was wrongfully convicted of first-degree murder in 1996. I was arrested in 1995 for a first-degree murder charge that I didn't commit. I went on death row in 1996, December.

The victim had won a Super Bowl pool that gave a thousand dollars. Someone heard that he won a thousand dollars. A woman named Christie Davis got the guy to come out of the barroom, and three guys came out of the alley, and I don't know if the robbery went bad or what, but the witness said no one robbed no one, that somebody came out there and started shooting and ran off.

The police said it was a robbery, but the only witness said it wasn't a robbery. So there is no ground for a first-degree indictment. The Supreme Court failed to do the right thing. Instead of them giving me a new trial or exonerating me, they just downgraded my charge to second-degree murder. They figure, we take him off death row, he'll be happy. But I was innocent. I was going to fight until the end, and I had a legal team willing to fight with me all the way.

I stood on death row five years, a total of ten years in prison. We went through several appeals. They were all denied. Finally, we found the FBI report. In the FBI report, it said they knew who killed the guy and it wasn't me. We took that FBI report and we fought maybe another year. So the Supreme Court finally gave me a new trial. The state, the D.A., didn't want to go back and have another trial because they knew they had the wrong guy from the start.

The truth came out. I can sit with you all day and tell you the errors in my case. In fact, I had 165 reversible errors in my case.

When I went to prison, my mother moved to Gretna and was blessed to get a house.[4] Since getting out, I've been living with my mother. I've been job to job. It's real tough 'cause no one wants to hear that you was innocent. All they know is that you were on death row.

---

[4] Gretna is a small city located on the west bank of the Mississippi River, across from New Orleans. See page 42 for a map.

FATHER JEROME LeDOUX

I was born in Lake Charles, Louisiana—extreme southwest Louisiana. Another thirty miles and you're in Texas. So you have somewhat of the Texas flavor there, but it's mostly still Louisiana. I was there until age thirteen, and went through seventh grade at Sacred Heart Catholic Elementary School. After that, I left and went to the seminary in Bay Saint Louis, Mississippi, to study for the priesthood.

We were cradle Catholics going back generations. My mother's family came out of Saint Martinville, which is virtually all Catholic. My father's family came out of a place near Eunice, Louisiana. I was an altar server, I lived in church, so my parents could not have been more pleased that I went to the seminary. They figured a better thing could not have happened to two of their sons. I'm the middle son. My older brother, Louis Verlin, is a priest in semi-retirement. And my younger brother, Nathaniel, Nat, who is six years younger, actually went to the seminary for a couple of weeks, but he got homesick and went back.

High school seminaries were the rage back then. You got a lot of candidates for the priesthood and the religious life. I belonged to the Society of the Divine Word, which is simply a translation of the Latin *Societas Verbi Divini*. One of my mother's nephews, Harold Perry, went to Bay Saint Louis thirteen years ahead of me. He became a priest and then in 1966 he was ordained the first Catholic African-American bishop of this century. There was one before him, Patrick Haley, but he was of the last century.

I did my theology there in Bay Saint Louis and was ordained there in the chapel with four classmates on May 11, 1957. I was twenty-seven years old. Afterwards, I studied in Rome, then taught moral theology and canon law in Bay Saint Louis, and in 1969, I was assigned to be the chaplain and teacher at Xavier University in New Orleans.

I was to report there on August 17. However, I did not report there until the following week, Sunday, August 24 because on August 17 a vicious hurricane, Camille, came up from the Gulf of Mexico and hit Bay Saint Louis. To date, it is the strongest recorded hurricane ever to hit the country. The winds exceeded 200 miles per hour. I stayed on an extra week at Bay Saint Louis since I was ready storm-wise already. Then I decided to drive to New Orleans. I went to Xavier University on August 24.

In early 1990, a job at St. Augustine Church became open. Father Bob Fisher was about to leave there, and my congregation had in mind not to staff St. Augustine Church anymore. We were about to withdraw from there, but they said, "Well, we'll take one last shot at it. Jerome is there, he's just doing some writing. Let him take it and he'll be the last SVD [*Societas Verbi Divini*] there. After that we'll withdraw." So I took over as pastor on July 13, 1990.

Tremé is the oldest African-American neighborhood in New Orleans, and because of Congo Square it is the most African in culture. St. Augustine was established in Tremé on November 14, 1841, and by late summer of 1842 it was finished. It was built in less than a year. The first gifts were scraped up by free people of color, and of course back then, it was big-time money. Bishop Antoine Blanc wound up paying the lion's share. The church cost all of $25,000.

So the free people of color participated in the construction. They had attorneys, physicians, politicians of every sort, artisans—mostly from Haiti—who could do anything in construction.

And when it was finished, the free people of color began to do what people did in those days. They began to purchase pews for their families to have on Sundays. When the white folks saw that, they said, "We cannot let these colored folks buy more pews than we're going to buy." The white folks began to hustle and bustle, and the white folks were here, the colored people there. It became known as the "war of the pews."

But the colored folks had that head start, and they wound up buying three times more than the whites. So the colored folks had one whole central pew for themselves, the whites had one whole central pew for themselves, and then the people of color had bought up both side pews—and they were half the length of the big ones, so together they made another third—so that means they had a two-thirds advantage. And the people of color, after having bought up those side pews, turned them over, gave them to the slaves. So for the first time in their history, they had their own spot and nobody could take that away from them.

SONYA HERNANDEZ

New Orleans is like the gumbo, the jambalaya—so many cultures together. It comes from so many places, and then all that "gumbos."

Like, you got black-Americans with Cuban, and then you got the Cuban with the white Americans, and all of that is in my neighborhood. And then you got the community from Honduras, then you got the Cuban community, then you got the Italian community, then you got the white-people community—that's Chalmette.

My husband's mama's black, his daddy white. In my country, Cuba, ain't no white and black. We don't worry if you black or white. That's up to you. It's a lot of mulattoes. That's what my kids are. My oldest daughter, actually, her brothers and friends, they call her "white girl" 'cause Amelia's white and she got the long hair. And Maria is different; she looks like she's Indian. Maria got the hair all the way to here. She just puts it up in a ponytail. Then Sonya, she looks like she's Jamaican. She's got the normal curl in the hair. She wash her hair and she got curly; she don't have to do nothing. You know some people pay for it, but she got it normally. And Johnny's got the white-people hair like his daddy.

I get paid by cleaning houses, but for twenty-five years I've been getting paid by doing tarot readings. And believe it or not, a long time ago, I said that New Orleans was going to get real bad. But my vision was not like a hurricane. I didn't see water. It was like a big tornado. My vision was like a humongous tornado. It was bringing all the houses up and down like God was playing, or the devil was playing with the houses and bringing them up and down on the storm. My husband say, "Don't forget that you're a visionary since you was little, so we need to be careful, see."

Usually when I say something, that something's going to happen, I just say it and I forget about it. I don't even talk about it no more. My mother used to tell me, "If in case that happens, you're going to feel sad that you don't say nothing about it." But my point is that not everybody listens to you. Some people think you're talking and they say, "She's crazy," which I don't give about it. I say what I have to say. So if you don't want to listen, that's okay.

KALAMU YA SALAAM

My father was a major influence in terms of how I view life and this story kind of encapsulizes how things went for much of my early years: I was about six or seven years old and this was right before Christmas. My father called my brothers and me to the table and he handed each one of us five dollars and said, "That's Christmas," and walked out of the room. We put the money in our pockets, looked at each other and said, "Damn. That's Christmas."

My father was in World War II and the Korean War. He came up very, very, very, very poor. That man walked from Donaldsonville out in the country to New Orleans. Walked. He made us grow food in the city—we didn't have gardens for decoration. I'll tell you what we did do. My father wanted a lawn, a front lawn with St. Augustine grass, and we used to drive out to St. Bernard Parish—the parish below Orleans—along the river, and he'd find spots where the grass was growing wild, and we had to dig square-foot patches and take them back and replant them.

My father was a medical technician, laboratory technician. He learned in the army working as a medic. When he got out of the army after the Korean War, he came back here and he applied at the Veterans Hospital for a job, and they said no. Because he was black, they weren't going to hire him. And he fought it all the way to Washington D.C. They forced the local veterans hospital to hire him. So he was the first black non-janitorial staff person to work at the veterans hospital.

I grew up in the Lower Ninth Ward, but I went to school wherever my mother was teaching. She was a teacher, and so for kindergarten up through fourth grade I was at Fisk Elementary School, which is uptown off of Tulane and Jefferson Davis. And then for fifth and sixth grade I went to Phyllis Wheatley, which is around the corner from Dooky Chase Restaurant. And then I went to Rivers Frederick in the Seventh Ward for seventh, eighth, and ninth grades. These were all public schools. There were no high schools, no junior high schools in the Lower Ninth Ward when I grew up because the city didn't care to put them there.

This was the late fifties, early sixties. You've got to understand, segregation, for all its evils, also made it necessary for our community to do for ourselves, because there was absolutely no assistance coming from anyplace else. And up through ninth grade I was taught primarily by black women, many of whom I now recognize were what we call "race women." So the education I got, was an education to prepare me to confront the world. They always told us, "you're going to have to be better, you're going to have to be better if you're going to make it."

I wanted to continue my high school education at McDonogh #35, but my brothers wanted to go to St. Augustine High School, a Catholic high school. The priest persuaded my mother that it would be almost the same price for three kids as for two. So the decision was that I had to go to St. Augustine. It was considered the best high school in the city available to black males at the time. During my high school years I became very, very active in the civil rights movement, including sit-ins, boycotts, door-to-door voter registration, rallies, and other demonstrations. I did virtually nothing at high school itself. My high school years were spent in the streets and in the library.

I went to Carlton College in Northfield, Minnesota. I only stayed up there two trimesters and left. The school was approximately 1,200 students, thirteen of us were black. And of that thirteen, eight were freshmen like myself. It wasn't so much being around white people that was the problem, but not having a lot of black people around. I saw the potential opportunities there but I also intensely disliked it. It had none of the cultural references and affirmations that I was used to getting in school. I remember Bobby Bland—Bobby Bland was a blues singer—had this magnificent song that had the line in it: "Soon as the weather breaks, I'm going to make my getaway." And that's the way I felt.

I didn't fully realize the importance of New Orleans until '68, after being in the army. One of the things about New Orleans is its great respect for street culture. And street culture encourages everybody to participate in one form or fashion in the arts. For instance, food becomes a social issue and not just a private issue for the immediate nuclear family. And as a result, when you're sharing food with a lot of people, inevitably your food will be compared to other people's food, so you try to do your best in terms of cooking. And so it becomes an art about cooking, and if you're around traditional, pre-storm—New Orleans people long enough, you'll hear almost every male, female, young, old, bragging about "my beans" or "my potato salad" or whatever. They don't necessarily cook every day, that's not their thing, but they can do a dish. It's part of a culture.

I am the oldest of three children. My other two brothers are in different professions, but we're all artists. I'm a journalist. I'm fifty-nine years old and I've been writing and publishing since 1968. I'm also a literary activist, so I do a listserv. The list right now is roughly around 1,700 direct subscribers; I don't know how many indirect. But that goes out every day. I send out ten messages a day.

My brother immediately below me, Kenneth, went to school and majored in urban planning and history at Columbia, and he's an entrepreneur now and he owns one of the major cafés in New Orleans. But his first love and his enduring love is music—he's a trumpet player. My youngest brother Keith Ferdinand is a cardiologist and is also a very good visual artist. All of which is to say, there must have been something in our upbringing that encouraged us towards a lot of things, but definitely the arts.

And in that regard, to say when I became an artist is difficult. I can pinpoint specifically when I took up photography, when I began writing, and when I found an interest in music, but I can't pinpoint for you when I became an artist, I can't say it. You come up with art. You come up singing in church, you come up dancing in the second line, through the streets and what have you. That's part and parcel of the culture, and it's expected that you would do that. It wasn't just savoring the culture as a thing to itself, but becoming an active part of a community of people that existed. For instance, I spent more time with Danny Barker—a jazz musician who played guitar and banjo—away from the bandstand than I spent, you know, going to his gigs. I would go to his house all the time.

And this kind of identification with the people who produced the culture is the singular thing of importance, because then you're not simply amassing cultural artifacts. To say that you have the culture, you love the culture, you're involved with the day-to-day living of the people who create the culture. Both my grandfathers were preachers. The one on my mother's side was a minister who had two churches at one time, had one in the country and one in the city. And the one on my father's side, he was what they call a "jack-leg" preacher. He didn't have a church or anything like that. But I can remember, up until the time I left the church, young people were encouraged to participate.

Before the storm, I was working with students based at Douglass High School in the Ninth Ward in a writing program. It's an independent program, not a school-board-administered program. We raise our own money. We taught Sonya Hernandez's whole family. Maria, Amelia, and Juan—her older brother who was killed—were in the program. Johnny and little Sonya were scheduled to be in the program the following year.

School had just started. We had been open for about two weeks, I think—something like that. We had a core of students that we had worked with over the years, may have been about seven or eight of them. The last two years before Katrina were very difficult for us. We reached the end of funding cycles from two of the major funders, so we didn't have much money, but we were looking forward to a really strong year.

KERMIT RUFFINS

I grew up in the Lower Ninth Ward. Me, my little sister, and my little brother, we would go crawfishing and crabbin' in that Industrial Canal—kind of close to where the levee actually broke—almost every weekend, and sell 'em to the neighbors or go boil them at home. And we always was into a lot of fun stuff, being kids growing up in the Lower Ninth Ward right on Jourdan Avenue, at the 1400 block.

My uncle Percy Williams would always come over on weekends and let us blow his trumpet. He plays trumpet with Irma Thomas right now, and he plays percussion with Irma Thomas, too. I always wanted to play trumpet, and finally one day we got home and there were two trumpets laying there on the sofa, one for me and one for my brother. And we joined the band the next day at Lawless Senior High School.

I was the lead trumpet player after one year of getting that trumpet. After about four years of marching in all the Mardi Gras parades, going back to the Lower Ninth Ward every night, finally I went to Clark High School and I just moved into the Sixth Ward area.[5] I just fell in love with all the traditional bands that would hang out there, all the bars.

You would see Vinny Jones, Uncle Lionel, Tuba Fats, Milton Batiste. The list goes on for all the great musicians that were just hanging around that area. I met Philip Frazier at Clark, and it all started with us playing at a party for the teachers. After the teachers' party down at the Sheraton Hotel, the teachers threw us out 'cause they was serving alcohol, so we walked down Bourbon Street taking the shortcut home, and some guy said, "Hey, play us a tune," and they threw us a lot of money. So we would go into the French Quarter after that every day, after the band rehearsed at Clark Senior High School.[6]

We started playing in Jackson Square, up and down Bourbon Street, for tips. After about three years, we realized that we could make money playing in the Quarter. We called ourselves "The Group" till we got out of Clark Senior High School. I think we came over to the name "Rebirth" in '83, from a guy that had the St. Thomas Housing Development. He said, "Oh, I want to manage you guys." He fell in love with us. And he said, "One condition, change your name to Rebirth." His name was Leonard. Leonard was his last

---

[5] The Sixth Ward is located in downtown New Orleans, adjacent to Tremé. See page 42 for a map.

[6] The French Quarter is situated between the Mississippi River, Tremé, and the Central Business District [CBD]. Along with the Warehouse District, the French Quarter and the CBD generate an estimated 95 percent of New Orleans's tourism revenue. See page 42 for a map.

name, anyway. Before we know it, we were playing in the Quarter and everything for tips, man. We had the hottest spot on Bourbon Street at seven o'clock till eight o'clock, Bourbon and Iberville.

We would just set up the whole Rebirth in the street, 'cause cars couldn't drive down. We'd have the audience from one side of the band all the way around to the other side of the band. We would play seven o'clock to eight o'clock and make maybe about seventy bucks apiece in one hour. So you know, we had it packed by then. Before you know it, we started traveling the world, man.

First stop was New York, then Tokyo, and then we started doing all those European festivals every summer up until now: Stockholm, Sweden; Pori, Finland; Montreux, Switzerland; Vienna, Austria; San Sebastian, Spain. We did Italy once. Only once. I can't wait to get back there. Rebirth did Africa for about six weeks.

I kind of owe all that to the elderly cats that I was lucky enough to hang out with during my early days, 'cause right away when I started playing with all those great old guys, they hired me on all of their gigs as well. So I was double-dipping and that's how I got the chance to hang out with Uncle Lionel, Tuba Fats, Danny Barker, and all those greats before they passed away. I got up there right at the tail end of all that. If I was lucky enough to grow up in that neighborhood, I would have saw a whole lot more, but it kind of worked out anyway.

Then I heard Louis Armstrong on WWOZ and that just changed my whole life. Probably it was "Sleepy Time Down South" or "Ain't Misbehavin'." But once I heard that, I was convinced that's what I wanted to do. I'd never heard a trumpet sound like that. The music sounded just so pretty. I'd never heard nothing like that come out of a trumpet 'cause I didn't hear Louis Armstrong on the radio until I was about twenty years old. Then I saw a video. I don't know if someone gave me the video or whatever, but when I saw that video of Louis Armstrong, I became more convinced. Then

I went out of my way to start buying and renting old videos of all the big-timers.

So it's like I watched them for about six years, and it was like I knew 'em. I watched Dizzy, then I met him. I watched Miles, then I kind of got eye contact with him while I was sitting next to Bill Cosby and he was playing on stage in Nice. I'm sitting next to Bill Cosby right here and Miles is playing on stage.

I always was lucky enough with Rebirth, being in the same hotels, living in the same hotels with all the greatest, and listening to the jam sessions until seven in the morning every night after playing a big show. They would do this every night and they're still doing it today. They play the show all day at the festival and then they go to the most popular hotel and play in the lobby till six in the morning, then they all go eat breakfast and then they take a nap. Then they play the festival again and they do that again that night, and that's what goes on.

DANIEL FINNIGAN

I ended up moving to New Orleans in April of 1996. I went there with my best friend in the world, Andrea Garland. I met her maybe six months before I moved. She'd lived in New Orleans before for a couple of years, and I met her in San Francisco. So we went down there to go see Jazz Fest and I just never left. I fell in love with it. It became my home.

I always stayed downriver of the French Quarter. When I first moved there, I was kinda just outside the French Quarter, and then as the years went I pushed farther back and back. And then maybe for the last four or five years I was in the Ninth Ward.

I'm an artist, which means I do other things to pay the bills. I paint apartments or bartend. I was a bartender for seven years in New Orleans. Anywhere from Bourbon Street–style clubs to small thirty-person jazz pockets. I kinda did the whole thing. You have to live somehow. I'm an artist, and it's difficult to make a living that way.

I lived the kind of lifestyle that you would imagine a bartending artist in New Orleans would live. There's a certain kind of underground culture, a lot of cool people, a big art community. So my life involved art, poetry, and fill in the blanks with debauchery. That's pretty much my life. If you can just imagine me going to work in the day, and doing artwork or going to poetry readings. New Orleans is a great place to make art, but it's not really a good place to sell it or make a living of it.

ANTHONY LETCHER

My name's Anthony Letcher. My word's real. What I speak is real.

In 1981 I donated my mother one of my kidneys, and I guess everything was successful for a little while. The kidney lasted six days. My mother's body some kinda way rejected it. My mother passed away and I went crazy. I went crazy, man. That's how I've been living for a long time. Sometimes, man, I be kind of like welcoming death.

But a lot of stuff has changed in my life, brother. A lot of things I used to do, I don't do no more. I got two nice grandkids. I got a good lady in my life. Her kid's cool. I'm cool, my sister's cool. I'm just a family-oriented person. All I want to do is take care of my family. I got a bad-ass son that loves his daddy to death. I got another son. That's one son I really gotta get tight with, man. I've been slacking off with the little man. There's a lot of things in my life. I've just been broke, hectic financial, but I'm cool, you know what I'm saying? I'm cool and I'm blessed.

My little boy, he's seven years old. He's begging me for a dog. That boy be on me so hard. I'm gonna get him one, though; I'm gonna get him one. I'll go to one of them things—what they call that?—Adopt-an-Animal. I'm gonna get my little boy one. He's in Atlanta right now, and me and his mom came to the decision she was going to hold him until the summertime. I have equal custody, so I'm gonna let him stay up there till summertime, and I'm gonna get him from here until whenever because I want to raise him. I ain't never had no daddy in my life, still ain't got him. But anyway, it's about me and my boy now. I need to try and look out for him before my time do run out. I want to try to make sure he's financially secure, just a little bit. Just have a little something-something in his pocket.

ABDULRAHMAN ZEITOUN

I was born in Syria in 1957. I left Syria around '73. Really, Syria this time in the seventies, there was too much politics, confusion.

In Syria, I had a brother who was a captain of a ship. I used to work summertimes after school on the ship with my brother, and we used to make trips to the United States. I was early-twenties when I come here to New Orleans for the first time. I was mid-twenties when I stayed for good. I happened to have a cousin who lived in New Orleans and I choose New Orleans because this is where he is.

After that, he headed a different direction, and I decided to start my own life. I got a couple jobs in the state here. I got a job in Baton Rouge. I stayed there a couple of years, from '89 to '92. And I meet my wife over there and I started my family. At first, I start working in construction, and I start work with a side job with used cars, and after that I start my own business in construction.

I have three daughters—Nademah, she's almost eleven now. I have Safiya, she'll be seven. And we have another one, Aisha, she just turned six. We live on Dart Street, uptown.

Hurricanes happened a couple times before. I never told my wife to stay. I always tell her to leave if she wants. She has family in Baton Rouge, and I always say, "You go. Go to Baton Rouge." And always I stay here in New Orleans. I never saw the hurricanes as something so serious. I believed in not giving up easily. I believed if I am there, if

I can do any help, sometimes you can save things. I mean you can do things might save you from big damage is what I believe, and it's why I stayed. Stay and see what happens. Something that will happen will happen. Nobody can stop it from happening.

FATHER VIEN THE NGUYEN

I was born in 1963 in Vietnam. I came to the U.S. in 1975 with my mother and my five siblings during the fall of South Vietnam. The Northern Vietnamese army was moving down and we were losing ground in the south. I was from central Vietnam, so as we were losing ground, the people were backing up towards Saigon. I was moving with them by foot with the rest of my family.

Saigon fell on the thirtieth of April. We were picked up by a merchant ship hired by the U.S. government. The ship had 10,000 people on it and it couldn't go through Guam with all 10,000 people, so it dropped off 2,000 in Subic Bay, the American naval base in the Philippines. So we were there for three days, and then we were flown to Guam. We were in Guam for two weeks, and then we were flown to Fort Chaffee, Arkansas. Then we were resettled in southeast Missouri.

I first moved to New Orleans in 1977, and I think I made the decision to become a priest around 1979. I studied for the priesthood in Covington, Louisiana, which is on the north side of Lake Pontchartrain. That was college seminary, and then I went to work at the Vietnamese refugee camp in the Philippines in 1984 to 1985. I returned and started my theological training in Notre Dame Seminary in New Orleans, and I was ordained in August of 1989.

Since 1989, I've been assigned to three, four different parishes. I became pastor here at Mary Queen of Vietnam three years ago, July 2003. The church is really at the eastern extreme of Orleans Parish. It's a personal parish, meaning that the parishioners can only be Vietnamese or Laotian or Cambodian—Southeast Asian, that is. It was established in 1980, and the church was built in 1986. It is the first Vietnamese-American-built church in the U.S. So the people dug deep to build that church. They actually sweat on the grounds of this church to get that structure up, and the majority of them are still alive. That was their blood and sweat.

New Orleans is home. I've been here more than two-thirds of my life. Vietnamese, you have to keep in mind, are agricultural people, meaning we tie ourselves to the land. And when do we tie ourselves to the land? When we bury our loved ones in it. We have buried our people here. We are tied to it. That's how it becomes home.

We have three priests here. Pre-Katrina we had some 6,500 parishioners. Our Sunday attendance was around 4,800 to 5,000 for Sunday. On any given day, we had early Mass at six a.m., maybe six-thirty. And then we might have a Novena right after Mass. That was in our day chapel, which was the original church. And then we'd return home. Normally people begin to come in to see us around eight-thirty or nine. People would be continually coming in to see us when they needed us, which could be for anything because a number of my people do not speak English, especially the elderly. So we would help them with anything from dealing with the courts and the police, welfare, Medicaid, Medicare, employment.

In the evening we had Mass at five-thirty p.m. And then from seven p.m. on would be meetings. We have some forty organizations and five choirs. There would be meetings, practices, and the meetings may continue until ten. And then during the school year we had our classes on Thursday, Friday, Saturday. Basically that would be the routine on weekdays. Weekends it would be a little different. There were more Masses, more meetings.

I've committed my life to this type of ministry. I have the opportunity to be closer to the people, work with people, and help them to make sense of what's going on with their life—their ultimate goal being salvation, and the will of God in between. Any time when a person comes to that realization, that's where I find satisfaction.

That sense of satisfaction is not always readily available. So a lot of times, even if I don't feel the sense of satisfaction, I just have to continue to walk on in faith, trusting that what I'm doing is correct, trusting that the Holy Spirit will guide me to do the right thing. So I guess satisfaction comes periodically as a highlight.

NARRATORS

Patricia Thompson is a mother of six. She lives in the William J. Guste Housing Development.

Renee Martin helped raise seven of her siblings in New Orleans. She works as a clinical nursing assistant and lives in the West Bank.

Jackie Harris is a native New Orleanian, and a founder of the Louis Armstrong Summer Jazz Camp.

Rhonda Sylvester was born and raised in the Desire Housing Project, and lives there with her niece.

Dan Bright was wrongfully convicted of first-degree murder in 1996 and released in 2004. He is a father of four.

Father Jerome LeDoux was born in Lake Charles, Louisiana. He is the pastor of St. Augustine Church in Tremé.

Sonya Hernandez is a native of Cuba, and a mother of five children.

Kalamu Ya Salaam grew up in the Lower Ninth Ward. He is a journalist and a teacher.

 Kermit Ruffins is a New Orleans native. He is a renowned trumpeter and performs around the world.

 Daniel Finnigan moved to New Orleans in 1996. He is an artist and lives with his dog Blue.

 Anthony Letcher is a resident of the Ninth Ward, a father of two, and a grandfather.

 Abdulrahman Zeitoun was born in Syria and moved to the United States in 1973. He is a father of three.

 Father Vien The Nguyen was born in Vietnam in 1963, and moved to the U.S. in 1975. He is the pastor at Mary Queen of Vietnam Church in New Orleans East.

NEW ORLEANS NEIGHBORHOODS

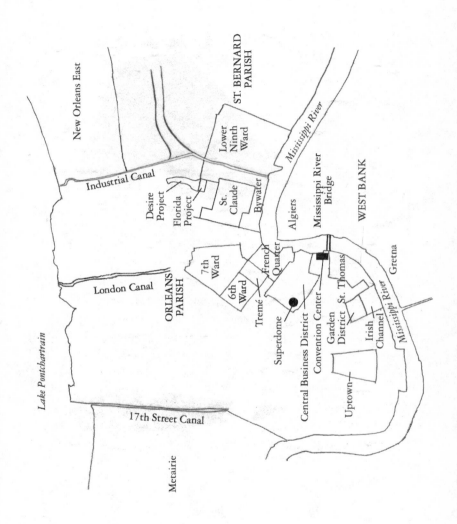

NEW ORLEANS AFTER THE FLOOD

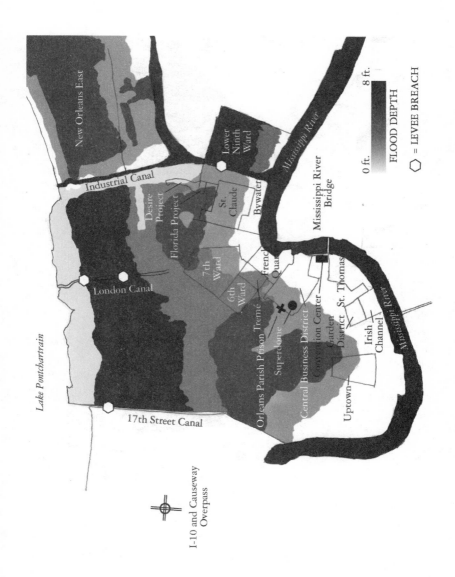

THE STORM

SATURDAY, AUGUST 27

• *Hurricane Katrina, the eleventh named storm of the 2005 Atlantic Ocean storm season, is gaining speed and intensity in the Gulf of Mexico. The National Hurricane Center (NHC) upgrades it to a Category 3 storm with sustained winds between 111 and 130 miles per hour.*

• *After striking southern Florida on Wednesday, Katrina takes an unexpected turn toward Louisiana. At ten a.m. EDT, the NHC issues a tropical-storm warning for southeast Louisiana, including metropolitan New Orleans.*

• *President Bush grants Louisiana Governor Kathleen Blanco's request that he declare a federal state of emergency, authorizing the Federal Emergency Management Agency (FEMA) to begin relief efforts.*

• *New Orleans mayor Ray Nagin and Governor Blanco call for a voluntary evacuation of New Orleans. Nagin announces that the Superdome will be made available as a shelter of last resort, but encourages residents to evacuate.*

• *80 percent of New Orleans residents evacuate the city.*

KERMIT RUFFINS

I can remember moving about a month before the storm, steady traveling, in and out of town, doing shows and coming back to New Orleans. We were playing these little festivals on Saturday and had one more set that we were gonna do. We did the set and we got in the car and we go to the hotel and we all say, "Man, we need to get home and board up our windows and get out of there. That's a big one going in." We flew home and we got home about three o'clock Saturday.

I was living right here in the Bywater. I can remember going home, packing a small bag, getting my kids all together, getting the dog all together, getting my fiancée. My fiancée is expecting right now; we were about a month away.

So I say, "Okay, we're leaving early in the morning, about four or five o'clock Sunday morning, and we're going to the house of an old friend of mine." And then I changed clothes, ran down to the lumberyard, stood in a long line with my truck, got about eighteen boards, big giant boards. Went and found some friends in the neighborhood and gave them a few pennies to put up the boards.

Then after the boards were up, I went barhopping. I think I might have gone to Vaughan's. I went down to all the neighborhood bars and being typical of New Orleans humor, said, "Hey man, this place will be underwater in the morning. You know how to swim?" The other one was, "Ahh, I'll see y'all tomorrow." You know, "It'll blow right over. I'll see you in a day or two. We'll ride this one out."

The stories were just so different, everybody telling me what they gonna do. "Well, I'm going to Baton Rouge." "Well, I'm going to Houston." "Well, I'm doing this." "I'm staying here."

My family and I left at about four o'clock, five o'clock. We went to Baton Rouge. We got to Baton Rouge right about nine o'clock Sunday night.

FATHER JEROME LeDOUX

Well, I follow the weather implicitly, whether it's coming my way or not. Even if a hurricane is deep down in the Atlantic and heading out to the Northeast Atlantic, I still follow it, which means I was well aware of Katrina the whole time, aware unfortunately of their predictions that Katrina would cross the southern tip of Florida, make a right angle, and go up the Florida coast to the Panhandle.

And of course the hurricane quickly dispelled their predictions. It simply never made a bend, just made a beeline across the Gulf of Mexico and by the time it was two-thirds across the Gulf of Mexico, everybody realized we have a monster, and at one point the monster hit Category 5. And pretty soon the forecasters realized this monster was bearing down on New Orleans, and hardly wiggling to the one side or the other. They kept waiting for a bend, a slight bend to the east, as most hurricanes do. As they approach the mouth of the Mississippi River, almost all of them have a little twist to the east—even Camille did that.

When they first spoke about the hurricane failing to make that turn to the Florida Panhandle I heard about it right away, so that would have been, I guess, Friday night. By the time Saturday came, we were aware that New Orleans was going to take a hit. But we knew that the hurricane was not about to make landfall before sometime Monday morning, so there was a window of opportunity there.

So on Saturday morning, I had a funeral. The woman, Mimi, had been lingering for six weeks, something like that, in and out of the intensive care unit. Finally, Mimi must have died around Wednesday, going into Thursday. We knew that the hurricane was not about to make landfall before sometime Monday morning, so there was a window of opportunity there. We had the funeral, and celebrated— just our big usual wonderful celebration with song and everything else. Then we put Mimi away in the cemetery and everybody was saying Mimi certainly knew when to go home—ahead of this hurricane. She knew when to go.

Amid all the good food being passed around and amid talk of the hurricane, many of the others were saying, "Well, it's time to get out." By this time they were seeing the hurricane as a big one, and it looks like pretty much of a direct hit, which we hadn't heard in ages, hadn't happened since 1965, Betsy.

So the people started rolling out, and of course they had time. They had all Saturday afternoon and they had Sunday to get where they were going; they knew that. I just went back to St. Augustine and started weighing pros and cons, realizing I'd been through many things similar to this before, realizing the floodwaters should not touch St. Augustine Church because we're only about a half-mile from the river, and the closer you get to the river, the higher the land. I figured we might get a little water on the street, but that would be it. The wind, we might get some roof damage. The other thing I thought of was that I did not want any looters to come in on St. Augustine rectory or church. And the last thing I knew, there would be people in the community who for one reason or the other would not be able to evacuate, and I figured, well, I'll keep them company.

So I just hung in and late Sunday afternoon I walked the area, the streets—this is Tremé, this is Governor Nicholls Street and St.

Claude, one block before the French Quarter—I could tell things were picking up a little bit. I walked the property, made sure everything was locked up, secured, turned all the power off, disconnected all the power in the powerhouse, and left the power on in the rectory and in the hall because I was going to use that. The caretaker, Frederico, was still in the hall with his brother Charles, so I left them up there on the second floor, and then as it grew dark, we still had lights and everything.

DAN BRIGHT

I thought, as usual, the storm was gon' turn or wasn't gonna be a big thing 'cause we've always been escaping major hurricanes, so I stuck around.

Saturday night they have this club in the Lake Forest Plaza, and I was going there when I was pulled over. The cop—city police—asked me to get out, asked for my license, ran my name in, and said I had a warrant. He's on duty, but I guess he's doing detail work for this nightclub. He's black. I had a warrant because me and my girlfriend, we had a fuss. My neighbors heard the fuss and they called the police, and they said it was domestic violence. It was a domestic dispute between me and my girlfriend. This was like a week before.

And at this time, the city was asking them not to bring in misdemeanor charges, but the cop was insisting that they bring me in. I don't know if it was the car I was driving. My car was a '97 Jaguar SJ-6, and it was given to me by my aunt. It was in my aunt's name because we never got the titles. Maybe that was the problem. I know what they thought: either they thought it was stolen or I was a drug dealer. It was one of the two. If a guy is driving a nice car, he better have a Armani suit on, and that's just the way it is. They see you driving a Jag or a Mercedes, they gonna pull you over because it's just New Orleans. They figure if you have the type of car, you have to dress for it.

So when I pull up in the parking lot—you have to remember, this is New Orleans, even the cops is corrupted and envious—his excuse to stop me was to say something about parking in the wrong spot. I wasn't driving, I was parked. He said I was over the line. This guy didn't even want to look at me. I asked him, "What you bring me to jail for?"

He just say, "I have a warrant."

I say, "It's a misdemeanor. You supposed to give me a summons to appear in court or something."

The bottom line is he brought me to jail for domestic violence, resisting arrest, and drunk in public. I don't drink. He brought me to jail and that's how I wind up in the predicament I was in for the storm.

My exoneration case is well-known down here, and these jailers have a lot of friends. And not only that, when the FBI played their part in the original case—you know, it was in the newspaper like once every week. And when you going against the FBI, man, it's like you labeled. So yeah, I'm always figuring that I'm singled out. Every time I'm around police, I feel like they're watching me, or they recognize me. That's just me. But in order for him to insist on bringing me to jail, he had to know who I was.

When the cop brought me to central lockup, the guard asked him why was he still bringin' in misdemeanors, and he didn't say nothing. He just looked at me and pointed at me and told me, "Go on up." So he left us there. So they didn't have a choice but to arrest me and to book me in. I couldn't get out because the bail bondsman had done left.

I was in Templeman III. Central lockup and Templeman III are the same building but different parts. You go to central lockup and they will write you in and they will bring you to the back, and that would be Templeman, and I was in the receiving tier. The cell is a two-man cell. When you go in this dormitory, there's an upper level and a bottom level. You got maybe ten cells at the top, ten cells at the bottom. Fortunately, I was able to get at the top level. But now I'm stuck in here, and the storm is coming.

FATHER VIEN THE NGUYEN

On Friday the twenty-sixth, that morning, as I recall watching the news, Katrina was a weak hurricane that just crossed Florida into the Gulf. Of all indications, it was heading towards the Florida Panhandle. I remember commenting that Pensacola just got hit recently and it hasn't fully recovered yet and there it goes again, another one.

Friday evening, we had a wake here for a major figure in the parish. For a layperson, that was the first time that we held a wake here in the church. She had held several positions in this parish and was a major character that built the parish.

So we held the wake here with approximately a thousand people. And then the next day—the burial was ten a.m.—we also had another thousand people in for the burial. So all of the focus was on that because the wake didn't end until ten, eleven p.m. So the next day, we geared up, we had early Mass, and we geared up again for her funeral. I had a conference call appointment on the West Bank, so what I did was, right after we buried her, I took the Chalmette Ferry to the West Bank for the conference call. And so as I was waiting for the ferry, I was just listening to the radio. And that's when I found out that the hurricane was heading this way. And so I continued to monitor that after the conference call.

I rushed back for our evening Mass, and as I was going back, I was listening to the news and it was more and more certain that it was heading this way.

That Saturday evening we also had a major feast celebration

because that was also Saint Monica's feast day and the Catholic mothers here take her as their patroness. So we had a celebration that evening for them. At that evening's celebration, I told the parishioners to get out. "Those who can, get out as quick as possible. Don't wait until tomorrow."

So a lot of people left, and the next day we had a six o'clock Mass and the message throughout for all of the priests was, "Don't preach. Just get through Mass quickly and tell them to leave."

SUNDAY, AUGUST 28

• *Hurricane Katrina begins the day as a Category 4 storm moving northwest from the Gulf of Mexico. However, at eight a.m., the NHC upgrades Katrina to a Category 5 storm, the highest rating on the Saffir-Simpson scale.*

• *Mayor Nagin orders the first-ever mandatory evacuation of New Orleans at ten a.m. CDT.*

• *Government agencies begin to evacuate. However, many prison officials evacuate without their prisoners, leaving them in gyms, common areas, or locked in their cells.*

• *During a teleconference with President Bush, FEMA director Michael Brown expresses worry over the New Orleans Superdome's ability to house disaster victims. During the same teleconference, NHC director Max Mayfield warns that the levee system in New Orleans may not withstand Katrina.*

• *By Sunday evening, approximately 25,000 people have arrived at the Superdome, where National Guardsmen have enough food and water for 15,000 people for three days.*

SONYA HERNANDEZ

The day of the storm, they started saying in the news about the storm coming bad. So I said, "I need to bring everybody home and try to get them safe. Maybe their family wanna go on and go to the Superdome."[7]

I used to drive all of the neighborhood kids around the city. "Mama Sonya I need a ride," they'd say. I used to bring them here, there, everywhere. And they called me when they was out there somewhere. So what I did, I bring everybody to their houses. Then I start working on my house, see what we was going do.

I was not worrying about nothing. My mind already was on the aftermath of the hurricane. Let me tell you why: because I was in Hurricane Andrew. In Andrew, my husband figured out what we was going to do and we got help five minutes later.

The news was talking about, "Katrina's moving this way and we don't think it's going to come to New Orleans." And then when Katrina was almost on top of New Orleans, then they start saying on the news that it would come to New Orleans and it was going to be

---

[7] The Louisiana Superdome is a large sports venue located in the Central Business District. It covers fifty-two city acres and has a maximum capacity of 72,003.

a major hurricane. They was talking about evacuation but they were saying, "If you don't feel safe, you need to evacuate."

We didn't went nowhere. We got some money. We borrowed some money and we bought a few things that we needed just in case, like flashlights, candles, canned food, a lot of bottles of water, and stuff like that. Diaper for my granddaughters. But about eleven-thirty a.m., the police come to the door and they said we have to go.

The police said everybody gotta go. My husband was there, he said, "I'm not goin' nowhere," and he hide. He don't wanna go. He don't want to evacuate. So he told me, "You go with the kids. I'm'a stay here because I'm not about to let nobody come and vandalize my house." He never run from no hurricane at all. So we left to the Superdome, but he got his cousins and friends.

My oldest daughter, she's got a friend—his mama and his grand-mama left him—so we got in the van and this boy called my daughter and my daughter said, "Mama, Ronnie by hisself." So I went all the way to Tulane and Carrollton to pick Ronnie up and then there was a line of police people telling the cars, "Go to the Superdome." I think it was too late. They should've done that earlier. I think that's why a lot of people died. Some people didn't know what to do, and some people don't even have no money to do nothing. Let's put it to you this way: You got a car, you gotta put gas in. What about if you don't got no gas in the car, if everything is stopped? Which bus are you going to catch to go to the Superdome? So actually, they should've do it early. By the time they was doing the mandatory evacuation, it was too late.

And a lot of people got trapped on the bridge across the Super-dome, 'cause when the hurricane was about to hit, they don't let nobody else get in the Superdome. So a lot of people go through the storm on the bridge.

When we got to the Superdome, we was searched like we was about to go inside jail. The New Orleans police was not there when we got there. It was the Superdome police who was there. It was like security guards. They was trying to run things. And they told the people, "Sit down on the bleachers." Everybody sat down on the bleachers.

KALAMU YA SALAAM

I was living in Algiers when Katrina hit.[8] I had the belief that it was going to be a bad storm, just from the projections and looking at the size of the storm. It was a huge storm. Many people do not realize just how large it was, even people in New Orleans.

It's funny, though, because I have this feeling that I will know when I'm about to check out. And I've had feelings that, "This is a dangerous situation that I might not make it out of," but I've never had the feeling that I was gonna die. I don't have a fear of flying. I don't have any of that. There must be a little bit of reptile in me, and I don't have certain nerves that other people have and respond to things. I just don't respond to it. I'm not a worrier.

My wife is an X-ray technician specializing in CAT scans. If she's on call, we go to the hospital, we go to the Veterans Hospital and ride the storm out in the hospital. And she was supposed to be on call for Katrina, but there was a bureaucratic snafu and her name was not on the emergency personnel list, which meant she couldn't bring her family to the hospital. So she asked somebody else who was on call if he would they cover for her, and he said, "Yeah, I gotta be there, I can't go nowhere, so yeah, I'll cover for you."

We evacuated the Sunday before Hurricane Katrina hit. Three of my children—I have five—were living in New Orleans at the time.

---

[8] Algiers is a neighborhood located across the Mississippi River from downtown New Orleans.

They all evacuated. The hurricane was Monday. We left Sunday morning about nine-thirty a.m. We went with some heavy traffic. I think we got to Houston at two-thirty in the morning.

FATHER VIEN THE NGUYEN

I guess about ten a.m. on Sunday, the wind was whipping up already. I told the people, "You can feel the wind now and the storm is more than 360 miles from here, so get out."

At nine-thirty Mass, I told the people that the Hurricane had reached Category 5—175 miles an hour. And the reporters were saying with that force, residential buildings would just collapse. So I told the people, "All of you are to leave, but those of you who cannot leave, I will open up the school building," because that's a newer structure, and also it has a second floor just in case of flooding, and then they could evacuate upstairs.

So I told them, "I will open it up at three p.m., but get out if you can." By noon, I was watching the news, and I believe that was when the mayor called for a mandatory evacuation. And a lot of people left but some of them still came to the school building.

The first hundred, hundred-twenty evacuees arrived that day. And I told them to bring food and water because we only have enough for ourselves. And so they did. They brought food, they brought water. And that was the day of the storm. Ten p.m. was when the wind was really kicking up. I was watching the news, but I knew that because I was trying to go to sleep and I can feel the wind really, not just rattling, but ramming the window. And my concern was whether or not my window can take it.

At about two a.m. was when I started to hear some dripping in my room. We still had power then, and I left my door open. Although I was dozing off, I was listening to the news as well. The wind was, again, kicking up even stronger, and the rain was driving. The force of the wind was driving the water through the top of the window sill.

So what I did was I found some paper towels, got a trash can, just to catch the water where it was falling through my window. About four or five minutes after four a.m. was when the power went off. So I called my assistant and I said, "It's here." I was upstairs and it was all dark. At about five a.m. was when the top part of my house, the second floor, was creaking as the wind pushed it. But it's interesting that throughout the storm, our phone lines were still on. Although there was no power, we have some of the low-tech phones that needed no power other than the lines—$5.99 Walgreen's special.

DANIEL FINNIGAN

Well, we didn't know that Katrina was coming for us until, maybe not the eleventh hour, but the tenth hour at least. The storm was Monday. Saturday was really the first that I knew that it was coming straight for us and it was going to be bad. Maybe some other people knew one day before that, but you know, living in New Orleans you always kinda half pay attention to these things: "Okay, something's comin' in the Gulf, what's goin' on?" But everybody had the impression that it was going to hit Florida. Sorry for Florida, they got hit bad last year. They always get everything.

But on Saturday we started thinkin'. Your ears perk up and you realize that somethin's coming. Me being me, I didn't try to do anything until Sunday and of course all the stores were closed, and everybody who was left was running around trying to find a store that was open.

I went to the bank. I had 150 bucks and I took it out and, to be honest, I was tryin' to buy cigarettes and stock up on beer. I had water. That sounds ridiculous after the fact, but at the time you don't know it is going to be all that. This was the first hurricane that scared me prior to it coming. George, I wasn't that worried. Ivan, I wasn't worried. I've never really been that worried.

Well, for one thing, Katrina was a Category 5. It took up half the Gulf. It was just a big scary storm that was coming at the last minute. I just had a sense that it was gonna be really bad, but I had no idea at all that it was gonna be anything of this magnitude. So normally in New Orleans, you have your "hurricane party" kind of mentality. A hurricane's coming, you get everything squared away. You board up your windows, you get your supplies, you do all these things, and then all you can do is wait, so you write slogans on the boarded-up windows.

On one window, I drew a bull's-eye. It sounds insensitive now, but it was a different climate at that time. It was, "You've done everything you can," so now you're, I don't want to say egging the storm on, but that's just kinda how people do it down here. I did that and I heard a phrase on TV, they were saying, "possible tornadic development." So I wrote, "Tornadic development, Horatio." I don't know why or what that means, but I thought it was funny. It wasn't funny after all.

I had another one that said, "Amnesty for the hounds, Katie." I'm a dog guy. It's like, "Do what you want to us, but let the dogs live." I drew a picture of Blue on another one. Blue is my dog. He's pretty much why I stayed. I don't have a vehicle, I don't have any of that. I coulda caught a helicopter ride out, but I don't wanna go anywhere without my dog. So I drew a picture of Blue that said, "Bad God, Good Dog." And then I heard on the radio, even before the storm, maybe on the Christian right or some radio station or something, they were saying, "Possibly New Orleans deserves it." So I said, "Down with the preachers, long live Gomorrah," and then on the last one I just painted a painting of a woman named Katrina.

So we got everything done we could. I helped JD and Sandy across the street put their boards up. We all put our boards up, and then it was just wait. There's kind of an excitement. I've always enjoyed the excitement of storms, the intensity, and you kinda have some butterflies. You don't know what's going to happen. This is supposed to be the big one. They're telling you, "Get out or you're on your own," because it's gonna be that bad. So it's exciting.

My boss had given me a bottle of Patrón tequila a couple days before the storm, just as a little bonus. I was working for a guy named Kim, up in the warehouse district; we were doing a remodeling project on a condominium. He was a good guy.

So anyway, I was hangin' out with my friend JD. He was with his girlfriend, Sandy. We drank that bottle of Patrón. We were just drinking and you're kinda anxious and just waiting to see what's gonna happen. So, you just try to mellow out. About ten o'clock that night the power went out in our neighborhood and the storm started coming in, just the outer bands. This is Sunday night.

When the power went out, we're like, "Okay, there it is. That's the first step. That's probably the last power we're going to have for a week." So we hung out until maybe midnight and then we all kinda went to our own little hideouts and kinda holed up, and just watched the storm start to come in. I maybe fell asleep around two or three in the morning. The storm had come in and it was windy. I woke up periodically through the night. The storm was getting pretty bad—a lot of wind, really bad wind, really bad rain. It still wasn't even the heart of the storm yet, but it was already pretty bad.

I'd look out the window, and I kept thinking that I saw a dog hunkered down underneath the truck parked in front of my house. I wanted to go out and check. Things can play tricks on your eyes and I guess your mind can, too.

JACKIE HARRIS

Well, on Saturday I had two meetings, one of which I kept and one I didn't. I came home and quickly went to the Internet to find a ticket to get out. And so I had to decide where I was going. Since we had an event with the Louis Armstrong Educational Foundation in New York taking place in November anyway, I would take this opportunity to go there to advance the date. I thought I'd be away for three days, four days at most.

I actually had to buy a first-class ticket, as poor and as cheap as I am. I hate to spend over a thousand dollars for a seat, but I got the last seat on that particular American flight. And so I flew out on Sunday. And the flight was leaving at six a.m. I left my house at two-thirty because I didn't know what to expect from contraflow and I was not going to be left.[9]

And when I get to the airport, man, there were so many people there trying to get out of New Orleans, they had already began to cancel flights and people were trying to buy tickets to get out, people were on standby trying to get out. Let me tell you, I was very happy to have had a first-class ticket. I flew out. I couldn't get a hotel room in New York. I think there were a couple of conventions and I couldn't get a room. And so Phoebe Jacobs, a friend, told me not to worry, that I could stay with her.

God is good, that's all I can say.

DAN BRIGHT

So I'm in central lockup and I'm like, this is a nightmare. I'm seeing death row all over again, like everything is flashing back. I don't want to see this no more.

I used the phone but I couldn't call no one because there wasn't no one to call. I called my family. They was about to leave and they tried to find bail bonds and they couldn't. They couldn't stay here so

---

[9] Contraflow is the reversal of all inbound highway lanes in order to expedite evacuations.

they had to leave. All of them have left, so now I have to stay here and wait the storm out.

I didn't sleep. I think the lights went out. After breakfast on Sunday we didn't see the guards no more. That's the only time we ate, that Sunday morning. They gave us grits, boiled eggs, and that's it. This was maybe like six, seven in the morning. So the guards left maybe like nine that morning.

See, every two hours or three hours, they'll come and count us. When they didn't come around to count, I'm thinking, "Where everyone at?" They didn't come. And then lunch came around, they didn't bring food then. I'm really worryin' 'bout "How can I get out this place?" There ain't no bail bondsmen. Living conditions is very bad. Anyone who knows about Orleans Parish Prison know how bad the living conditions is. It's filthy, filthy. You know, it's just rats, roaches, spiders.

I hear guys hollering for the guards to come. They wanna eat. Some guys might want to take a shower. They don't come. It's just total chaos, everybody hollering, banging on things, tryin' to get their attention. No one comes.

RENEE MARTIN

I was living on the West Bank. I had a one-bedroom apartment because my son had died and I couldn't live in that house no more. There was too many bad memories. I wanted to be alone, but I was real depressed because I had lost him.

He had yellow jaundice, liver problems, and I didn't know. I don't think he believed it because he never complained about it hurting. I was there when he died. It was hard on me. I remember when he was sick for a week and he was throwing up. He couldn't keep his food down, so I thought that maybe he was dehydrated, so I went to the store and got a lot of liquids, but he still wasn't able to keep nothing down. Then his eyes started getting yellow.

I said, "Your eyes are yellow. In the morning I'm going to bring you to Charity Hospital." He said, "Okay, mom."

I thought he was going to be all right. I went to sleep. Later on, I woke up, and I took a shower, and I got dressed. I went to check on him, and my baby wasn't even dressed. I was tryin' to get him dressed. I am talking to him and I'm struggling. I thought he was just sick. So I called the cab to come and pick us up. I had a pad laid on the floor, and I laid him on it. I noticed he wasn't moving at all. His stomach wasn't even going up and down. I put my ear to his chest, trying to hear a heartbeat. I checked his pulse and nothing. Put an ear up to his nose to see if there was air. Nothing.

So I called the taxi driver back and told him to cancel the cab because I'm not sure if my son is dead or not. I don't even know. But I think I might need the ambulance. He kept me on the phone. Called the ambulance.

He had turned eighteen on March 1, and he died April 7, 2003. He had two kids. My granddaughter's birthday's August 6 and my grandson's birthday is September 20. That little boy looks just like him, acts like him.

I was dealing with deep, deep depression. It was hard on me. I used to get sick a lot. I wouldn't eat. I wouldn't go nowhere. I wouldn't talk to nobody. I was giving up. My daughter, she would say, "Come on Mom, you can't give up. You can't give up. What I'm supposed to do if you die? I'm here."

And I'm like, "You're right," but it was sticking in my head to do it. She was right. I guess I wasn't thinking. It was hard. I was depressed, really depressed, you know?

I was doing a lot of unhealthy things to my body: not taking vitamins, not drinking no water, not eating the right food—I might eat junk food and stuff, drink liquor or beer, smoke cigarettes. I used to throw up a lot because I was weak, and my daughter tried and make me eat. She'd cook and the food would be too heavy on my stomach because I'd gone so long without eating. Then I was going through a lot of pain. I had a back injury, but I had back surgery twice and the doctors put me on medication. I suffered a lot of pain, and the medication that they had me on, I had to take them two at a time. They had me addicted.

If I didn't have the medicine, I'd get sick. And when I had the medicine, I'd get sick. And I knew that all of my problems were because of the medication. It was too strong. A doctor puts you on medicine, says, "Stay on this regimen because of the sickness," but they don't tell you the side effects, and the side effects had me where I couldn't walk. My daughter had to pull me around. She had to bathe me. She had to do everything. I don't like to feel where I need help. I knew what I had to do. I had to wean myself off that medicine. And I was doing that. And the night of the storm I was sick. I was very sick. I had gone almost two weeks without taking my medication because I was tired of being sick.

We didn't really take the storm seriously because we were used to having storms heading our way, and they die or they get there and turn another way. On Thursday, it was flashing on the news that we had a storm heading our way to New Orleans. They didn't have nobody coming around saying, "Y'all need to evacuate." If they would have, I think it would have been a little more smoother. But Saturday they were saying it was heading straight to New Orleans, as a Category 4. I'm like, "Oh well." Sunday, it was a Category 5, and that's when we were really started taking it serious, and I left from the West Bank where I live, and went into New Orleans.

I decided to go in the city for shelter. I thought I'd be more safer coming on that side of the river than on the West Bank. The West Bank is always known for flooding real bad. I stayed with one of my friends in the city right off Canal Street. Just us two, but there were the people in the neighborhood, like the neighbors and stuff. It was the morning. It was Saturday morning. I couldn't hardly walk. I was sick, but my friend had went to the store to get candles and stuff, and they had nothin' else on the shelves. We didn't have no candles or anything.

The newscast on TV telling us that we had a Category 5 building up, coming our way, that the eye part of it is headed for New Orleans area. It's a mandatory evacuation. Everyone must get what they need and pack up and leave. But everybody didn't. It was mandatory evacuation but a lot of us couldn't afford to even leave. The storm came on Sunday. We watched TV and everything that night, and then it started raining all that night.

I also called 911 and told them that I was a sick person and I was alone and I didn't have no way out—could they please send, you know, a policeman or somebody to get me? They told me that someone would come out but it was, you know, pretty full and busy and I waited and I waited. I called like nine times. After like five times, they told me that there was too much water to even travel to that street.

PATRICIA THOMPSON

When Hurricane Katrina hit, I was in a state of desperation. I was doing work for my church for two hundred dollars a month. We were getting paid once a month, the last day of the month. The hurricane hit August 29.

I know you've heard all of this foolishness about the people that just did not want to leave: those are bald-faced lies. I had one dollar in my pocket. I did not have a vehicle, so there was no way for us to get out. It was two people living in my house when the storm hit, me and my youngest daughter.

My son went with his girlfriend and her family, and my second-oldest daughter and her kids left with her job—she's a supervisor at a convalescent home. But my oldest daughter, my third-oldest daughter, my fourth-oldest daughter, and my baby daughter were also stuck in New Orleans.

We was hearing on the news and everything that the hurricane was coming. I was watching the meteorologist on the news, listening at the radio and everything. I remember seeing one particular weatherman who had a very, very worried look on his face, and he was explaining that what we were about to encounter we were not ready for. And if I could understand what the man was saying, then I knew the mayor, I knew the governor, and I knew the president knew what time it was. We got a mandatory evacuation order less than twenty-four hours before the storm made landfall. Less than twenty-four hours.

I know the race card was being played. I don't know exactly what percentage of the city had evacuated, but there were masses and masses and masses of black folk left in this city. There were some whites, but I guarantee that for every white person they had in New Orleans, they had a few hundred blacks.

So anyway, once we got the mandatory evacuation order, right now you're like crazy, you don't know what to do, you can't evacuate, you don't have any way. So now this leaves desperation. The whole city is like one big riot. People are trying to get water, people are trying to get food. People are trying to steal cars, whatever they can do to help themselves and get out of that city.

ABDULRAHMAN ZEITOUN

Sunday night I didn't sleep.

Late at night it starts, the winds start getting stronger, stronger. The wind and the trees moving, a very strong wind, many things flying outside. I didn't go outside. The roofs start blowing away—a few pieces here, a few pieces here, and the water starts coming in. It comes inside the house, and I start using a container to catch it because I have hardwood floors. I try to save it. What I did, I opened holes in the ceiling to make the water come through one place instead of too many places. And I never give up all night, and the rain stopped finally early in the morning.

MONDAY, AUGUST 29

• *Heavy rainfall hits the coast of Louisiana in the early morning hours. At approximately six a.m., Hurricane Katrina makes landfall as a strong Category 3 Storm in Buras, Louisiana.*

• *The Superdome loses power as the storm hits New Orleans. It begins running on emergency generators, dimming the lights and shutting off the air-conditioning.*

• *At 8:14 a.m., the National Weather Service warns of a breach in the Industrial Canal.*

• *At nine a.m., the eye of Hurricane Katrina passes over New Orleans. The Lower Ninth Ward is already under eight feet of water.*

• *At eleven a.m., the first reports begin coming in that the 17th Street Canal has sustained a 200-foot-wide breach.*

• *As search-and-rescue operations begin, Michael Brown urges emergency services and civilians to wait for orders from state or local authorities before acting.*

• *At two p.m., city officials confirm levee breaches.*

FATHER JEROME LeDOUX

I was checking the winds, going back and forth. It was getting on four o'clock in the morning, Monday morning, August 29. I did not fear winds, figured the winds could do some damage, not much. After all, the church on October 9 would be 163 years old. The hall is seventeen years younger, built in 1859; the rectory built in 1890. Now they had been through all these huge storms. I figured, well, this is not going to do any more damage than those storms did.

At about 4:45 a.m., the power was still on, lights still on. I turned everything off, laid my head down and went peacefully to sleep, slept five, almost six hours. When I woke up the hurricane was moving in, it had made landfall, and I just stayed inside from that time, kept my watch through the windows, watched out for neighbors and so forth. Of course nobody belonged out there. And then when the hurricane came into its full violence later in the day Monday, I heard familiar sounds. The whine of the wind at such high speed has a certain sound, and then when the winds gust higher than usual, they make a lurching, wrenching noise.

So between the rectory and the hall, every once in a while there was this wrenching noise, it would go like *rrrrrooof, rrrrrooof, rrrrrooof,* and then you'd get that smoother sound, sort of an express-train-like sound of high, high wind going by. So that went on for hours. You could hear the winds and I kept listening for debris. There are three covers on the church roof, heavy wooden covers coated with copper on the top. I did not know when they blew but all three blew off. I found them the next morning—two out in the parking lot and one closer in on the opposite side of the church. Half the copper blew off the steeple of the church bell tower, and many of the asbestos shingles blew off the top of the church roof. I could not really detect that until the next morning.

DANIEL FINNIGAN

I woke up at about seven in the morning with water on the floor. For some reason, I haven't graduated past the college level of sleeping with the mattress on the floor—and I'm six-foot-three, so usually my feet hang off the end—so I wake up with wet feet. I looked down and I'm like, "Oh crap, it's comin' in. This is bad." So in the three or four hours that I slept, some dramatic turns had taken place.

I got up and jumped. It's like goin' from a dead sleep to an adrenaline rush. We gotta get things goin' on, gotta do this, gotta get the pets upstairs. Quick, quick, gotta get my artwork, gotta get all the bottled water up there. Maybe those things should have already been done. I probably shoulda had all that stuff all ready, had all of my ducks in a row. Luckily, I knew where everything was. It took me fifteen minutes to do everything I needed to do. But I remember going and looking out the window, and the storm was just raging at that point.

There was debris flying through the air—shingles and pieces of wood and things. I looked out the window, and at that time the water was maybe four inches in my apartment and I looked out and I remember I felt kind of shocked, because it was about a foot higher outside my house than it was inside my house, which meant that it was seeping through the cracks in the doorway or under the house or whatever. That kind of startled me. So then I really kicked it into gear.

In the fifteen to twenty minutes it took me to move myself and my pets and my paintings upstairs, the water rose about a foot and a half. And then I didn't know if it's gonna keep rising or not. So that was pretty scary.

You're in a "go" mode. You're just doin' stuff, you're gettin' stuff done, you're gettin' the things done you need to do. You don't have time to really stop and think. Actually, during that time, when I had already woken up and I was in the process of getting my stuff together, my friend JD came from across the street into the garage and yelled into my apartment, "Daniel, are you awake? Wake up. Get up." Their house across the street, their roof had blown off and they lost everything. You can see sky from their living room and bedroom. So they came over here. They had to wade through probably three-and-a-half, four feet of water in 150 mile-an-hour winds. They had to wade across the street in that with their cat, and the cat got away. The cat bolted, but they ended up gettin' him. He came back.

They were headed across the street here for refuge because we're all friends and this house fared well. The roof held, the structure held. It was fine. There are other houses around here that didn't. There's a house a block away where the whole side of the house was blown away. All you have are rafters and a water heater hanging out in the middle of nowhere, by the pipes on the third floor.

At that point, I came up here and we watched the storm. And we were excited because it was raging and it was big, and we were watching the house across the street, the shingles just rip off two hundred at a time, and slam into the next house. And then you'd see the plywood being ripped off.

So at that point, we didn't understand that it was going to be everything it was. I was scared to the point I'm thinking, "Man, this is bad. I'm probably not going to be able to work for a week. How am I gonna pay my rent 'cause I can't work for a week?" At that point, you don't know that it's gonna be so far beyond even worrying about that. So we watched the storm and just kind of waited. We weren't enjoying it, but I guess you could say that it was some kind of thrill to be in something that's that powerful.

So then the storm dies down, and people start coming out on their porches and asking how everybody was faring. "Did you fare okay? How'd you do?" Whatever, whatever. The storm, the winds, and rains died down by the afternoon sometime, I believe. Before nightfall, the water was off Dauphine, and it receded all the way back, maybe a block away from my house.

So Dauphine was really the first completely dry street. Parts of Burgundy were dry and parts still had water, but everywhere beyond there had standing water and the water quit receding and it was about a foot deeper for every block you went.

At that point, we still didn't realize that it was everything that it was going to be. I remember at one point when the street finally went dry, we said, "Hooray, Dauphine's dry. We're okay. We're saved."

ABDULRAHMAN ZEITOUN

With the hurricane I was okay. Everything went smooth with the hurricane. Monday, when the wind stopped, I cleaned everything. I see the branches, trees down, water in the street, a couple feet of water. I say, "Okay, it's a good time to go check it out, see what's happening out here."

I decide I will go around in the canoe. Go outside.

I am a contractor and what happened a while ago, one of my customers was moving out of state, and he called me to do some work with his house, and he's selling his things. And I asked him, "What you do with the canoe?" and he said, "I'm selling it if you want it." And I bought it. When I brought it home my wife said, "Crazy, what are you going to do with it?" I used it probably two, three times. It's good exercise. It's relaxing too. I just take the kids for, you know, sport. The kids didn't like it.

On Monday, I say it's time to take the canoe for a ride, check out what happened. I take my canoe and go around the block. Two trees were down close to my neighborhood. I just go around the block. I don't wanna go further. I see a few power lines down, and I come back home. Rainy weather, quiet, no more wind, sprinkling lightly. The wind is down. I see no people; it was really quiet. When I got further from my house I see people sitting outside, not many.

Something confused me. I didn't know what happened. I have been here, like I said, from '73 and we had a few floods, but this area never floods. The area where I live now had like two feet of water in '95, and the other one small flood we had came from rain. That day, I saw a flood.

In the late evening time, though, the water start to leave. The water started pumping out. Middle of the night, we have no water in the street anymore. The water is gone. Monday night the water is already out. I sleep quietly Monday night. Everything going well.

I had phone in my house. I called my wife in Baton Rouge and said, "Everything's over. We have luckily no damage." And I said, "If you want to, you can come back."

RENEE MARTIN

That storm spread over us for twelve hours, just tearin' it up. And it got real bad, it got bad, it did. We could hear the roof, and you can hear stuff hitting against the house like flying debris, but you couldn't go outside because you had this stuff flying. It was bad. I was scared. I just stayed in a corner most of the time, praying and hoping that I'd come out alive.

I was in my friend's basement apartment. It was a real low first floor, and I was laying on the sofa bed the next morning after the storm died down. I felt wet in the bed. I felt cold and wet. I went to get up and I stepped in water. When I stood, the water was to my knees.

We was running around the apartment trying to save the computer and stuff like that because of all this water. We could hear on the radio they were saying that the main levee had broke, it was flooding, and the water was rising. "You need to get out if you could get out," and stuff like that. I said, "I'm leaving."

The car was covered up with water. It was leaking transmission fluid, gasoline. So the water was oily and dirty, and cold. I had no other choice but to leave because the water was rising and it was filling up. It was getting too deep in the apartment, so I had to leave all that and walk through the water and go to the next building.

I had grabbed a pillow and a blanket and walked through the water, and went to the house next door, which was on the second floor, and they already had left, evacuated. I stayed up there on the porch. All that day I was sitting up there, and you could see the next house over, there was a couple. They had a generator. They had to pick it up off the ground because it was getting wet, and they put it on the porch, and they set up there. Across from us, this lady and her son were on their porch. Everybody was just watching the water. Everybody was asking each other were we all right and stuff.

Then we lost electricity. The phones went off. The electricity went off. I had a little fever because I was still sick. I was going through withdrawals from not taking my medicine, and I wasn't eating.

So Monday night, I stayed on that porch. It was gonna start getting dark, and I was laying on that porch in the dark, and the mosquitoes were biting me. Oooh, I got so many bites.

It was scary. It was dark. You couldn't see anyone. You could hear people hollering, "Help, help." And all you can see is the stars, so many stars in the sky. More than we saw before when we had electricity. That's the only light we had, the stars. And it was just so close, so close to me. I just laid on the porch and watched the stars.

And to me, this might sound crazy to other people, but to me it was like God looking down at us and talking. We don't hear no voice but he's talking. And to me it was like everything was going to be all right and my baby, my son who had died, is going to be with him. And I always felt like I'm gonna be all right. And I don't have no fear.

FATHER VIEN THE NGUYEN

Monday morning all my computers were gone, so I couldn't retrieve the telephone numbers of my relatives. But I had memorized one of them in California, so I called him to let him know that we are okay, we are still here in New Orleans East. And then I asked for my older brother's number. He had evacuated. So I called him and let him know that we were okay. People were calling in constantly, and I knew that some of the nuns were still here. They were in their house.

I was waiting for the eye of the storm to pass because in our previous experience when the eye passed, things would calm down for fifteen minutes to half an hour. So I waited. Ten a.m., the sky lightened up a little bit, but prior to that it was all dark and windy. There wasn't much rain. The droplets were very small.

Ten minutes later, it got dark again so I called my brother and I asked him, "Where's the eye?" He said, "It just passed you."

So during that time, some more people came in. I knew of more than a hundred who were in the building. But other than that, I knew that there were others at home but I could only take care of those who were here. The sisters came in. They walked through all of the rain, and came in. And they were taking refuge at the house.

So the power of the storm surged through continuously until

about two-thirty p.m. Periodically there was a gust but it wasn't a major issue. Throughout the storm, the people were calling here to find out what's going on, and also requesting that I locate their loved ones who had remained. And so in all of that, I was taking down the addresses that I needed to pick up the people from. And so by two-thirty p.m. Monday, everything died down. My people began to leave the building and I drove the van around checking the water.

The streets were flooding, but really just minimally. The one right out front probably had about four inches. So I went around to survey the damage. The damage was quite extensive with all the trees and roofs, but again, there was no flooding. About five-thirty, I went out again and as I was driving, I thought to myself the water seemed a little bit higher, which should have been just the opposite.

I went inside. Someone in the house made the comment that the water seemed a little bit higher. And someone else said, "No, it went down." But what I did was I went and marked the water line on the way into the house, on the concrete, and waited. Sure enough, within fifteen minutes, it was moving. I mean, we saw it creeping up.

And so I went to my car, cranked it, and listened to the radio and I heard that some of the levees had been breached. And that's when I said I need to bring my people in. Within three hours, the water was so high that as I was driving around, the water came up and blocked the headlights of the fifteen-passenger van.

Finally, at about eight-thirty p.m., I went to bring the sisters in and the rest of the people. The water was too high for us to go. So I went and borrowed a boat to bring the people in because we didn't know how high the water will rise. Given the speed of the water, if it continued unabated for the night, it would reach our second floor.

I borrowed an un-motorized boat, and another man and I rowed the boat. We didn't have proper paddles but we still paddled with what we got. We went to find one family because I had heard that the wife had just given birth a week before, and someone told me she had decided not to evacuate, not with the infant, knowing that it would be some fifteen, twenty hours to get to Baton Rouge. Well, I went over, and we went and knocked on the door. No one answered.

When we determined that no one was inside and we went back out, the boat was gone. We had pulled the boat onto the ground to keep it from floating away. By the time we turned around, that area was also flooded. I mean, it was within ten minutes. Luckily, we found the boat on the other side of the street, stuck against a fence.

I went back and stayed with the people at the church, just to prepare them for the night. At the end, what we did was we had Mass here at night. At that point, more people had returned because of the flood. So suddenly, we had more than a hundred people.

RHONDA SYLVESTER

We never thought nothin' about the storm 'cause we was in the projects. When you done been in New Orleans all your life and you done had as many storms that hit, and when you live in a housing project, you think you can stand it. We thought it was safe there, wind-wise. They said the risk factor was gonna be real high but you know, the projects, the bricks that been there for a long time have seen some things. So that's why we stayed there during the storm.

Before the storm hit, the lights went out. We had a little water but we didn't get no floodwater inside, nothing was broke. We stand it, we weathered the storm.

It was me and nine of my family members, including several young kids. We was on the first floor. The problem was that the water was risin'. That's what we were afraid of. We didn't know what was goin' on, why this water was risin'.

As the water rose, we went to the third floor. Well, we noticed this water just kept rising. So my sister said, "I think we better get these kids and get outta here." The water was about a good four feet before we left outta there. So we went to the other side, to her daughter's house—she lives in the project too, the B.W. Cooper. They didn't have no water on that side. It's on Martin Luther King and Erato. And we went over there 'cause they didn't have no water. We went there that Monday evening.

ANTHONY LETCHER

We're standing right there in the Ninth Ward during the storm, so we can see everything, so we really think people got out. We can look out on Luisa Street and we're like, "All right, well, shit, man, I see all this water rolling like this here, so ain't nobody in the houses," you know? So me and my Aunt T on the porch, and we're just like chillin', just lookin' at all this hurricane, Katrina tearin' it up. We're right there just lookin' at it. So we stood out there for a little while I guess, right on our porch 'cause she lives in a two-story home, and we're looking out at the weather.

Man, the next thing you know, we heard something from a distance, "Hey!"

I stood up, my Aunt T stood up. She looked at me, she said, "Anthony, you heard that?"

I said, "Heard what?"

She said, "I thought I heard somebody."

I said, "Heard somebody where?"

My Aunt T looked around, man, she said, "Oh Lord Jesus! Oh Lord Jesus! Look at them two babies down in that water, Lord." Just like that.

So I look down and see the kids in the water. They said, "Help! Help!" The kids was hollerin', "Help!" So I pulled off my pants, and in my underclothes, jumped right in the water. Everything was haywire, man. And I don't know what I was thinking about. If you know me, I'm a low-life motherfucker. I'm thinkin' about me and only me. But

I don't know what happened. I saw them two babies, I just lost everything. I didn't think. I didn't care nothing about life or death or whatever. I just knew I had to go jump in and get them babies, man.

Man, I start swimmin' around with them kids. I can think about it right now, but at that time I wasn't thinking. Seriously. It was a reaction. I guess you can say that. I'm not one to say reaction, but that's probably what it was. That's probably what it was, man, 'cause I thought nothing for myself whatsoever. I didn't think. I guess it was a reaction. I didn't think.

And my Aunt T, like, she went off then. She panicked and everything when I jumped in the water. "Oh Lord, Lord! Jesus! Boy, you can't swim in that water."

Man, the wind blowin' like seventy miles an hour or whatever. I say, "I'm all right, I'm all right, I'm all right," so I swim out to the little kids. As I was swimming over there, I was trying to think, "What can I do, what can I do?" Then I had a good idea. I saw this long four-by-four board.

I got a little smarts. I know that board is gonna float. So I got the board and treaded over to the kids, the little girl. I actually told the girl, I hollered and told her to hold on to a telephone post because she was the one that was really in trouble, as far as in the water. Her brother was a good strong swimmer. He was all right. He was sturdy, brother man. He was like egging me on, you know what I'm saying? He was fifteen years old. I'm forty-two. He made me get a little power. Because I was like conking out in that water.

I made it there. The little girl, she was about fourteen years old, she was real scared. I see her brother and he said, "I can swim," and I said, "No, we got to work together. If you swim at me, you're gonna put a lot of weight on me, so let's try to work together by you being a strong swimmer," because you know, I'm tired and forty-two years old. So I kinda like paddled over to the kids, and got everybody situated. The little boy's in the front, the little girl's in the middle, and I was in the back. Man, I had about two, three cramps. Lord, Jesus I don't know how I got through that, man.

But it all went good. The kids was all right, everybody was all right. And when they got on the porch, the little girl, she was so messed up, she was saying, "Oh my mama, my mama, all them down in there." She had, like, two more sisters, a little baby brother, the mama in an attic a couple blocks away. And one of them was pregnant, big pregnant. I knew we was gonna have to go get a boat to go try to get the rest of the people.

Anyway, this lady Miss Ruth lived in the corner house. She was an older lady and lived with her brother. I don't reckon his name. My uncle Richard said, "Man, go down there and get that boat. They got that boat in their yard, man." But, I mean, we didn't think much about the boat that he was tellin' us to go get since we saw another boat across the street.

It was a little skiff, a little boat submerged in the water. We know we had to get that boat outta there. The boat had a huge motor on it and we couldn't move it, so I'm tryin' to get this here motor off this boat manually. I tell you, I tried everything to get this motor off this boat. This motor would not come off this boat for nothing in the world. I'm talkin' 'bout nothing. I'm in that boat, and I'm pulling, and I'm huffing, and I'm puffing. Man, that motor wouldn't come off there. I stood in that water for about maybe two hours and a half I guess. Me and my cousin Aaron, and the little boy who I had rescued. Man, we couldn't get the motor off.

So we kinda like maneuvered the boat toward the ceiling of a house. We were able to pull the boat up onto the ceiling, but as we were pulling the boat up on there, I guess you could say a miracle happened, or something good. Still, today, my cousin, my Aunt T, and all of us now, we still be trippin' off that right now. As we were maneuvering the boat up onto the roof of the house, the motor that we was trying so desperately to get off, came off. Man, don't ask me how. I tried everything I could. We were pulling the boat up, face-up. It wasn't upside down, to the side. Pulling like you normally pull a little boat in the water, out the water. It wasn't no way the motor was leaning where it could've fell off, just come off. I don't know. I guess God was with us, man.

Then all these motherfuckers were in an attic, so we got in the boat and had to paddle two blocks, you know what I'm saying, to go get their mama from out the attic. We got there, put them in the boat, and brought all them down by my Aunt T's house. And my Aunt T, she took over, man. She was takin' care of everybody, man.

So man, we went in the stores and shit. We did a little lootin' too, but we was doing it for a good thing. We went down to get food, and fed all the people that we had got. I ain't gonna say I wasn't thinkin' about my money, 'cause that's what I was tryin' to get. Like I was telling you about myself earlier, I'm an opportunist. I'm thinking about some money. I wasn't thinking about saving nobody. I'm thinkin' about my pocket. I guess somethin' else happened. Somethin' else got in the way. Guess it was a little bit more important than money. After I started getting them people, man, I forgot all about money. That was insignificant. It was something bigger than that, and brother, it felt good in me, you heard me?

I know at one time, I used to be a dirty motherfucker. But getting them people, brother man, it felt good. It brung out the beast in me. The power of the beast. A survivor, you dig? And this one time in my life—actually, the second time, because I donated my mother a kidney when I was seventeen—it made me feel good to say I did something good. Not even thinking that I wanted to do nothing good, you heard me? I just did it.

Man, I tell you, I rowed that boat for about three days, man, around that whole thing, hollering at people. People callin' me in the boat, "Anthony! Anthony!"

I said, "Whoa, who there?"

"Man, what's happenin'?"

"Hey man, we're just rowin' around, brother man. Come on, man. Y'all wanna come? Y'all wanna come?"

A few people came, a lot of people just stood on top of the roofs, man. I guess eventually helicopters did come 'cause that's what I heard, but me and my cousin we probably got about forty people from out there, at least. My aunt, she said about fifty. But I don't know. I think that may be exaggerating just a little bit.

But out of all them people we got out of that area, a lot of older people, we missed our neighbor Miss Ruth. Man, I felt so bad, brother man. Man, all that while, Miss Ruth was in there. Her and her brother. We didn't know. The water came in so high, so fast we didn't even realize they had people there.

DAN BRIGHT

Late, late—maybe early Monday morning—maybe like four or five. Hard wind, very hard wind. Lights went out in the jail. I was on the top floor. We can look out the window. They had these little portholes that you can look out, and see the rain, the wind blowing, and the water starting to rise.

It was early. You can see the water is constantly rising. You gotta remember, we're stuck in these cells. Guys on the first level, on the bottom level, man they hollerin' and screamin'. No one comes. They were hollering for the guards to come. Begging, pleading. You had guys who had broke windows out, burning sheets and blankets, flagging them to try to get some attention. In fact, helicopters was flying over, and guys was holding blankets out the windows, burning blankets to try to get their attention. And no one came and help them.

The water had done got from chest-high to chin-high. So guys was on the top bunk with their head stuck out the ceiling to get air.

They couldn't hold their breath that long. So everybody, the whole tier's hollering. You had men that you thought was kids down there hollering, because that's how they sounded.

The lights had done went out, so you can imagine being in this water, in the dark with this water constantly rising. Only thing we had to do now is to break out. We wasn't trying to break out just to be breakin' out of jail, we breakin' out to save our lives.

One guy got out. I think it was the tier rep. I don't think they locked the tier rep's cells. The tier rep is the guy who represents the tier. All the complaints go to him and he takes them to the corrections office. His cell was upstairs. He got a mop wringer, and he went to prying the cells open with the steel rods from the wringer. And those cells, they slide backwards and forwards on hinges, so you can also kick on 'em just enough where they can get off the hinges, and you can squeeze out the bottom of 'em. But you still had to kick on this door maybe like two hours and whoever in your cell, your cell partner, he got to help you kick. You take turns. If your ankles don't break you be all right. But you got to remember you kicking on a steel door. I kick a little while, then he'll kick. You don't want it to come off, you just want it to give way a little bit so you can push it off its hinge and ease up out it.

Then they used this mop wringer that the guy got, and busted a hole in the cell wall. We used the mop wringer 'cause it's made of real thick, thick plastic, and it's got steel rods through it. If you keep banging on something with this thing, it'll crack. Once we knocked a chip in the wall, we took the mop wringer loose and chiseled through the concrete. The rods are about the size of a dime or a quarter around. It wasn't like chiseling out of the walls. It was chiseling to the next cell.

It's like a moment of panic. I can't really explain it. The mind is very constructive if your life is in danger. You can basically use anything that's strong to get out. And you gotta remember it wasn't no five or ten minutes. It was over a period of hours. When we did it, we saw it working and we just kept doing it. You bust a hole in that wall, the guy would come out. Now, you got to go in that cell and get the other guy out. All the cells is next to each other, so you got to knock holes in those cells to get those guys out, and some guy was breaking out through the door, kicking on the door like we was kicking.

You got old guys in these cells, too. They couldn't kick on those doors and we couldn't help everybody. In fact, they had an old guy, well, to be perfectly honest with you, I don't think this guy ever made it because this guy had a heart attack in there, and he was just laying on the bed not moving. You had a bunch of guys who didn't get out, that we couldn't help.

The guys at the bottom were just hollerin' and screamin'. The police had left. No one was in Central Lockup, no one. We had to go down to help most of 'em. When you go down, the water is maybe up to my chest. So we had to go under there and try to help them out, then come up for air. These guys are on that first level. They're scared to death. They think this water gon' continue to rise, but the water stopped maybe to your chest but they had no knowledge of that water gonna stop.

The police ain't gonna tell you that. They will lie and say that they got everybody out, but they're lying. Now if you would go in that jail, if they haven't patched those holes up, you would see what I'm talking about. They got holes all through the wall. They hurry up, they tryin' to cover their tracks. Lotta guys drowned in there. They gonna cover all that up.

The rest of us got out Monday night. We didn't see a guard until we got out. When we finally got out, that's where the guards were at, outside. They were sitting there on boats. Just sitting there waiting. They know we were gettin' out. If you got out and you made it, they will put you on a boat and bring you to Broad Street.

They have the Broad Bridge right there, and that is how all of us got onto Broad Bridge.

I say about a thousand guys escaped, but they couldn't go nowhere. There was just too much water, so they was just giving up. They might swim two blocks and come back. The police weren't even really much going after those guys. Whenever they come back, they'd just put 'em on a wall, tell them stand on the wall right there, and when they get room on a boat, they'll put us on the boat and bring us to the bridge. "Put your back to that wall right there and don't move till the boat come back."

The water is chest high. You walk to the boat. You gotta get in there yourself. They're taking three to a boat. The guards didn't say anything. They didn't want to be there. They was quitting, like, "I'm gonna check on my family." They were tryin' to find boats for theyself to go, to leave. And they bring us to the bridge, the Broad Overpass. That's the name of it, the Broad Overpass on Broad Street. That was Monday night.

TUESDAY, AUGUST 30

- *There are between fifty thousand and one hundred thousand people left in New Orleans.*

- *80 percent of the city is underwater.*

- *The Army Corps of Engineers assigns army Chinook helicopters to drop three-thousand-pound sandbags to repair the breach in the 17th Street Canal. These attempts fail.*

- *Reports of looting begin surfacing.*

- *President Bush cuts his vacation two days short to address the crisis.*

RHONDA SYLVESTER

We slept till Tuesday morning. My family and I had gone to my niece's house in the same project, the B.W. Cooper, around the corner from me. We noticed the water just kept risin'. We didn't know what was goin' on because we didn't have any lights. The storm had passed and everything seemed like it was all right, but the water kept rising. We didn't have a plan, and the city didn't have an evacuation plan so we had to evacuate ourselves. We were sitting on the steps and everybody was coming by saying that the buses were coming on the West Bank.

We got all the kids together. My little grandbabies, they were a week old and fourteen months old, and my sister's grandbaby, she was three months, and we put 'em in buckets. You know the buckets you buy to store stuff in? We put 'em in there. We had the little kids in the buckets. We also had a five- and a four-year-old with us because the lady who lives upstairs she had two kids. We got a mattress 'cause the mattress floated and we had them on there. It was a queen-size mattress.

We was told to go across the Mississippi River Bridge and someone was gonna pick us up. The street was Erato, the street that we had to walk up to get where we was going. I am 5'2", and the water was to my shoulder. I can't swim but I think I was more afraid something was in the water. Stuff was in the water. Big ol' nutria rats. I'm talkin' 'bout big as babies. I've seen a nutria rat big as my grandbaby. Plenty of ants. Thousands. You know ants sit on top of water, and they just will sit there in piles.

There were dead bodies floating everywhere. There was a dead body where someone had put the man in a plastic bag, his whole body, and they had tied him to this post. It was just so sad. I never thought I'd experience something like this.

We were trying to get across the river because they didn't have no water on the West Bank. Our side had all the water. So we walked all the way to the Mississippi River Bridge. We was pushing the babies in buckets, and it was so hot, and people was pushy. It took us at least a good seven or eight hours because we had to keep stopping. Oh, that was a far walk. I never walked that far in my life. I can't even say how many miles. That was a long walk.

Then with a one-week-old grandbaby and a fourteen-month-old grandbaby, we walked across the Mississippi River Bridge. I guess they was comin' to the decision where the bus was gonna arrive there, so we got across the river and waited under the bridge. They just was throwin' the food to you like you was dogs. That was under the bridge where we was. They was throwin' it off a truck. The food was on the truck and we was in the crowd, and they just was throwin' the water and the food off the truck. I don't know who they was working for. I didn't really ask who it was but I know it was done. You never know how your life gon' be. One day you could be all right and the next day you could be down. And that was a hard hit for us, I'm telling you.

The authorities over there were telling us that they was gonna take us somewhere where we could get us a good night's rest, a hot shower, and somethin' to eat. So we're under this bridge, and everybody's fightin' to get on a bus. Everybody's afraid. It was devastatin', somethin' I never experienced in my life. We stayed there about seven hours.

The three-month-old, my niece's baby, she had had the heat

stroke. So these people had stopped on the bridge. They was so nice. Their truck was full, but two of the people got off the truck to let my niece and her kid in so they could take the baby to the hospital. So they drove her to Baton Rouge, her and her kid. When they got the little baby to the hospital, she was all right but they said she had had a heat stroke. It was too hot out there for her. That's why her eyes was rolling in the back of her head. And after that, they found a shelter in Baton Rouge and they put them in a shelter. But we were split up from them for three days. We didn't find out till like three days later where they were.

SONYA HERNANDEZ

When the storm start hitting New Orleans, the tarps on the top of the Superdome, you could see they were flying. And the water was all in there. It looked like it was raining inside the Superdome. Then after the storm, the ceiling tiles was falling on people. They was falling on people's heads. Then I think something broke or something. It was a fire all the way in the top. I know it was smoking real bad in there.

It was amazing how in a powerful city like New Orleans, how they're gonna have one place, the Superdome? How are they going to fit the whole entire city of New Orleans in the Superdome? They over-filled the Superdome. They was bringing people through the street, through big cars, big Navy cars. And it was overcrowded in there. So people was sleeping inside on the ramps. The people was inside on the field but not some parts of the field because it was wet and the roof was falling.

My daughter was holding my granddaughter Kayla and I was hold-ing my grandson Angelo and we was interchanging because Angelo's big. Angelo's four years old but he's fifty pounds, so, big boy. I carried him for a little while, then my older daughters did. So it was six kids. My grandson is four years old and my granddaughter, she's one.

Then my oldest daughter, she walked away around the Superdome and she came back and she said, "Mama, we should move from here to the entrance ramp." And people start saying everybody has to move from the bleachers and go to the ramp 'cause everything was falling. So we moved to the ramp. I got a small place inside on the ramp and I put all my kids in there. There was all full of families, all the ramps.

The storm passed and everything passed and then we was thinking that we was going back home. But it was not like that. They don't let nobody get out the Superdome. Water was through everything. Water was all over.

It was devastating. It was my four kids and my two grandkids in the Superdome. We had only like a change of clothes, just in case, and when we got changed the next day, what was we gonna use the other days? And how we going to wash what we was having on? It's not fair how we was treated in there.

At first, the first or second day, we had lights. And then after that they cut it off and it was like a backup generator. It was real dark in there. The people was trying to survive in there. They had broken in stores to get bottles of whiskey and stuff. They actually was selling the whiskey for cigarettes, for underwears, for everything. That was like a city with no law in there. I'm talking about the beginning, before the National Guard.

The floor had all kind of situations 'cause they got everybody together. Families, with men by themselves, women by themselves, and kids. I mean, for me, that was terrible. You can't sleep because you're scared your kid's gonna get raped or something.

When I start seeing a lot of men by theirselves, I was very concerned 'cause not all minds are good. When I started seeing a lot of people that actually I don't know where they come from, I was worried. I tell you what I was worried about: seeing the men, grown men. If you're a woman and if you don't got no kids, you would be worried. Let me tell you the naked truth. Twentysomething-, thirty-something-, fortysomething-years-old men by themselves means something 'cause I think by that age you're supposed to have at least a bird, somebody next to you. My grandma used to say that the lady is different because sometimes the lady's a nun or something. But my grandmama said, by the time the man is thirtysomething or fortysomething years old, he's supposed to have at least a gay guy next to him. But in the Superdome, it was thousands of lonely mens walking around drinking, doing everything. I'm not going name what they was doing. That's not my job. That's the authorities' job, but I can tell you it was out of control. That includes everything.

They got all the bathrooms on the first floor. They was stopped. How? I don't know. It's three women's bathrooms and three men's bathrooms. The whole line was stopped. They cut everything, the water in the whole Dome off. Now what?

They did have a lot of military jeeps with a lot of water. But I don't even know how many thousands of people was in the Super-dome. They was giving one bottle per person. They come in the morning and the afternoon, and in between they sent little cars. There was little cars with like ten packets of water and soon as the men walked from the truck four steps, he already was out of water. The people was already getting there. Then we was eating military food.

They was feeding the people like once a day. They got a micro-wave in the back and then they got food, but it's like dry. It's food that is already made and they put it in little sacks. And it's actually good. I'm not going to lie. It's a light-green plastic bag, and you put a little bit of water and it boils and you put it back. And that was amazing; I haven't seen that before in my life.

RENEE MARTIN

The weather was like a tropical breeze blowing. I was cold because

I was wet. Monday night I had stayed up on the porch until I went to sleep. By the time I woke up Tuesday morning, the water had got higher because we had a breach in the 17th Street Canal, which was like five blocks from where we were.

The water pump cracked. It wasn't working. It was a brand-new water pump that they built, and they didn't have the other water pumps on, which I think there were like seven of them. The brand-new one cracked, so we had so much water. And I didn't know how much higher that water was going to be coming, and when it's dark and you can't see, it's scary looking at that water because the water was too high for me to stand up in and try to walk through.

There were some guys, some people riding around in canoes and small boats rescuing people. It was like private-owned boats, and then they had some like, wildlife officials riding around rescuing people.

They had electricity in some areas because I remember one boat with a man and a dog, and another boat that had three ladies on it, they were saying that they had come all the way from Metairie.[10] And they had heard about the bridge, and they came out to save some people because they heard about it on the news, that it was flooding, and it was still coming up.

I had a big white towel and I was on my porch flagging it and calling for them, "Hey, hey." Finally, a man came and got me. I remember him as "the Man with the Dog." He was a white male, about seventy-five years old with a brown dog. He was like a hound dog.

It had to be like around noontime. I was so happy to be removed from that area because I didn't want to be there another night, in that dark, and getting bit by mosquitoes.

He asked me what I was doing there by myself, why I didn't have nobody else with me, where I came from. I told him the West Bank.

---

[10] Metairie is a community under the jurisdiction of Jefferson Parish, located west of New Orleans.

He said, "What in the world are you doing over here?"

He picked me up and he put me in the boat, and he picked up a girl, her husband, and her mama.

I was hearing that they opened up the Superdome again. It was forced to be open because there was so many people stranded, didn't have no other choice. They didn't make any kind of arrangements for us to evacuate, so we had no choice. Everybody who stayed home, they knew to go to the Superdome.

They opened up the Superdome for the first time when Hurricane Ivan came in 2004. They opened it at the last minute, but I mean, everybody got in there and everything. The storm passed by, wasn't that bad. But on the way out of the Convention Center and the Superdome, people were coming out with the sofas and the tables and stuff like that, and the mayor really got upset. To me, it was like he said, "I give y'all somewhere to stay and look what y'all did!" That was the truth. That's what I would have said.

So the Man with the Dog took us to the Superdome area, but he couldn't go all the way. They had bodies in the water. They had fish in the water. They had, like, big logs blocking the street, so we had to walk. The water was, like, right over my knees. It had started to begin getting the smell in the water. They had leaking gas in the water from the cars.

It was scary because we had bodies and we had to walk through these bodies, but you had no choice. It was either stay on the boat in the water or walk through all of that and get up on that ramp where everybody else was. And we wasn't the only people. They had lots of people coming from different areas who had tried to survive the storm from home, tried to ride it out. We were all walking from different areas.

I didn't have nothing. All I had was a pillow and a blanket, and by the time I got to the Superdome I didn't have that. I was looking for someone that I know, my family, my kids, but I didn't see nobody. All I had was me. I did have a little wallet with my ID just in case. I was thinking, "What if I die? How they gon' know who I am?" So I had my ID, and my Social Security card in my pocket.

When I got to the Superdome ramp, they had so many people out on the ramp and they had so many people inside the Dome that you were trapped. Part of the Superdome roof, it was tore up from the storm. It had rained inside there. It was a mess, they had people that were dying. A lot of them were like children and babies. Well, all ages. A lot of them was overheated or dehydrated. Some needed to be on a machine, like they had people who were diabetic on dialysis. Different situations. And the Superdome wasn't equipped for that kind of stuff. They just opened the doors and let people in.

I couldn't walk too much because it was so packed full of people, and it was pushing and shoving and everybody was panicking, and I didn't want to go too far inside because I didn't wanna miss a ride if a ride came. I was more like on the edge of the ramp where the railings were, so I can see what was going on, you know, see if anybody was coming.

I got to the restroom area and I didn't want to stand there long. You can hear people screaming and hollering. It was a lot of crime, and yelling "help," and people dying. It was crazy. They were doing crazy stuff. They were stealing from each other, fighting, having sex. I felt like we was in a place called Sin City and Satan was going to take us all.

People was pushing and shoving all out on the ramp, as well as inside the Dome because we panicked. We don't know what to do. We don't have no one to organize nothing. We're just on our own and taking our own thoughts on what to do. And you have to fend for yourself because you are in the middle of different things going on, you know?

And me, I was by myself. I mean, I was with a whole lot of people that I didn't know but I wasn't with family or friends. So

I had to mingle with people that was there, who was trying to do the same thing. It was like we're clinging onto life, so we're clinging on each other. That's all we had. We didn't know each other, but we know we needed to be together because we was all suffering and going through the same thing.

We were dehydrated. They had no changing clothes; I had to stay wet. And I had to wind up sleeping with those clothes on and drying in those same clothes. We couldn't use the bathroom. We didn't have no food. And I started dehydrating real bad. You had children, and the children were like, "I want to eat, I want to eat!" You know, they're starved. You hear little boys, they tell you they wanna eat. They're hungry, and there's nothing to eat.

You have to step over a baby, you gotta walk around a lady who said, "Oh, I want something to drink so bad," and she just lie there and that was it. And people were scared. Some people when they go into stuff like this, it's so hard on them that they start panicking. You know, what can you do but try to assure them that it's gonna be all right? Don't give up. Just hang in there.

After doing that for so many days, a lot of people were dying. I thought I was going to die too because I was sick, and I wasn't using my medicine before I got there. And it went on for three days, four days till when we did get food, we got those MREs, the military-ready food. It was good, but I couldn't hold it down because I had been without food for so long.

ANTHONY LETCHER

It was Tuesday, the second day of the storm. I went to Gentilly, which was higher ground so it was dry on Broad and Michoud. It was hectic, man, everything was going on—lootin', robbin', jackin'. Man, all kinds of stuff. Brothers walkin' around with Uzis and shit. It was off the chain over there, you dig?

I knew a lot of cats. So I'm over here, doin' my thing, whatever I do. I ain't even gonna go into that there. That's another story, another chapter in my life. Anyway, I'm over here doin' my thing, and it got kinda late. Then, there weren't any lights. It was dark, and I knew I had to make it back home. But I also knew that I had maybe about two, three miles of water in the front of me.

I know y'all ain't gonna believe this shit, but God as my sacred judge, I grabbed a piece of board—basically the same board I had to get those two kids with—and I stroked all the way home. I'm talkin' bout like two, three o'clock in the morning. I'm tellin' you, I heard brothers say that they done got bit by something, something that snatched their leg and took 'em underwater. I actually saw 'em in a hospital with teeth marks, when one dude told me somethin' bit him in the water. I'm tellin' you, man.

I stroked all the way home on that board. Nothing touched me. I didn't run into no obstacles like telephone wires, or brushes, or trees. And I tell you what, I had sailed those miles for two days, back and forward. All kind of obstacles that I had to avoid, but I'm in the dark. Pitch dark. The only thing that I can use for light was the stars. I'm lookin' at the stars findin' my way home, all the way home, and ain't touched nothin'.

I didn't run into no telephone wires, no trees, shrubs, brushes, whatever you wanna call it. No bottles, no cans. Man, it was smooth sailing. Nothing touched me, nothing bit me. Man, I scared the shit outta my Aunt T when I went strokin' up on side of her little building. I said, "Aunt T."

And she jumped outta her skin, she said, "Boy, where do you come from?"

I said, "Aunt T, I swimmed all the way home."

She said, "Boy, no you didn't."

I said, "TT, ain't nothin' touched me." Said, "Man, it was straight."

I tell you, I got some weird shit that happened in my life. But I guess God was with me. When I came for the hurricane, man, I had the wrong things on my mind. I really did. I was lookin' at it for an opportunity to try to make some money. Yes, I am an opportunist. Or at least I thought I was.

ABDULRAHMAN ZEITOUN

Tuesday morning I got up late. I was upstairs in my bedroom. When I got up, the water was still below my house. My yard is above the street like two feet and a half. My house is above the yard two feet. I see the water like a river into the city, coming the wrong direction. I never go out there Tuesday because the water is coming in.

I like to see where the water will stop. I know the water will come in and continue rising. I don't want to leave my house before I know how high water will stop. Tuesday, continue rising slowly. I think it got to even with the house floor and the next day, after like noon, it stopped rising, got three feet inside the house.

Just in my house, I start to elevate things. First thing, I go inside my house, take my children's clothes, move them to second floor. Start moving everything I am able to move to the second floor, electronic things. Downstairs, elevate all my couches. Something that I cannot carry upstairs, I leave it in place. I sacrifice one couch to save one couch. Like, put one couch on top the other one. Dining room table, I put all the chairs on top of the table. I lift the mattress, I put chairs between the mattress and the bed, and it come up about four or five foot above the ground. I start trying to do things.

Every couple hours I come down, check where the water would be. We lost electricity when the water rise past the electric box, Tuesday. When you can't do anything about it, when you can't stop it, you just watch it.

DAN BRIGHT

I was on the Broad Street Bridge from Monday night up until Thursday with nothing to eat, no water to drink.

But the guards from the prison, they was drinking water. They had cases of water and they wouldn't give us a cup of water. They wouldn't give us nothing. They was taunting us with the water. They was givin' their dog water. They would take a bottle of water and pour it in their dog's mouth before they give it to us. They were right there with us, they didn't care, they didn't care at all. Majority of 'em were white, and some of 'em were black. I'm not a racist person. I don't look at color, I look at financial status. If you poor, it don't matter if you white or black, you gon' get mistreated in Louisiana. You might get some favoritism if you're white, from another white guard or somethin', but if you don't have nothin' we in the same boat.

Wherever you sit at, you couldn't move. They tell you you can't get up. So you sittin' on this hot concrete. For four days you can't move. You had guys defecating on theyselves, urinating on theyselves. You couldn't move. They thought you were gon' try to jump in the water and swim off. But the bridge is surrounded by water, so even if you trying to go somewhere, it's all water. There's nowhere to go. And if I'm not mistaken you can go on the Internet and see this bridge, with the prisoners on the bridge. It was on CNN. So now you're just stuck in that one position. You got guys faintin', catchin' diabetic comas and seizures and heat strokes. Then you had guys, on the first day, Tuesday, they couldn't urinate. They might feel obligated to let you stand up and urinate over the side of the bridge, but most of the time they said, "Nah, sit down, don't move," so guys gotta urinate on themselves, defecate on themselves. It was a nightmare.

Guys were just fed up, tired, aggravated. Guys were like ready to say, "Just shoot me, get it over with. It's too much suffering."

You couldn't do nothing. You just got to take it all in. You had guys drinking that filthy water. You had guys actually drinking that water on the streets. The guys would like take their boots or their shoes, and tie a string on it and throw it over the side of the bridge and get some water and reel it back in. I just had to tough it out. I wasn't gonna drink that water.

They're making us all sit in lines along a path. There's maybe a hundred guys on this line, a hundred guys on that line, and they're walking through this path with their guns and their dogs so the dogs can just snap at you at any time. It wasn't like they was lookin' for drugs or anything. They were just bored, so they did what they did. Put fear in guys. And they were big dogs, German Shepherds or somethin'.

You had inmates gettin' fed up, so one guy might stand up and say, "Man, we want some water." They'll shoot him with a rubber bullet or a Taser gun. Rubber bullets, beanbags. The next day, maybe like a day after, you got the Department of Corrections officers from Angola and Hunt coming out here to help out. Now, they're comin' down here with an attitude 'cause they don't like people from New Orleans no-way. They shootin', they sprayin' mace on everybody. It's random.

I seen two guys get Tasered. Then after they Taser you, they hog-tie you. They consider you anywhere from three to four hours, and if you keep protesting, they figure you gonna start a riot or you gonna get everybody to help, to stand up against 'em, to rise up. So they gonna try to deny you that.

I'm thinkin', "Just stay calm and stay out of their way," because if you shoot me with a Taser gun for no apparent reason, I have to defend myself, and I don't want that because I know what's gon' happen. If you shoot me with a rubber bullet or hit me with a billy club, I'm gonna have to defend myself. So what I do, I just stay to myself and hope this would hurry up and get over with.

I'm thinkin' we gonna die on this bridge, either from starvation or dehydration. No one care. These people is gonna go on a killing spree and kill everybody on this bridge. They was looking for a reason to shoot someone, especially the guards. You have to remember these, the ones comin' from Angola and these other parish jails, these guys are like, excuse my language, backwoods hillbillies. All they do is hunt. I knew 'em because I know how they operate from me being around them in Angola. And all I'm saying is all it gon' take is one person for these people to go shooting us. They had some guns. They had assault rifles. They had handguns, they had shotguns. They had the right equipment if they want to slaughter us. They had the right equipment.

FATHER VIEN THE NGUYEN

I've been a Boy Scout all my life. I'm used to camping; I'm used to this type of thing. In doing my reading, watching the news and all that, I know what we need to do for preparation. At the same time, I travel around this country and several other countries, so experience is one thing. And also, I was placed here to be the leader of this community, and so the situation required that I have to step up and take care of my people. Simple as that.

And so we continue with the rescue, with the boats going out. We found more flat-bottom boats. The boats were going out. And by Tuesday, on the news, I'd heard of some looting. My people at that point were staying in the rectory. Some gathered on the stage we use for outside gatherings and for the bands whenever we have our festivals. I asked the men who were here to go and gather all of the flat-bottom boats because if we needed to rescue people we would have the boats available, and also to prevent people from looting because if there were any looting, it would be very difficult to drag anything as they wade in the water.

So we brought in most of the boats that could be brought in here. Also, Sunday night we had evacuated an invalid who had to be tube-fed and had to constantly have air flowing at her. So she remained upstairs with a generator going at all times for her. She was my worst concern. There were some other elderly who could not walk, or only walk with walkers, something like that. Some were downstairs, but most of them were upstairs.

Throughout Tuesday, I listened to the news and I walked through these areas to the three locations to inform them of the news periodically. I used the car to listen to the radio. I remember listening because I was still thinking that within a few days the water would be pumped out. And Mr. Nagin came up and he was saying that power would be restored. I was listening to all of that. But then, there was that breach that they were talking about and they were talking about the Corps of Engineers were going to use the three-thousand-pound sandbags to stop the flow. So we were all hopeful. Everything was fine. I informed the people of it.

And then, Tuesday evening, I heard that the water just swept the sandbags away. At that point, I said, "We're in deep trouble." I told the people, "Be prepared to evacuate." I told the people to get ropes ready if the water gets too high. Get the boats, tie all the boats here. If we need to get on the roof of the church, then some of us will climb up and use the ropes to pull people up on top of the roof. So that was the plan.

FATHER JEROME LeDOUX

Tuesday morning there was no power. I peeked out and there was a bit of water. Nobody had any business going outside Monday. You had to be insane. So Tuesday morning I began to assess the damage. I could see that half the copper'd blown off the roof, and I checked for things I would recognize and maybe nobody else would. I looked to the live oaks, and of course some had broken branches—not too many, they're strong—and I looked to see whether the live oaks had their leaves. They had their leaves and I made a mental note: this storm was nowhere near the wind velocity of Camille, of 1969. Camille, with sustained winds of over 200 miles an hour, stripped every single leaf off the live oaks, left nothing but twigs.

I nodded, said, "Mm-hmm, the wind itself has not caused much havoc. The only question is whether there was an effect on any of the levees."

There was a bit of water in the street, not that much, and as I looked toward the Quarter, no water, because you're going up toward the river, and when you get across Rampart Street, no water, just a little wind damage. So I began to walk around and ran into some neighbors. We began to talk, and of course by this time it sounded like Vietnam—helicopters constantly, every minute of every hour, Blackhawks, the big Jolly Green Giants, the big Huey, big double-rotor helicopters, the big heavyweights.

So a number of neighbors were down the street on Governor Nicholls, and we hailed one another. The triplets were there, young ladies who belong to St. Augustine Church—they live right around the corner on Tremé—they were home, and some other people came walking up from around and we exchanged notes. And we could tell there was trouble in the Ninth Ward, because you could actually see the movement of the water from the Ninth Ward towards us from the Industrial Canal area. We knew that folks down there had issues.

You could see a current coming at you; you could see flowing water. St. Claude was just low enough to have water up to the curb, and one neighbor actually waded part of that water, must have waded a half-mile or so towards the Ninth Ward and he said, "The water is flowing this way, the trouble is in the Ninth Ward."

And of course not too many hours later there was the other issue, the water was coming from the lake into the 17th Street Canal, and at first they thought the water had simply breached the top of the canal. But what actually happened was that the foundation of the levee was not built on the proper soil. In fact, some of it was built on peat, which is not suitable soil for foundation on levees. Part of the levees—in fact where the break occurred in particular—was on unstable ground and what gave way was not the top. The foundation buckled and when the foundation buckled, the top broke. You had a breach in the top and the water came over into the entire area around the 17th Street Canal, the Lakeview area, and that same water from the Lakeview area ran down Robert E. Lee and the other streets feeding out, and then ran over to the other side out towards the Superdome.

PATRICIA THOMPSON

My family and I rode out the storm in the William J. Guste Housing Development. I don't know if you've ever heard, but projects are good for things like natural disasters, because you got bricks. I was on the second floor in the Melphomene Housing Development, now known as the William J. Guste.

I knew a lot of people in the city so people were bringing us water and food. Even though there was no electricity at this particular time, the water in the houses was still on. I could cook breakfast, lunch, and dinner. But when the water went off in the house, it was next to impossible. That's when I realized we just had to find a way to get out of that city.

When the mandatory evacuation order was given, we were told to go to the Superdome, go to the Convention Center, or go to the I-10 interstate bridge. So what we would do is we would go out in the evening, right before it got dark, to try and get rescued. We'd walk about a mile and we would sleep on the street, but at first light, me and the twenty-one other people in my family would walk back to my house at the William J. Guste.

We were leaving in the nighttime because it was still early in the week, and we still had meat at home that kept for the first few days so I could cook for my family. And for the first few days we didn't see anybody with food outside. You had to help yourself.

If I'm not mistaken, the man that owned Wal-Mart got on the radio and he said to open the stores. My daughter Troylynn, my daughter Gaynell, and another young lady Amber, they went to see what they could get. At this point, it's not stealing, it's survival. But while they were in Wal-Mart the police came and they started shooting in the place. It's dark, there's broken items all over the floor, there's glass, and they're in the place shooting. And the police are shootin' because they want the people to get out so they can get what they want.

I lived directly across the street from a police substation. And I tell you, the goods the police were bringing into the police station in the back of their personal vehicles, in the back of their police cars and trucks! You name it, they were stealing it, and the residents were getting blamed for it. I seen the stuff that they had. I seen guns. I seen TVs. I seen computers. I seen some of everything from my back window.

DANIEL FINNIGAN

There were five of us in the house. There was JD and Sandy from across the street. There's Alex who lived up above me, and his girl-friend Danielle. The day of the storm and after the storm, there were probably fifty people left in the neighborhood in our immediate vicinity. The day of the storm, really nothing bizarre was happening. We just kinda knew that things were messed up, there was flooding, we could see where the water stopped receding. We could see that there was a lot of flooding across St. Claude. We didn't know what was happening in the Lower Ninth Ward.

Our location on Dauphine and Mazant—I'm three blocks from the Industrial Canal, which is the dividing line from the upper Ninth Ward and the Lower Ninth Ward—was the first dry street after the storm.

We had no idea what was going on up in the Lower Ninth. We knew there was still water there, but you don't know 'cause you don't have any means of gaining that information. There was one station that was on everywhere on the dial. It was 870 AM, and that was the only thing that was comin' in—the emergency radio or whatever. The whole city was crippled. So that was weird and that plays a part in your own mindset and how you handle things.

It still seems like everything's okay or gonna be okay, and it's not gonna be this massive chaotic thing that it became. We were just expecting, "Okay, anytime tomorrow the Red Cross will be here with water and things for people. The police will come back, or the army will be in here and they'll be doing their thing."

We have a little neighborhood meeting and we talk about the things that we're gonna have to think about—security, food, water, sanitation, things like this. There were still quite a few people here. There were probably twenty people who attended that meeting. I say meeting; it wasn't like some grand formal thing. It was just neighbors and you talk and then like, "Okay, here's the deal. This is what we have to think about." There were probably about twenty people and there were people walking around. Most people did evacuate, but there were many people who stayed. To be honest, I didn't take the neighborhood meeting that seriously because I wasn't mentally there yet. I wasn't to the point where I thought we were in that big of trouble, which it kinda turns out we were.

Later that night, my neighbors and I heard somebody screaming up the street, just yelling and screamin' bloody murder, so we went running over there with our bats or whatever we had 'cause we thought somebody was getting robbed or whatever. But it turned out to be somebody that lived right there and he was screaming, "The levee broke! The levee broke!"

When we heard that screaming, we didn't know if he was full of shit or not. We knew that he believed it because he was scared. So that kind of put us on edge.

There were already some people that were coming over from the Lower Ninth at that point. And Dauphine was the first dry street so this was kind of the passageway. They were walking towards the Convention Center, Superdome via Dauphine Street. We were just sitting up on our balcony just tryin' to survey the situation and get a sense of what's goin' on. The next day is really when the looting started.

At first we started seeing people with looted things. Everything from food to tennis shoes. I remember the grocery store up the street on Mazant and Royal, people were looting that immediately, the very next day. It's just called Mary's. It's a good store. The people that own it are good people. People took everything and we were very kind of cross-eyed and looking down on that 'cause we were like, "Come on. That's our neighborhood store. That's ridiculous. There's no need for that." But I think the people who were doing that saw something coming that we didn't. That was all food and all water, and things like that.

KALAMU YA SALAAM

I watched television constantly while we were in Houston. And that's saying a lot for me because I don't look at television. Unless there's something specific, like maybe the Super Bowl or the NBA Finals or something like that, I don't even turn the TV on.

I can distinctly remember it was Tuesday during the middle of the day, CNN was showing random snapshots around New Orleans during a break between reporting. One of the pictures that was shown was Circle Food store which is on North Claiborne and St. Bernard. Circle is an old, old store. It has French doors on it, and the shot showed water near the top of the doors. The French doors are about ten feet tall. When I saw that I said, "It's over. The city is flooded." I'm fifty-nine years old, and I've never known water to be that high at that location. When Betsy happened, the flooding was confined to the Lower Ninth Ward. This was not anywhere near the Lower Ninth Ward. When I saw the water there I said, "This is a serious one, the city is flooded."

At that point, most of the reporters weren't from New Orleans. They had no idea. They were just covering a disaster. They had no idea of the geography. They never put it together. For instance, the media never reported that St. Bernard Parish was completely flooded. St. Bernard is a parish immediately adjacent to Orleans heading towards the Gulf of Mexico. I don't believe there was a house that wasn't touched by flood waters in St. Bernard Parish. They were completely flooded out. You never heard any of this. And this was a predominantly, overwhelmingly, white population. Poor and working-class whites, but overwhelmingly white. This was never really reported on CNN. We have a population of twelve thousand Vietnamese in New Orleans and nobody even knew. We have the largest population of Hondurans outside of Honduras. Nobody even knew.

I heard that the situation with the police had broken down and by then CNN was reporting the "looting." Well, it was twofold with the so-called looting. For one, people had nothing. And two, which has never been explained to anybody: nothing that was in any of those stores was ever going to be used. All of that was going to be trashed anyway. In fact, I talked to someone who was associated with one of the insurance companies and he said that there's an odd wrinkle in the insurance thing, that if they had given away the items, they couldn't have gotten any compensation for it. But if they let it flood or people stole them, they could get insurance compensation. Why would they try to stop people from taking things out of the stores if the things can't be used anyway? To what end? If the city is as bad as you say it is, what's the purpose of stopping people from taking shoes?

By Tuesday night, it was just about over for the Lower Ninth. People were going in, in boats, rescuing people off of rooftops, bringing them to the St. Claude Bridge and then depositing them there.

I spoke to one of the guys that was doing this work, a fireman, who was from the Lower Ninth Ward—lived there all his life, was forty-something years old. And he said, "So, when we made this run to rescue people—what turned out to be our last run—when we got back to the bridge, they told us we have to go in 'cause there was no more light and, 'We can't guarantee safety, and if you can't guarantee safety you're not gonna save anybody. You're gonna endanger people.'" He said, "Okay."

I said, "Well, what happened?"

"Well, we got on the fire truck," he said. "It really hurt when we had to leave the people there, but wasn't nothing we could do."

I said, "Wait a minute, what do you mean 'the people?'" I said, "These were friends. These were family members. These were people you grew up with."

He said, "Yeah."

I said, "What happened?"

He said, "Well, we went back to our base."

I said, "What happened to the people?"

He said, "I don't really know."

I was angry about that. I was really angry.

WEDNESDAY, AUGUST 31

• *Mayor Nagin orders the 1,500 members of the New Orleans police force to abandon any search-and-rescue operations in order to focus on stopping widespread looting.*

• *Lt. General Steven Blum, chief of the National Guard, orders the first deployment of 3,000 troops over the next twenty-four hours.*

• *New Orleans residents have been advised to go to the Mississippi River Bridge, where buses are waiting to take them through the drier West Bank. However, on Wednesday, city officials in Gretna—a small city across the Mississippi River in Jefferson Parish—order armed police to block any evacuees from crossing over the bridge.*

• *Over 3,000 people arrive at the Morial Convention Center, where they have been told they will find food and transportation.*

• *FEMA and Governor Blanco announce a plan to begin evacuations from the Superdome.*

ABDULRAHMAN ZEITOUN

The second canoe trip was Wednesday around afternoon. Really, I just go around to Claiborne Street, see who is there from my tenants, and see what's going on that way. It is where I used to live, originally.

When I left my house, I was seeing trees lying down, things blown over, a mess. And the water was up to the stop sign exactly. Six feet up. I continued on. I think two blocks up I saw my friend, one of my neighbors. He's wonderful, he's a friend of me and my wife. I saw him outside on the porch and I started talking to him and he first asked me if I had a cigarette. I said to him, "No, I don't smoke."

He said, "Then can you take me somewhere to get them?"

I say, "No place open at this time."

So we talk and I ask him if he wants to take a ride with me. He said, "You can take me to check on my car."

He had his car, his truck, on Nashville. I said, "Okay." I said, "I am going to check on Claiborne if you want." Soon we pass, see his truck, and we continued going up on Nashville, and we go to Claiborne. Couple blocks up, after we crossed Fontainebleau, we saw a lady and her husband sitting on the porch. They say, "We need to get out of here, we need help," and I said, "We'll get you some help." They not look like desperate. He had two-story house. We left them saying, "We'll get you something."

We saw a few more people. One doctor, he is at Walmsley and Fontainebleau. He needed help but he said he could wait some more, and also two others. Really very quiet after that. We hear this quiet noise and we stop to hear, to see where the noise come from, and we start following the voice and we got to very small house, few houses before Claiborne, one-story house, and have like green awning, I remember. To go closer, I have to jump from my canoe, jump to the water, and I open a screen door, go to the porch and I get to the house. Inside, I see one old lady, remind me like my grandma. Her dress full like a big balloon, floating in the water, and she's on her back holding to her furniture.

I drag her by her shoulder, and brought her outside through the door. No way to put her in the canoe. To save her would be to drown her if I tried put her in the canoe, because it would flip no question. And I take her to the porch to try to go get some help. We went up to Claiborne and see one of the boats with a fan—airboats. I see them back and forth, plenty of them on Claiborne, and no one stopped. I tried to get in his way to stop one of them, turn him around. I know how to control my canoe against the waves, so that it doesn't hit me in the side.

Anyway, no luck. One of them stopped and say, "We'll be back." After that two guys with a fishing boat and I said, "Look, we have a lady with some problems. We need some help." He said, "Okay." Really, the guy's a very big help. We come to the house and we try to get the lady out of the door, but no way. She's very heavy. First, we try to carry her.

We tried to put a piece of furniture to climb on it, and she said she can't use her foot. I mean, very tough situation. It's also a very small boat and what happened, when you push, the boat not too big so when two guys try to push, the boat start leaning. What we did, we ask if she have a ladder in her garage. One of guys in the boat, he swim to the garage because she said she had ladder in the garage.

I'm holding her and the other guy in the boat, he's the one jumped to her garage. We got the ladder, like a stepladder. We put it against the boat to climb. When we tried to make her climb ladder, she can't. One of us decided we can lift the ladder with her together. What happened, 'cause I'm in the water by myself, I grabbed the ladder from the bottom and the guys from up there picked up the ladder from the top and we got her up there. I never asked her name but I know where she lives.

We tell the guys we have two more who need help. And we made our way back to Fontainebleau to get the other old couple, the one we saw first time, and we hear somebody else scream from between those places. The voice come from a small side street between Octavia and Nashville. We have to go around inside somebody's yard to get to the house. We got two people like in their eighties. These people already like in good house. I mean, easy to help. We go back to get the other ones.

First lady still in the boat. We finish with them, we brought them back to Claiborne and took them to the hospital. It has gotten early evening, like close to five or six o'clock. Dark.

I come back, go to my Claiborne house. I saw my tenant, he got excited, said, "I can't believe someone come to check on us." He is very happy to see me. This is what he tell me, he said, "You're very good to come to check on us." I ask him if he need anything. I find a case of water; I grab it for my canoe. When I find his phone working I call my wife from there.

I go to my house. Really quiet, nothing. Darkness. We didn't have light. I spend the night over there. Same night I started hearing the noise, the dogs.

RHONDA SYLVESTER

On Wednesday, when we crossed the Mississippi River Bridge, we stayed under the interstate for a little while to rest. Then we walked by Lakeside Shopping Center. We was under the bridge because that's where the buses was pullin' up at, under the bridge. Harry Lee, the sheriff of Jefferson Parish, he arranged it. It was really set up for his people over there.[11] He was trying to get 'em out because they didn't have no water and stuff over there. But it so happened somebody told us walk over there and we probably could get on the bus. Our sheriff, our mayor, they hadn't arranged anything. They let the buses go underwater instead of savin' some lives. They could have saved some lives if they made an evacuee plan, but they didn't plan.

It was disorganized, I'm telling you. They wanted it organized so they was pushin' people down to get on the bus. People crying, fussing. Irritated. Just everybody wanted rest. The sheriff department hollerin' at 'em, cursin' 'em out. At one point, they shot in the air because people was pushing to get on the bus. I don't know, they said it was some kind of pellet or something they shot in the air, but whatever it was, it was a loud *boom*. And it scared everybody because everybody was pushin' to get on the bus. Everybody was afraid that they was gon' get left. Everybody was panicking 'cause they know all this water was coming. So everybody was just tryin' to get a way in.

Then at the end they organized. They lined us up and let us go, instead of everybody pushin' when the bus come. When we first started out it was like three buses every two hours or three hours. So if you don't get on that bus, you have to wait an extra hour to get on the bus. And we was the last ones to get on the bus 'cause they was pushin'.

They told us they was gonna take us to a place where we was gonna take a shower, eat, and get some rest. They was gonna take us to a hotel, but then they informed us that they wasn't takin' us to the hotel till the next day.

---

[11] Jefferson Parish is a suburb of New Orleans. It is located to the west of the city and is connected by the Mississippi River Bridge. It includes Kenner, Gretna, Harahan, and Westwego.

They took us on the Causeway/Mandeville exit on the interstate. They put us off right there on the interstate 'cause the interstate was blocked. We had to walk under the bridge where they had water, mud, and when we got there we stayed there for about twelve hours. And it was horrible. It had been raining. They had dogs, feces. They had some unbelievable stuff. People were sick. It was terrible.

PATRICIA THOMPSON

I had two other sisters and a son that lived on the other side of the Mississippi River Bridge. Over across the river is Jefferson Parish. Where we live was Orleans Parish. Jefferson Parish was nowhere near in the condition that Orleans was. Jefferson Parish is run much stricter than Orleans Parish. It's a better community to live in. It's got better drainage systems, and everything is better across the river. So in New Orleans, looking like a war-torn country, if you could just get across the bridge, you could get to safety, and I had family members over there—any of three houses we could've gotten to. My sister has already told me, she said, "Pat, you all just try to get to us. The lights are on over here. You all try to get to us."

Before we were rescued, we attempted to try to cross the bridge. Lo and behold, this is where we met with the resistance. The guns weren't pointed directly at us, but they were raised. We were told to turn around or risk being shot. The police! The police told us this. They told us, "Turn around or risk being shot." We tried to ask questions, but everybody was hush-mouthed. It was like, "Turn around or get shot." That's the way we were treated trying to cross that bridge.

It was twenty-two people from my household, but there were masses of people trying to cross that bridge. But you see, the sheriff, Mr. Harry Lee—and I say Mr. Harry Lee because I can't even tell you what I'd like to call him 'cause he's an egotistical, racist, ignorant somebody—he definitely has no love for blacks. It's just blatant. The politicians have been doing what they want to do and getting away with it for so long now, it's the normal thing to do.

Like I said, we met with resistance. We stayed up on the bridge for awhile, but we had reservations about trying to cross it again because they had already told us if they seen us again they'd shoot. They had police all over the place. They had military all over the place. FEMA was all over the place. And nobody was doing anything to help us. They were just there to keep us in line. They boxed us in that city. They wouldn't let us out. They said if we tried to get out, they'd shoot to kill.

Let me tell you something. That is nothing new for New Orleans. The police been doing that. The police has been doing that. And I hate to say it, but the black police are just as bad as the whites. That's the way I read it, anyway.

RENEE MARTIN

Everybody in the Dome was mad.

The mayor wanted people to evacuate, but a lot of us couldn't evacuate. I mean, everybody don't own a car. Everybody didn't have means for transportation, no money to travel. But the city of New Orleans has cabs. They have schoolbuses, charters. They have public-service buses. They have planes, trains, boats. If it's mandatory, and he knew the city of New Orleans is under a Category 5, he should have thought about all those transportations, and let those people out. *You* got out, so you should've helped us out.

My sister lives on the West Bank in Stonebridge, and she said that the Sheriff's Department came around and were able to knock on each door, and took them on buses to where it was mandatory. They went house to house and moved them. But look at the area she stays in. Her husband, he is a seaman. He works on ships. She is a manager of the Jazz Fest. She books concerts for Jazz Fest.

Our area didn't get that. We just know from TV, on the news, that it's mandatory, must leave now. How you gonna leave if you don't have no money? Even if you have a car, if you don't have no money, you can't get no gas. So if you have five dollars to buy gas, you can't take a chance and leave with five dollars.

So you gonna have to fight it out. And that's why a lot of us got stranded. They planned the evacuation for some areas like I said, but they didn't plan it for a lot of other areas. It made me feel like a conspiracy at the time. It's a racist thing. All of us was overlooked. God didn't overlook us. We went through it.

I think some people look at it in a spiritual way. Some people look at it like Democratic and Republican way. Doesn't matter how you look at it. To me, you can look at it all ways, different ways. I'll never wanna stay like that in my life again.

They government's like, "New Orleans has all these low-income people keeping us down. We have to have so many tour sites, and get money in, keep the city going. So we're just gon' target this area here, and let the water come in, and don't even try to help anybody. Just open the Dome for 'em, and there you go."

Even while we was there for them days, that's too many days for people to—especially babies and elderly or sickly people—be stranded for that many days with no food, no water, no proper care for sickly people, elderly people. If you're gonna open up the Dome, make sure you have the equipment there because you have to think about different people with asthma, you know, different problems.

It's a horror story, really.

It goes from being a storm by Mother Nature, or an act of God, into a horror. To me, it's a combination of having an act of Mother Nature and then an act of man.

FATHER VIEN THE NGUYEN

People were continually coming into the church grounds. I guess at that point there were about two hundred people. And we were preparing food for them. A deer had drowned, and as it was drowning, one of the boats that were rescuing people caught it and brought it back here. And so I went and cut it up, and prepared the food. We were barbecuing the deer meat, and some people brought out hamburger patties and shrimp, and whatever else. But I assigned the ladies who were here to cook together, so that we can ration the water, the food, as well as the propane because we don't know how long we're going to be here.

I remember someone from the fire department came. At about three o'clock, I decided that I need to doze off a little bit. Just as I was about to do that, someone called and said that somebody's here to see you. So I went down, and this guy said he came in to evacuate us. There were four boats, bigger boats—Wildlife and Fishery from Texas, firemen.

And so I explained that there's an invalid on the other side. One of the men went over, surveyed, and as the boats were coming in, he went up and I thought he was going to be able to take her out but he said he can't because she needed a med-evac. And there was no way they could bring her out on those boats.

I told the people just to go. We agreed that I can't leave the family with an invalid here because the daughter also could not move around. She had to use a wheelchair or hold onto something to walk. And the husband was here, and the son was here. I remember looking over to the husband's face. He didn't frown, but he just didn't know what to do. So I told him, I said, "I will stay with you."

So those were the four boats. They loaded them on the boats. They told us that they can only take the elderly and children. So those who can walk would have to wade the water and walk out with them to the Chef Menteur highway. And so some of our people did. I guess by about five-thirty or six p.m., everything was done. Everything became quiet. You have to imagine that there were two hundred people here, and suddenly there was only me and that family in the school building. Everything got really quiet, and everything was dark. So a few people came in later, after everyone had evacuated, and I said, "They're gone. You might just have to wait here until tomorrow."

There were calls in between then and the next day, two days. Someone, and I cannot recall his name—he's a son of a state representative or someone, who knew me from one of my parishes and he was trying to get the state trooper to send in the helicopters. I was talking to a Texas representative who's Vietnamese to explain the situation because we didn't have that much gasoline left for the generator for that lady. So he was doing everything possible to do that, to help us out.

It was Wednesday night when the state trooper called me and asked me how deep the water was, and if there was enough open ground. And I told him how deep it was, and he said, "It may be too late for us to come out now, but we will rescue you tomorrow if we can't get in tonight." And so we waited all night for the helicopter to come. It never came.

THURSDAY, SEPTEMBER 1

• *Buses from the Superdome begin arriving at the Astrodome in Houston, Texas. By the end of the night, the Astrodome reaches full capacity.*

• *Violence, looting, and lawlessness spread throughout New Orleans. Only a few thousand National Guard troops are in the city. In response, the military increases the main deployment of troops to thirty thousand.*

• *Governor Blanco announces that National Guardsmen have been given shoot-to-kill orders in order to control "hoodlums."*

• *The state of Louisiana's Homeland Security Department denies the Red Cross permission to enter New Orleans, fearing that the Red Cross's presence in New Orleans would pose a safety hazard and also encourage residents to stay in the city.*

• *A majority of the seven thousand prisoners being held in Orleans and Jefferson Parish jails are relocated to Hunt Correctional Facility—a male-only, maximum-security prison in St. Gabriel, Louisiana.*

ABDULRAHMAN ZEITOUN

Thursday morning, the water dropped one foot back. Some people think that it was like the water start pumping out. But I know, I am familiar. See, I'm born from islands. There is a Syrian island close to Tripoli named Arwad Island. My grandmother lived there and that is where I grew up. So I know that when the sea level high in the ocean, we got one foot above the sea level from the wave pushing the water inside the city. When the sea come down, the water go back reverse to the sea, back to the level of the sea.

Anyway, I wake up in the morning, I go to the house where I heard the dog bark the night before. I knocked on her doors to see if anybody's home. Nobody there. I shouted. She's my neighbor, I know these people. I knocked to see if the dog can come to me, no dog want to come.

What I did, I got a sixteen-foot-long board I saw between the two houses, and I make it like a bridge between the two houses. I walk on it to the next house.

I feel like I'm doing something. When we feel like we're doing something nice, you feel like you have the courage to do it. I walk across and I open the window. Two big, large dogs. One of them come to me, the other one run away inside. I afraid the one not come to me. The one he come to me, not afraid of him, because I feel like the one who come to you means he want you.

One is very black dog with very long hair. I'm not familiar too much with dogs. Like Labrador I think. The other one, very long hair like floppy. I don't trust the one who don't come to me. I trust the one who come, and I give him water and some food that I have. And I go back again, get some more food, put it inside for him, inside the window because I know he no want to come out. And I left.

I go to take my canoe. I left to go to Claiborne. In the evening when I come back, also I stop by the house and brought the dogs some food. Not easy for me to go back and forth because I climb a ladder to go. I don't want to get them down. I'm not sure what would happen with the water.

FATHER VIEN THE NGUYEN

Come Thursday morning, early in the morning, I heard some knocking on the door and I thought I heard a man's voice calling me. And I knew him, and I thought to myself, "Why didn't he evacuate? I told him to leave." Well I went down, there's more than him. There was another person. What they told me was that as they were brought out to Chef Menteur Highway there was assurance that they would be brought to either the Superdome or the Convention Center and there was the Red Cross there with food and water. So they didn't need to bring anything except what was essential. And so they left and what they told me was that no one came to pick them up. They were out there all night, just out in the open. Three hundred fifty, four hundred of our parishioners.

Well, there were some invalids as well so there were wheelchairs and everything on Chef. And they left them out. Infants and children. They left them out on Chef highway overnight. Had I known that, I would not have allowed them to leave because we had what was needed here. There was no supper, so they went without supper, without anything.

Some of the people came in to see me and I told them, "Now bring the cooking utensils, the propane, and all of that, the water. Take 'em out there for them. Take some instant noodles. Bring rice. Bring the food, everything out." Also, I told them to get some of the fifty-five-gallon drums that we have, and bring hammers and nails and set up toilets out there for them.

Two of them had a boat to come back to get me. I couldn't. I stayed here, and I directed the operation. But I guess about noon, someone came in and said my people were struggling, or even climbing on each other to get on the military vehicles that had come to pick them up.

I had heard what was going on at the Superdome already, and at the Convention Center. So when I heard that they were fighting to get on the trucks, I was concerned because here, it's just them and they're like that. What would they be like when they get to the Convention Center? So I decided to go out to talk to them.

When I got to Chef, they were loading the last of the people there onto trucks. The military there—I think they were National Guard from Texas or something like that—saw me coming, and they didn't know who I was, so they were leveling their guns ready. I said, "I'm the pastor. I'm here to see them," and I told them, "I'm not leaving with them, but I'm just here to see them off."

At the end, I told my people to go, but protect each other. And then I turned around. The man who was driving the boat said he and his wife wanted to stay with me. I said to them, "You go ahead. And I'll just drive the boat back."

I had never steered a motorized boat before. I asked him how to operate that and he told me, he said there's a lever. You pull it forward, it'll go forward. You leave it at the center, it will remain idle. You push it back, it will go back. And I said, "Sure, fine."

So slowly I got the boat in. It must've taken me about half an hour to get from Chef to here on the boat because I didn't know how to steer. And I remember crossing the bridge, the Bayou. It was kind of funny because I don't know how to swim.

Well, I was concerned, certainly. I had to remain at the middle of the street as much as possible. Otherwise, if it goes over into the Bayou there's no way I can get out. That's why it took me half an hour to get in. It was really funny because steering, you know, just like when you learn how to drive a car, you think you are turning but actually you're just tensing up your muscles. Or when you turn, you think it's not enough. Actually, it's too much. I was just zig-zagging. It was so funny.

When I drove up to the church, there was a Vietnamese policeman who remained, and he came out and I said, "Mr. Tuoc, you know how to turn this thing off?" I forgot to ask how to turn it off.

The motor was still going. He climbed up, he didn't know how to turn it off. So I was looking. We were fooling around. I said, "Maybe that button. Why don't you try that?" And he pushed it, and sure enough, it went off. So we brought the boat to the back and pushed it into the backyard where we have a little fish pond because we don't want people to steal our boat just in case we need it. So with the policeman here, it was really good. He'd been in and out, and he basically stayed throughout.

I called Texas again, the state representative, and told him of the situation. I said the gas is really low. We can make it for another day, but that's about it. And without that, the woman will die. So he told me he will do whatever possible.

Thursday night it was dark. I got two phone calls. One was a wife, the other one was a daughter—the wife of one man, and the daughter of another man—begging me to go find their father, and their husband. They gave me the addresses. It was 8:30, and I remember it was totally dark. I had the boat, but there was no way.

The water was so high that I couldn't figure out where the roads were. There was no way I was going to drive that boat out at night to find those people. I told them, "I'll try tomorrow."

I had no idea whether or not I could find them.

DAN BRIGHT

We prisoners don't leave off this bridge till Thursday morning. We went on this bridge Tuesday night.

They had buses on I-10 lined up, but we couldn't get there, so they built a scaffold, and they forced all of us down this scaffold. Now you got to remember, you got handicapped guys out there, you got guys afraid of heights. From the Broad overpass, it is like an eighty-foot drop, and we're not experienced in climbing up and down scaffolding. But they forced us to go down. They didn't care if you didn't want to do it.

On the bridge, there was a lot of hatred, like towards the inmates. You had to walk down, and the guys who couldn't do it, they set them on that side, and after everybody who was healthy enough to climb down the scaffold, they'll take the old guys and put 'em on boats, and bring 'em around.

They put us all on buses Thursday and bused us to Hunt Correctional Center. I was just ready to go lay down. We think we gon' get some food, some cold water. And it only gets worse. The nightmare continues.

It was a prison football field. Each correctional center has their own football team, and they have their own field. And we were sleeping on their football field. They didn't even have restrooms out there. If you had to defecate, urinate, you had to do it right where you at. So you imagine defecatin' in front of maybe like twelve hundred people on a football field.

They didn't have pillows. All they gave us was one blanket to sleep out in the open. You have to remember Louisiana's made out of swampland, so at night everything get marshy. This blanket's soaking wet, you soaking wet sleeping on this ground. Morning time, it's burning-up hot. And you got the gnats, got mosquitoes.

They didn't give us showers. They set up these big ol' spotlights they put over around the field. And they have this pipe, they got a pipe that comes out the ground, a faucet. That's the only water we had. We didn't have any cold water, just faucet water that come outta the ground. There were two of them. You gotta wait in line. You drank out your hand. Drink out your hand or put your head under the faucet, let it run in your mouth.

You got the guards that's outside the gates, with the assault rifles, the hunting guns, waitin' on you to try to escape. They got this field, they're patrolling it. It's like you're a wild animal in a cage. They didn't come in there, they didn't step foot inside that gate. They didn't wanna do anything. They didn't care. In fact, they was like, laughing. It was all a game to them because, you have to remember, in this state, no one likes New Orleans. New Orleans is like a outcast to other places. That's how they look at it. They figure everybody in New Orleans is troublemakers. And I'm'a tell you, anywhere in the prison system, the guards do not like any inmate from New Orleans. They don't like 'em.

They would get in this crane and lift theyself up over the fence and just throw sandwiches. If you get one, you get one. If you don't, you don't. That's too bad. That's how we eat. And if you don't jump, you don't get your sandwich, you ain't gonna eat. They was treating us just like wild animals or something.

Everybody was on that field. They had federal prisoners around state prisoners. You got guys with all different types of charges: murder charges, armed robberies, rapes. Then you got guys like us with misdemeanors, obstruction of sidewalk, trespassing, tickets. Everybody's equal; put everybody in this one yard and lock us in there.

You got Len Davis in there, the crooked cop who was on death row. Anybody who follows the news know who this guy is. When they found out who he was, they took him out. Maybe like twenty guards came all like fully armored. Hurry up, came and snatched him, and got him out of there. He was gon' get killed 'cause they had guys plottin' on him, they was gon' get him. Homemade knives, shanks and everything.

I saw stabbings. Guys would go around jacking guys' blankets from them, stabbing them, beating 'em up. You had gangs out there. Gangs was formed like, "We going to stick together. This ward going to stick together, this ward going to stick together."

All in all, everybody was basically fending for themselves. You got federal prisoners on one side of the field, and most of those guys in federal prison is under the protective custody. So either they snitched on somebody, or they don't want somebody to know they there. So now they all form in one group. It's like a gang now. So you have all kind of people out there.

You had guys like this going around, jigging guys for their tennis shoes. You gotta remember, all our shoes was wet, so if somebody got some good tennies, yeah, right. And then you got some sick guys out there, man. You have a female guard who's in the watch tower, and these guys masturbating on the tower, where the women can see 'em at. So you're being disrespected from all angles now. And in prison, doing that would get you hurt. It'd definitely get you hurt if you masturbating in front of another man. That's called disrespect. So you being disrespected from all angles, man. The inmates is disrespecting you. It's horrible, man.

And when some of the inmates broke out of Central Lockup, they went in the property room also, and so they had guns. I saw two guns on the field, on the football field. I seen this. It was, if I'm not mistaken, it was Glocks 'cause I know they was plastic. They was real guns.

This is facts also: in Central Lockup, the guards broke in the property room and took all our money and jewelry. My daughter called my phone and one of them answered it. Answered my cell phone. That's how I knew that they were stealing. And when he ask, he tried to get my daughter to give him the number so he could know the number of my phone. That's how I know they was breaking into the property room.

So this was worser than being on the bridge. We went from worse to worser. The guys is calling the guards for help—the weaker guys—and the guards is laughing, like, "Get it how you live." That's what they say.

ANTHONY LETCHER

This young black guy was in the news, Alpage. He's a young guy, went to college, made it out at a tryout for the football in New Orleans, and blasé this, blasé that. But his name is Alpage. Anyway, I got his grandmother—big lady, like a 400-pound lady—out of the water.

His grandmother was so big that they said a helicopter had to come and get her and her family. But we really didn't know if they had came. My Aunt Gayle and them, they was the last ones to leave the house. Everybody had to get out. The police wanted everybody to evacuate out. We stayed over in the Ninth Ward for four or five days, but it was time for everybody to go. So my Aunt Gayle did all she could do for the lady, and we tried to make it to higher ground. We could see the water's not receding, so we got to go. So I started paddling everybody to Gentilly.

But they was the last ones. The mama, two daughters, the daddy, and a little kid. They was like the last ones. And nobody wanted to leave their mom, even though she was a big lady, kinda senile, Alzheimer's, with all the trimmings. You dig? She was old.

So we all left, and they finally said after maybe a day or so, that the helicopter came and got them. And we learned that they was in Baton Rouge somewhere. They was all right. They sent word to my Aunt T, and my T related the message to me. They said God bless me and stuff, and I was glad to know that they was all right.

Alpage called me up, "Man what's happenin', bro?"

I said, "Oh man, what's happenin' boy?"

He said, "Man, I heard."

I said, "Heard what?"

He said, "Man, I heard you went and got my grandmother, my grandpa, my two aunties, and my little baby cousin."

I said, "Yeah, bro."

He said, "Man, thank you."

He was grateful. His family made it out, they was all right.

Let them tell it to you, because they're gonna remember me, and not that I'm looking for them, I'm way somewhere else. God bless them. I was glad I was able to help. I ain't looking for nothing in return, nothing. Well, maybe a little thing from God.

Yeah, man, I believe. I ain't trying to go down there. I mean, just speaking hypothetically, if there is whatever there is down there, I don't want to go fuck with him. I will let him do him, and I'm'a do me. I've been thinking about that too. What would God say to me? He's saying, "You're kissing up." Maybe I am, I don't care. If I gotta kiss the man's butt to get on up there, I'm willin' to do that 'cause I ain't no angel. I done did a lot of fucked-up shit in life.

That water was hectic, a lot of people lost a lot of shit. A lot of lives got tossed around. Ain't but the grace of God all my family got out of it, nobody got left behind, killed. We're not mourning deaths. So that's good. I rather mourn my property and my $157 Timberland boots. I rather mourn them than have to mourn a person's death. That's cool with me. God is good. All my family's straight, man.

RHONDA SYLVESTER

We slept under the I-10 interstate at Causeway for ten hours, with dogs, all kinds of feces, with people laying in mud. My son and my daughter-in-law had their week-old baby, and a fourteen-month-old baby with us. They just told us go wait. We were sleepin' on the interstate, some people sleepin' under the bridge.

You know how people haven't taken baths in days, how they gon' smell. Then they had dogs under there. Then they had food people had left open far before we got there. It was just waste. Smelled like pee-pee. I felt homeless, helpless. That's how I felt down there. I felt homeless. And even in the life I lived at one time, I never was homeless, but I know what it is to be homeless now.

I think that was the lowest part of my life, and before I came here I had some struggles. It wasn't easy livin', tryin' to live. But that was the worst. And I kind of reach out to people. I know how it feel to be homeless now 'cause we felt homeless. We'd gone from the Desire Projects, to Jefferson Parish, to the interstate, and hadn't had a bath in three days, and hardly eaten anything. It just was sad.

When we got under the bridge by Causeway/Mandeville, that's when the Red Cross was out there givin' out the food. But we didn't get anything to eat. We had a week-old grandbaby and put some blankets around him, but we was on the interstate. We slept on the interstate till they got ready and put us on the bus.

A lady came around and she noticed that we had a little bitty baby, so she told my son and my daughter-in-law, she said, "Come with me. Since y'all have these little kids, I'm'a get y'all on the bus first." I don't know who the lady was. They had a lot people doing different things for people. She was like the security that was surrounding the place, 'cause they had security out there. My son was trying to get me to come, so I told him, "Don't worry about me. Just take these kids and go. And I'm'a find 'em when I get there." So she got them on the bus.

PATRICIA THOMPSON

Like I said, every day the twenty-two people in my group were going to these three places they told us to go—the Superdome, the Convention Center, and the I-10 causeway.

We're trucking back and forth through all this gritty, grimy, disease-infested water every day. And I'm not ashamed to say, some of those stores that were open, we went in 'em. It was survival of the fittest. People were dying all around us. We were sleeping next to human feces and urine. All around you, watching people die, watching them scream for help. You're calling 911, the operator's telling you there's nothing they can do to help. You can't get any assistance from the police. There are helicopters; there are cops everywhere. Nobody would stop to give you a hand or so much as answer a question. And for a week, we went back and forth, trying to get rescued, then have to get up the next morning and start all over again.

We seen buses, we seen FEMA trucks. One night in front of Convention Center, about three to five hundred buses were just paraded by us real, real slow. Everybody knew at that point they expected us to bumrush the buses. That would give them another reason to get rid of a few of us. I mean, very, very slow, almost a crawl, they paraded past us and not one stopped.

On another occasion during the time we were across the street from the Convention Center, these cops—I don't know if they were police, but they were all in black, they had these guns, and they were banded real close together—they came up the street, and they were screaming all kind of obscenities, and all kind of racial slurs. And they were pointing guns at folk and demanding you to lay down.

At this particular time, I had really gotten tired of using the restroom on the sidewalk, so I'm trying to get across the street into the Convention Center to use the restroom. At this point, these cops, whoever they were, they came up the street, they got these guns with the lights on them, you know, they pointing them at people saying, "Sit your so-and-so so-and-so down before I blow your so-and-so head off, you black so-and-so."

I mean, God. At that point, it really felt like I was in the Twilight Zone. They're treating us like criminals. But everybody had to adhere to what they said, so once they passed me, I pretty much stayed low, in just about a crawling position, trying to get across the other street to get into the Convention Center to use the restroom.

What I seen when I came out I will remember for the rest of my life. I swear, God be my judge. At this time, I'm crouched trying to get back into the parking lot. I see everybody on the street and everybody in the parking lot. Everybody is sitting on the ground with their hands in the air. The cops are stationed in different spots, with their guns aimed on people. I look at my five-year-old granddaughter, Baili McPherson, and the light from one of the guns was actually on her forehead.

My oldest daughter, Gaynell, she's like, you want to go ballistic when you see someone do something like this to your child but you can't do nothing because, guess what, you and your child both might get killed. Baili is sitting with her hands in the air. And she's just past afraid, she's terrified. And she's asking her mama, Gaynell, "Am I doing it right?" because even the babies know the police kill in New Orleans. So she's asking her mama, "Mama, am I doing it right, am I doing it right?"

We're just sitting there, they talking to you crazy, talking to you bad, cursing you out, all kinds of stuff, and you got to take that shit sitting on the ground with your hands in the air. Finally they left. Now, once they left, people really go into a state of panic.

People don't appreciate the way they just been treated. All you can do is talk about it among one another. Anyway, we just sit there and we endured. We slept on the street that night again, and at one point I remember a young lady was holding a baby, and the young lady just dropped. Somebody grabbed the baby. I don't know if she was sick or what. We wind up bringing her back around, thank God. People were screaming for water. We had one of those big bottles of water that goes to the water coolers. People were like, "Miss, please, just could we use this water?"

I was like, "Use the water," 'cause where we were, there was no help, we had to help each other. I had to let them use that bottle of water and just pray to God that we would get more, and try to bring that young lady back around.

Another young lady was afraid to go into the store to get her baby milk. From what I could understand, the baby died. But I didn't see this with my eyes. I didn't see the child die with my eyes. I had talked to the young lady when I first got out there because the baby was constantly crying, and she told me the baby needed milk. I said, "Well, every store in the city is open, why don't you go in and get your baby a can of milk?"

She was afraid of going into the store. She was afraid to get in trouble with the police. I said, "Girl, the *police* are looting."

FRIDAY, SEPTEMBER 2

• *President Bush makes his first tour of the Gulf area, stopping to make a speech in which he says, "Brownie, you're doing a heck of a job" of Michael Brown's performance as FEMA director. He also laments the loss of Trent Lott's lakeside home in Pascagoula, Mississippi.*

• *Armed National Guardsmen enter the New Orleans Convention Center— where thousands of hurricane survivors remain—for the first time.*

• *Governor Blanco orders that out-of-state medical practitioners be temporarily allowed to work in Louisiana to aid the recovery effort. However, FEMA does not allow medical staff without FEMA certification to treat disaster victims.*

• *President Bush signs an aid package of more than $10 billion for immediate use in relief efforts.*

• *Across the street from the Astrodome in Houston, the Reliant Center opens its doors to evacuees.*

DANIEL FINNIGAN

We had our block under control. When I say under control, it wasn't a "control" under control. It was chaotic and kind of panicked, but we had weapons and a few people on this block, and we made no bones about it.

New Orleans was a dangerous place before the storm. I've been robbed at gunpoint twice. And I know people who've been shot, and just about everybody's been robbed. And I don't say that in any negative way against New Orleans because New Orleans is a great city with a great soul, but it was a dangerous place. There's a lot of guns here normally so in a situation where you have zero authority and you have a lot of strife and desperation you don't have to be real smart to figure out that that's a dangerous scenario. And that played a role in all of our fears. You would see people cruisin' around kinda scopin' out the neighborhood. If a car load of four people drives around your neighborhood for four hours, you know they're looking to loot. They're looking for what they can get and what they can take. So we made no bones about havin' guns. We have 'em too. If y'all want our stuff go find an easier block.

This is an odd thing to talk about, but there was a corner store up the street that we chased looters off for three days. People were tryin' to get into it and we would run them off and scream at them and say, "This is our block! You can't do that. Get the fuck outta here. That store is gonna stay untouched."

It kinda sounds funny in a way that we were all so scared and worried about the people, and that we were packing a gun instead of water but at that point, we didn't know about the horrors that were goin' on in the Ninth Ward. You're seeing people coming by with things—tennis shoes, designer shirts, and food and water, or whatever. We thought none of that was necessary.

We'd hear on the radio that people were up in the French Quarter partying, and we're back here holding an SKS rifle defending a store from being looted. We're in this weird, very tense, post-world scene back here, while there are people sitting on bar stools in the French Quarter. It kind of pissed me off. If I lived in the French Quarter, I'd probably be there too, but it didn't mesh with what was going on. It was just too disjointed.

I was thinking that we would be the first neighborhood to see some kind of relief and ground forces and things like that. But three or four days had gone by, and there was still nothin'. There's still no Red Cross. I mean, I live three blocks from an army base, and another two blocks or three blocks from a wharf that's made for ships to come in with things. And the army base, it's made for army people to be there and come there and do army things.

It would have been a totally different experience had there been some security down here. There wouldn't have been as much panic. There wouldn't have been the robberies and the beatings, and you know when I say that, don't think of Hollywood. In your head, it felt very much like that sort of thing. It built to that. It built to that sort of *Escape from New York*–type movie kind of panic. But obviously that's Hollywood. It wasn't like that. You weren't seeing beatings out your window.

It was real. The reality always differs from the way it's portrayed.

I don't know why, I don't know. It's hard to explain. I was scared. I'll just say it like that.

On the third day of chasing looters off from the store, and still no relief, well, we quit defending the store. At that point, we are also realizing that these people walking through our neighborhood are desperate and they need help. The Red Cross station is the corner store at that point because these people are thirsty and hungry and broken people. What kind of person would you be to stand in front of this place with a gun and tell people they can't have the stuff that they need when our own government isn't bringing them the things that they need? They need water. They need food. They need these things because they've been on their roof or in their attic for three days, and they probably just lost loved ones and they have to walk miles to get to what's supposed to be a sanctuary.

I remember when Bush came in on Friday, he flew right over my house. Well, it was either him or his decoy. It was definitely the Presidential Marine 1 helicopter that flew right over this house, about a hundred feet up. He did his tour and everything, and I thought, "Okay, I guess now it's a big deal." And after Bush made his visit, then the sky was filled with helicopters, like insects—they were everywhere. The whole sky was like a blender, it was insane. Double rotors, Chinooks, smaller ones, coast guard, army, whatever. So I guess that would mean there would be something like fifteen above my halo at any time. I used to like helicopters. I don't mind not seeing helicopters anymore. It's not that exciting anymore.

So now there were helicopters everywhere, and we're thinking, "Okay, now it's gonna get done." But there was still no ground presence at all. I'm not saying to speak of, I'm saying at all, back here. And it just doesn't make sense to me.

So we left the corner store alone. I think it was a safer thing to quit defending the store. It kinda made the block more of a target. There's a store right there that still had stuff in it, and desperate people will do what they gotta do. So that store got looted. I took some things from that store myself 'cause at that point, everybody needed stuff. I had water for a couple days. The main thing I wanted out of there was the pet food. Many people left their animals because they thought they were gonna be gone for a couple of days. So I had about ten to fifteen dogs I was feeding. I just went and found 'em. I didn't go far. I had just this general area. I had about ten on Mazant Street from Royal to Burgundy, and then a few more off Dauphine. One over on Lesseps. That's just something that I do. I like to take care of animals.

And I didn't have any dog food. I wanted that dog food, so I went to the store and took all the dog food and fed all the dogs. I also took some things for myself as well. That's not something I like. Even though at that point they were saying on the radio, "It's okay. Go ahead and take the stuff from the stores," that was scary. That's when we realized, "Well God, I guess we're not gettin' any help." I think it was the announcer who said that the word was that the authorities were saying to go ahead and fend for yourselves. If you need supplies of necessity, go ahead and take them.

But I'll be honest with you, whether we heard that or not we still would've taken stuff from stores. Because at that point it was a necessity. When something gets to be a necessity, you don't wait for the government to say it's okay, especially when they're still hundreds of miles away.

The people staying with me all ended up leaving on Friday. I was on my own from Friday night on. I wasn't able to go with them because there wasn't room for my animals, for my pets, and I didn't want to leave them behind.

RENEE MARTIN

I was still alone, waiting in the Superdome. It was hard. We didn't have no doctors. No police are organizing anything. We had soldiers came in there, but when they started comin' in, it was like they were comin' to kill us, I thought. That was Friday.

They came in and they had these M-16 rifles like they was ready to use them. And they was marching in like soldiers, one after the other. And I thought they was gonna tell us line up against the wall and shoot all of us. I did. It was scary.

I told them, "Please put the guns down. Don't point the guns toward us please. All we want to do is get from out of here."

And one of the soldiers said, "Ma'am we here to rescue y'all." But I still was afraid because I thought that Bush ordered them to leave Iraq and come all the way to New Orleans and free us people at the Superdome, and they felt like they had other people that should have been doing their job in New Orleans. So by them having to do it, they was kind of upset about it and they said, "Well, we gonna solve the problem, just kill all of them."

The choppers came down with soldiers, and they had baskets. They put us in the baskets and flew us to I-10. I-10 highway in Metairie.

The National Guard was doing the airlifting. I was confused. I was afraid. I was desperate to be rescued by somebody but at the same time I was afraid. I thought all the time that it was the end of the world, that I was gonna die.

It's scary because you think the basket's gonna pop, and you're gonna fall in all this water again, but you're higher. You're way up there. So I was holding on. I was cold, I was wet. And you're look-ing down, but the propeller's spinning and it's too much wind so we can't hear. But we were still happy because we'd moved from the Superdome. We didn't know where we were going. They don't tell you where you're going. You just know you're going away from that water.

I was scared. I thought they were gonna kill us. One of the soldiers, he said to me, "Ma'am, we're here to help you." But I didn't wanna believe him 'cause it's like, "Where we goin?"

And they say, "We don't know where you're going."

But I'm like, "You come and get us, you should know where you're flyin' the plane."

In a way, you take your chances leaving with the National Guard, so that's what we do. We gotta take that chance 'cause we either gonna die there, or die with them. It's crazy.

They dropped us off on the bridge by I-10. Then it was long, long ways, like miles and miles of so many people. We got there, there were so many people already there. That's all you could hear. Choppers flying day and night. Choppers flying everywhere. You're all saying to people, "What about us? What about us?" And they was pulling people from the outskirts of New Orleans, saving them, and leaving us. And we want to know why. We're watching y'all flying back and forth. Here we are being like, "When y'all gonna come up and help us?"

We were so glad to see that we wasn't taken somewhere where nobody was. They had CNN news out there. Lots of them. They had thousands of people there. But everybody was so tired. We didn't have nowhere to sleep. We slept in the road, in the middle of the highway.

The Red Cross fed us and everything. We had eaten the military-ready food. Some trucks had, it was like, spaghetti and meatballs that was already fixed. And they had sandwiches, stuff like that. I tried, but I couldn't hold it in. But they gave me Gatorade; I had that. I drunk that pretty good.

I didn't get no sleep until I got to the I-10. I felt a little more at ease because I had seen the news out there, the Red Cross people out there, the sheriff's department out there. So I know nobody gonna really do us nothing. But at the Superdome, I wasn't tryin' to sleep.

That night, three hundred school buses came from Baton Rouge and Lafayette. I was listening to the radio. And they took a lot of people to shelters in those areas. It was three hundred buses lined up, so that's a long stretch. So then when we came over, we asked to find out where we're standing, but we still wasn't allowed to get on those buses because they were supposed to keep going and pick up the people in the front of the line that was like three or four miles ahead of us. But the door's open and we got on the bus because we still wanna leave too. And the deputy made us get off the bus, and we got off the bus.

And no more buses came. So all night, we're like, "No bus gon' come out." And they're like, "They'll have more buses comin'. They're comin'." But that's just to keep us calm, you know? But they didn't have more comin' so we had to spend the night out there.

KALAMU YA SALAAM

I'm in Houston watching the news and I'm putting things together based on what was reported, and also what wasn't reported. Tuesday was bad, and we expected Wednesday to be a little bit better, but Wednesday was worse than Tuesday. Thursday, things were even worse than Wednesday.

The troops did not come into the city until Friday afternoon. I figured out what the problem was. They waited until they had enough troops so they could come in and apply the whole "Shock and Awe" routine and take the city back. They needed 30,000 armed troops with weapons at the ready. They didn't feel they could do it with two or three thousand. And they couldn't get what they felt was significant firepower here until Friday.

Within two days after the troops arrived, the Superdome and the Convention Center were all cleared out. People were forced out by gunpoint. People think that the rescue mission was not a military mission, but this was a military operation. People with guns telling you what to do, when to do it, where to stand, what not to do. Everywhere.

RHONDA SYLVESTER

When everybody on the interstate finally got on the bus, they went to sleep. Everybody was quiet. They was tired. The bus we was on, they stopped and some people were able to buy some food and some people didn't have any money to buy any food.

They really had people lookin' out for each other. They had different restaurants where we stopped at, like Burger King, Popeye's. They had a truck stop and I don't know how, but they had found out that we was from New Orleans, and some people just come and buy people food, or the food place would give so much food away just to feed the people. They was real nice.

Then when we got to Houston, the buses had to line up. There was like a two-hour process because they had to register everybody on the bus. You had to get this bracelet. It was like two hours for us before our turn. The Astrodome time, that was hard. When we walked in, I had got this vibe. They had so many people and less space. And they said that they was gonna close because they didn't have enough room for any more people.

They check you in and get all your information. They tell you go take a shower, but they didn't have no towels, no clothes to give you, and they didn't have no more mattresses. They had ran out of mattresses. My son was in there. The two kids were sleeping on a rollaway bed. They had got there in the wee hours because they had left before me. I said, "Where y'all sleep at?"

He said, "We sleep on the floor."

They had covers for 'em but they didn't have more mattresses. And when we got there they said somebody had got raped in the bathroom in the Reliant Center. They had a raper man around there, so we left.

I left them there and told 'em that morning I'd be back to get 'em. We went over to the Motel 6 on 34th Street. My sister paid five hundred and something dollars for two rooms for a week. The next day, we went and got them and we all stayed. We all slept in two rooms. It was my sister, my sister's three kids, her three grandkids, her and her husband, me, my boyfriend, my two grandkids, and my daughter and my son.

Everybody got along pretty good 'cause we be the type. We're a close-knitted family so we always have looked out for each other.

PATRICIA THOMPSON

We were picked up that Friday night from my house. It was my grandbabies, that actually got the attention of the people flying overhead. We had tried to flag them so much, we had just given up. For about a week, we had been going out trying to be rescued with no luck.

So one night, we were all sitting in the house. Everybody was tired, everybody was dirty, everybody was disgusted, and tempers were flaring. Everybody's just sitting on the floor in the dark, we don't know what to do. And the next thing we knew, my grandbaby Bailey—at that time Bailey was five years old—and another grandson, Charles Parker, were on the porch. One had a flashlight, the other one had this white cloth, and these kids were yelling, and flashing the lights, and waving the cloth, and before we knew it the 'copter was blowing things off the wall. It was like pandemonium. But this was a welcome sound. The kids had actually got that 'copter down.

They had to make two trips to get all twenty-two of us out, and from there we were brought to the causeway. We were airlifted in baskets. Once we got to the causeway, we still weren't rescued that night; we were rescued around six o'clock the next morning.

On the causeway, we had to sleep on the street again. It had almost got to be commonplace by that time. Early the next morning is when the buses started coming in. You still was going through all kind of havoc and hullabaloo because everybody was trying to get to safety. Everybody was trying to get on a bus.

SONYA HERNANDEZ

My husband came five days later when we was in the Superdome. In the storm he stayed home. He had said, "I'm not going nowhere. You go with the kids. You leave me alone." He got two half brothers. They're his brothers on his daddy's side. In New Orleans, I was living on Villere, and his brothers, they was living two blocks from my house. They was having a battery TV, and they was watching on the news what was going on. When my daughter Maria got out of the Superdome to look for her daddy, they come. They come with him and all that to the Superdome and we all left together on the same bus.

They bring us in the bus all the way to Texas. When we got to Texas, we was denied. They was having a lot of people already. We went to Dallas. They don't want us. We going to the Astrodome, they don't want us. We not even get out of the buses. We was in the bus for twenty-three hours.

I think the governor of Texas, he talked to the governor from Oklahoma and asked him for help. They stopped the buses and they come inside the bus and they explain to us that the government of Texas, they don't got no more room so we was going to Oklahoma. And believe it or not, the people from Oklahoma, they was very concerned. But they said we're going stop every two or three hours 'cause they got churches and people in different places of half of Texas and in Oklahoma, and they was already waiting for us. They got food, hot food. They got clothes. They got hygiene things. Full of water. They was worrying about, they really was worrying about the little kids. They was giving the kids toys, and diapers, and formula, and little baby clothes, stuff like that.

Two people died on the six buses. Two of the people, two old people died. One lady died I think from the asthma. Another man, they said he died in his sleep. He was sick or something.

When we got to Camp Gruber they stopped all the buses. Before we get out, they come inside the bus and the men say we was inside a military base, and this is like a federal territory and everything. First they say, "If anybody is sick before we search you and all that, we want to know if anybody got any health conditions so we can move them off first 'cause there's two people died already.

"If you guys think you got something wrong, we're not going to prosecute you guys for this if you leave it in the bus. If you bring it and we search you and you got it, you're going to jail."

I feel like we was in jail. We was about to enter jail—a prison or something. I think it was like a prison entrance. They was talking nicely, but at the same time they was being mean. My kids, they was like, "What's going on?" So my husband looked at me, and I looked at him, and then his brothers, they was sitting in front of us and they looked back like, "What really's going on here?"

Finally, when we got off the buses, they make us pass through the military tent, and then we have to take everything off, not the clothes but, like, if we got jewelry and stuff. Like when you go on the airplane, that's exactly what they did. Take your shoes off and all that. A shakedown. And then after that, like I told you, they was speaking nice but they was being mean at the same time. They was saying, "If you guys cooperate with this, soon as you guys finish we're going let you talk to the Red Cross people and they going help you, and they going bring you guys to your dormitory."

The dormitory was a military dormitory and we was lucky the first day 'cause they put all my family in one room. I think it was like thirty individual beds in each room. So they put my family of eleven people in one room. I was real happy about that because they had everybody all over the place in there and you didn't know who to trust.

ABDULRAHMAN ZEITOUN

I'm in the canoe every day. I leave my house. I don't want stay in my house. When I leave my house with the canoe, make me feel relaxed. It just make me forget about, you know. Friday, I go make phone calls. I got a couple calls to go check on houses for friends.

One professor, he's my neighbor where I live, and it happened his wife was my wife's really good friend, and he called me about checking up on his house. Him and his wife wanted to check on his house and I said, "Okay, I'll go."

Friday, I go to Tulane University and what I did, just I come there to get idea of what's going on in the place. And I walk around and I see a few trees inside the yard. They have Spanish tile; some of them were gone. I mean, I got idea what I want to tell him. To give him what he wants to know.

And when I walking around, this guy Nasser come out. I said, "Whatcha doing here?"

He said, "I come here to visit someone. I stuck here, I can't go anywhere."

Nasser was supposed to speak to someone there. In '95, '96, he come to the city and he start working here and going back home to Syria, back and forth, and he worked with me for a couple times. He worked with me like a painter. It happened he's by the university. I go to check the fraternity, and it happened he's there.

I said, "Okay, you wanna stay here?"

He said, "I want to leave."

I said, "Okay, let's go." From there we left.

And really, I stopped a couple places like by the post office, by St. John, and Orleans, and I saw helicopters lifting people out, take them to places to leave the city. And I said, "You want to leave now? I can take you there now."

He said, "Not now."

My neighbor actually from three houses away, I am passing by and I see him call me, asking for help. I said, "I'll try to get you some help."

He asked me if I have any water. I did, I have like maybe half case. I gave it to him.

My way back, I see a man with this one old lady sitting on the porch. And he called me with my name because he know me. I usually stop by and say hello to him. And sometimes he needs some help, and I help him. And he said, "I need to get out of here. I need somebody to help." I said, "Look, I know. I can't get you in my boat, or I would."

I went about fourteen blocks to where there's a hospital. When I got to the hospital, I see like a few military guys there in the front alleyway in the front of the hospital, all of them with guns. When I come across them, they're, like, ready to shoot. There was this very unfriendly, very rude guy there. And I spoke to him and he tell me, "We can't help you. You have to go to St. Charles."

I said, "Why not call somebody?"

He said, "We can't call nobody."

I said, "How come?" He talked at me like he's scared of me. I don't know how to explain it.

Really, I expect from them to offer to help. I believe these guys in the city to help. I see boats back and forth. I come there. If I know these people are not for this purpose there, I never go to them. I mean like if you're drowning and someone, he say, "He want to save you, give him your hand," and he never take your hand, how you feel about it?

If it's my enemy, he asks for my help, I will give him my help. At this time, nobody looks for who you are or what's your background. Doesn't matter who. This is how we feel.

I left and go back to the guy's house, up to Napoleon and St. Charles. Take me at least half-hour, because with the wind. It was raining; I make it there with the canoe. I see a few people who work for Red Cross, and one guy, he asked if I need help. He said, "Go to this guy," and I go to him. He's the one helped me. And I told him I have an old man.

He said, "Okay, give me his name."

I give the address, his name. He write down in his pocketbook, notebook in his pocket. I said, "When you go?" He said, "Like an hour." It's early, before noon. Believe me, I trust them. When someone wants this kind of work, I believe he go do it. This coming from government. It's something serious.

When I come back, and I go to the neighbor, he's still there. He's in a wheelchair, you know. He can't use his legs at all. I feel very bad. He's sitting on the porch with the rain, waiting for the help to come.

FATHER VIEN THE NGUYEN

So the next morning, we were still waiting for help to come to the church. I told the man with the invalid wife that if people come, just tell them I'm on my way out, and I'll be back. Mr. Tuoc and I went out to find the men whose families had called the night before. We found one man, the man whose wife had called.

The man was inside his house. He had lost his job six months, eight months ago, and he was so depressed he didn't want to leave. I went in, and I told him, I said, "Your wife and your children are looking for you. They were crying all night, last night, calling me. So let's go."

He didn't want to go. I coaxed him into going. He asked me what did he need. And I said, "Just bring your papers, and leave everything else behind."

And so we got the papers, put him on the boat. And my thought was because all of my people had evacuated, I could get some pictures so they would know the condition of their home. So I said, "Well, let's go around and take some pictures," just so that when we evacuate, people would be able to see their homes and community. So I took pictures of the houses, the streets, the level of flooding, all of that.

By the time we came back, it was about, I guess it was about ten, eleven a.m. when we returned, and I remember looking and seeing the husband of the invalid woman. He said, "Father, I don't think anyone is coming to rescue us." And he looked totally dejected. So I said, "Don't lose hope yet. Let me make another call."

I called Texas again and conveyed the need to the representative. I heard some motors going outside, so I went out. There was a boat coming in to rescue us. And so we went out and I said, "Well, thank God I called the Texas representative. That's why you were here."

This guy said, "No that wasn't why we were here." These two guys were from Lafayette. They came with their flat-bottom boats, and they had been rescuing at other places for several days, from the very beginning until then. They had run into a deputy sheriff from Jefferson Parish. His home was on this side of the city, so he jumped on with them, and they came down this way.

It wasn't because of the state representative, nor the state troopers, nothing. Just by accident. I mean, eventually we would have been rescued anyway.

So they brought the woman out to their trucks waiting on the highway. There was no ambulance, so they waited, and they were putting ice on her, but she seemed more and more stressful. So we just opened up the truck bed and placed her on there. With her son holding the umbrella for her; they just took off to catch up with an ambulance. The man and his daughter stayed behind.

Now I wouldn't have minded going to the Convention Center to meet my people, but the only problem now is I would not be going up there alone. So the policeman asked the driver of the other truck where he was going. He said he was going home. Where was home? Lafayette.

So the officer said, "Can you take the pastor and these people with you?"

He said, "Sure, I can take them."

The man's wife is Catholic so his wife located the priest in Lafayette, and told him I was coming that way.

I remember passing through Chef highway. There were still people walking around, just looking dazed. I'm talking about the victims. And they're just dazed and the devastation was just tremendous. I saw the buildings collapsed. And as I was passing by, a house had burned down but the fire was still going at full blast from the gas-line pipe, and the man who was with me said, "That's one of our parishioners' house." And I didn't have a chance to take a picture. I couldn't because I was sitting on the other side of the truck.

We arrived in Lafayette close to midnight. I took a shower. I was joking with the priest because it was a week before that I took a bath. I told the pastor—I was joking—I said, "Man, I almost drowned in there."

He said, "What happened?"

I said, "Hadn't taken a bath for so long, didn't know how to do it."

SATURDAY, SEPTEMBER 3

• *After touring the New Orleans area, President Bush addresses the Katrina crisis from the Rose Garden, pledging an additional seven thousand troops to aid the cause.*

• *Louisiana's Office of Homeland Security reports that approximately two thousand people remain in the Superdome. Buses are diverted to the Convention Center where almost twenty-five thousand people remain.*

• *Governor Blanco declines a federal takeover of the Louisiana National Guard, thus also prohibiting active-duty troops from entering New Orleans.*

RENEE MARTIN

It was Saturday and I was listening to the radio and they had five hundred tour buses coming from Houston. They was parked a couple of miles away from where I was on I-10, but they was waiting for the okay to come through. But the bus driver said they stood there overnight, all that time. And they didn't get the okay to come through, so they didn't get the okay till that morning. And it was like six, close to seven o'clock in the morning.

They only allowed ten of them in. I was on bus number six. But there was so much pushing and shoving, Lord, it was hard to get on the bus. But I was determined. I wasn't gonna get left again and spend another night out here. So they let us on the bus, and ten buses loaded up and started out down I-10 coming to Houston.

Oh, it was comfortable. We had a bathroom on there, and the bus driver was real nice. He talked to us. I was right in the front, the first seat by the door. I was the lady waving on CNN news. I was relaxed. I was so relaxed because I felt like the closer we get to Houston, the more I'm out of danger because I thought that the military in New Orleans would kill us. I believe that. And then, also when I was on the I-10, I know that it was still flooding, and I thought if we stay out there another night, we all gonna die in the water. It was scary all the way until I saw "Welcome to the State of Texas."

We came up to the Astrodome, and when we got off the bus, we had to get off the bus one bus at a time because we had to register and they had to give us a wrist-band, and a serial number, stuff like that. And we had to go through medical and all that.

It went smooth. It was just so many people. We had to wait for our time, but it went good because all you have to do is tell them who you are, where you're from, what kind of problems you have, what kind of medications you take and they were there. It went real good.

They allowed us to take showers, eat, all of that, gave us clothes, gave the children toys, little portable baby things, blankets, pillows, everything. It was like a parade. It was like, "Over here!" "Throw me that!" And I couldn't get nothing. There was so many people, and when they throw it, if somebody on the side of you, they jump and they grabbed it. So I didn't get any clothes, but I had toiletries. And I went upstairs and I got me something to eat. It didn't make any sense to take a shower. I had no clothes. But the next day I was up early 'cause I didn't go to sleep. I hurried up and got over there, and got me something to put on. And it was too big but it was clean. And I took me a shower.

They had thirty showers, all in one room, and we have to share that with twenty-nine other women. It wasn't too cool, but you didn't really care. You wanted to get clean. I wanted to wash my hair. My clothes was dirty. I took a shower, put on the clothes I had got, and I spent a lot of my time sitting outside the Astrodome. A lot of us was sitting outside because we wanted to see who was gonna get off the next bus because a lot of us was displaced from families and friends and stuff. So we were looking for our family and friends, and all that time I still didn't find nobody. I didn't find nobody till I left the Astrodome.

PATRICIA THOMPSON

Saturday morning is when we finally got on a bus. With all the pushing and shoving going on on the causeway, we were split up on different buses. The twenty-one people that were with me went to three different parts of Texas. I remember when we all finally got on the bus, I remember looking out the window and saying, "Lord, where to now?"

My grandbaby that was like four months old got sick. College Station had the best facilities to treat the babies so their bus came to College Station, Texas. Me, my third oldest daughter, her husband, her three children, and my youngest daughter, Ariel, went to New Boston, Texas. My oldest daughter and her family were in another part of Texas.

They were asking us in New Boston if we wanted to relocate because we had already been told that the lights would be off in New Orleans for at least thirty days. So I'm like, "I don't know, and I'm not making a decision until I get back in touch with my family members because we are a very close-knit family. And all my kids have is me. I don't have a husband, and they're not in constant contact with their father. I'm all they got." I'm like, "I'm not making a decision until I get together with my kids. Y'all can either bring them here, send me where they are."

So what they did, they sent us all to College Station. Once we got up here, we were all taken to a place called Christ United Methodist Church. One of these ladies' husband, Gene, had some real estate. Gene took us around to a few of his houses, and said if we liked what we'd seen, he'd give us the key without money, without even getting the first dollar from FEMA. God bless this man. He just gave us the keys, and he just waited for us to get FEMA money. Most of Gene's houses were $550 a month, and he lowered the rent to $400 a month. He gave us those keys and just told us to get back with him once we got the FEMA money up and running. He gave us time. He was true to his word.

ABDULRAHMAN ZEITOUN

Saturday I brought my tenants and my friends to my house to have barbecue. I have a flat roof, and I brought my charcoal. My wife, she had left everything in the freezer, and we started cooking before it started melting. She had fish, she had shrimp there, had chicken, all kinds of stuff. I tried to cook all of them. I cook how much I can, how much fire I have. I have all the friends, the one I brought from the University, Nasser. He eat with us.

I have my tenant, and I had my neighbor next door. She have a German shepherd dog, we saved it. She left behind. I'm going there to feed 'em and I saw her in the water just holding on for her life in the tree. I found her up there. Very happy when I found her. She was soaking wet. Really, I feel very good. She come all the way here to the house to get her dog, and then she's very, very happy to see her dog, and believe it or not, her dog very happy to see her.

I give the guys to take away home with them, and also I have neighbors who refuse to come, and I sent them plates to go. And also, next morning, I feed the dog.

That same night we have the fire. One whole block caught on fire. Talking about around eight o'clock at night. The fire made the whole area light. Very strong fire, maybe six houses in the fire, almost a full block. I saw the fire because I have my office building, my warehouse next to the fire exactly. And I have one idea in my head: in my store, my warehouse, I have my paint supplies, my shoes, my office there, all my work supplies.

I go there with the boat. My tenant, he comes with his boat and we go there. And I go there and circle the place. And really when we were there, I have one lady, her house across the street from the fire, and the people screaming to help her. We tried to help her—we don't want to go through the fire to go to her house—but somebody come before us.

There was a very beautiful house in the corner. A few years ago, I was supposed to buy a house in the middle of the block. All of them, all of them burned to the ground. It's very sad. And also the fire station two blocks away. No engine there. Nothing. Empty.

I feel like I'm lucky, and at same time I feel sad about that. You feel like you're okay, although you see somebody else is not.

SUNDAY, SEPTEMBER 4

• *FEMA announces that the Superdome and Convention Center are completely evacuated. They anticipate more evacuees will arrive, but they will be bused out as they come.*

• *Patients from the top twelve New Orleans hospritals have been evacuated to 563 shelters in ten states.*

• *All told, approximately 42,000 residents have been evacuated from New Orleans.*

• *New Orleans police kill at least five New Orleans residents on the Danziger Bridge after those residents opened fire on government contractors hired to repair the 17th Street Canal.*

DANIEL FINNIGAN

On the seventh day, the first cops that we saw came through. They were driving slow with the blowhorn, saying it's a mandatory evacuation and to proceed to the school yard for an immediate airlift out of the neighborhood. So of course I flagged them down, stopped and said, "What's up? What are you guys doing?"

They said, "Man, your city's dead. You have to leave. You have to leave. Your city's dead." And, you know, that hurts.

There were five people in my house. I think it'd almost be better to go through something like that alone because you'd only have your own fears to deal with. But when you have five people, then you have their fears to deal with, and then you have the fears of the people up the street to deal with. And I think all that kind of feeds off of itself, and it's easily overblown, and that's where panic is born. And I'm not saying that we panicked. Panic is when you let your own fears scare you, you know? It's okay to be afraid, but don't be scared. Everybody was an adult, and everybody was cool, but everybody handled their fears in a different way.

It's strange now because with every day that I move past this, some of the behavior seems more absurd. Why was that so scary? Why was I trippin' so bad? You second-guess yourself. Was that really necessary?

Did I need to do that? Did I really need to do that? Why did I do that? But there are also things that I know I did right.

The main thing is, there was no way I was leaving my dog Blue. Not a chance. I would have handcuffed myself to him if I had to. There was just not a chance I was leaving him. And there was really no reason why I needed to. I was on dry land. I didn't need to be rescued; I just needed the people around me to be helped. That's what I needed and that's what they needed. I was doing okay.

DAN BRIGHT

I was on the Hunt Correctional Facility field for four days, from Thursday until Sunday. The buses was coming in and out every day, gettin' guys, bringing them to other facilities, places. That's how I wound up at Rapides Parish Prison in Alexandria, Louisiana.

They're taking so many of us off the field, bringin' us to other prisons around the state. Wherever, however you got in the line, that's where the buses was going at. Everybody would line up and just get on those buses. No one knew.

They put us in a dormitory, maybe like fifty guys. They did feed us better, much better, but it's very small portions so you're still hungry. We didn't eat solid food in, what, eight to ten days, so the little food they're feeding us we appreciate it, but it's not enough. And you have to remember, these prisons already have inmates in there, who live in this parish, so they still have to take care of the regular inmates. So now they're not gon' take food out their mouths and give it to us. So we gotta get the scraps.

I was in Alexandria a month. A month, month and a half. You know, this is all confusing. I'm still in a daze. You have to remember, I'm confused, I'm angry. I had not been convicted of anything. I was exonerated from death row. It's like a nightmare.

As soon as I got to Alexandria, when they find out who I was

I was singled out. They were trying to put me in isolation 'cause they didn't want me around nobody else. I had been on death row so I'm being picked on, and beat, and cursed out. They right here in my face screaming and hollering. They called me nigger, city slicker, killer, death-row killer, all kind of stuff, man. I was sent to the hole.

In fact, some of them thought I was still on death row. Now how can I be on death row and I'm in here? So man, it was all kind of stuff going on.

FATHER JEROME LeDOUX

Sunday, none of my parishioners were there at Mass time, which was usually ten o'clock, so I was in the kitchen fussing around with something, probably barley green and something else, and two ladies called me. I could hear them calling so I said, "Hold on," dried my hands, ran out.

"Father, we want you to pray with us." Of course this is shortly before the usual Mass time. I said, "Well, give me a few minutes and I'll be right back," and I ran back to the kitchen and got that straightened out and went back, and by the time I got back to the front door of the rectory, not only were the two ladies there, there might have been a total of a baker's dozen or so people out there. So I greeted them, walked right past towards the church, unlocked the church. They knew to follow me, and some were sitting in the regular part of the church, I sat at the piano stool, opened up the piano, and I motioned for them to come and sit where the choir usually sits. So they all sat there, and when they were all settled, I began to play "Amazing Grace."

Wherever there is something—you heard it after 9/11 for instance; it was prominent there. You hear it at the funeral of great people. I call "Amazing Grace" the National Anthem of Mourners and Victims of Tragedy. After the final verse I thought a minute. I was about to lead them in prayer, and I held back and I said, "At this time I'm sure you have a prayer in your hearts." And one by one they just prayed, and I call it the most magnetic, the most riveting church service I've ever conducted. Everybody was deadly serious and so very thankful, and so very beseeching of God's mercy, and, well, you could tell this was not a regular Sunday service group. I sort of estimate, looking over the group, that a number of them had not darkened the threshold of the church in quite a while, and you could tell they did not know exactly what to do. Then one got up, shook my hands, then walked out, one man; then a second man got up, shook my hands, walked, and just as mysteriously as they made the scene, they faded off back into the morning, very quietly.

THE WEEK AFTER

[MONDAY, SEPTEMBER 5 – SUNDAY, SEPTEMBER 11]

• *Monday: The breach in the 17th Street Canal levee is repaired.*

• *Tuesday: Mayor Nagin orders that all people remaining in the city should be evacuated, by force if necessary.*

• *Wednesday: FEMA begins distributing $2,000 to each family affected by the storm.*

• *Thursday: Questions surface about the credibility of FEMA director Michael Brown's resumé.*

• *Friday: Secretary of Homeland Security Michael Chertoff removes Michael Brown as manager of the Katrina relief effort. A week later, Brown resigns as head of FEMA.*

DANIEL FINNIGAN

It was Labor Day Monday.

Well, at that point it was pretty much a skeleton crew. Just about everybody had left. It went from maybe forty people in the neighborhood to about ten, if that. It was really a ghost neighborhood.

Somebody, I think his name is David Thoreau, he had been coming by and hanging out with us up here on the porch, and he had two vehicles. He offered me a ride out with all my animals, so I took it. We were afraid that it was going to be a situation where they were going to come and arrest people and forcibly evacuate you from the neighborhood. And there were actually some cases where that did happen, so I wasn't going to take the chance of being forcibly evacuated and having to leave the animals behind, so I took the ride.

I fed all of the animals. I knew that if they were forcibly taking people out, saying mandatory evacuation, that you have to go, then they're obviously not gonna be letting people back in. That was clear. You had animals trapped in yards who had to be let go, so I let them go. And I own up to that, full-on. I hope the owners of those animals understand that that's why I did it. Because the SPCA [Society for the Prevention of Cruelty to Animals] and the Humane Society weren't allowed in for three weeks. Your pets wouldn't have made it had I not freed them. I hope you can get them back somehow. But, you know, I hope that you understand that that's why I broke into your house and let your dog out.

I had a guy who pointed a gun at me. Well, he didn't point it; he pulled it out and said, "What the fuck are you doing?"

I said, "I'm going in there to feed that dog. There's a dog trapped in that house. I'm going in there to feed him and let him go."

And once he understood what I was doing, he said, "Okay, that's cool," and he let me go ahead and do it. I almost had to leave one dog behind because it was just too heavily fortified. At the last minute— I was leaving in, like, an hour—I went back over there, and I had to break into the house so the dog could get out. I crawled through fire ants and got all bit up, but it made me very happy that I was able to do that because it was something that was bothering me that that was being left. So once I did that, once I was able to wrap up that one loose end, then I was able to leave and feel okay about leaving.

I hadn't slept in a week. An hour a night maybe. You know, you would just stay awake until you just physically couldn't keep your eyes open, and you'd basically pass out for an hour and get up. You weren't eating. You couldn't really eat. It was definitely a place to leave at that point. But 49 percent of me really wanted to stay because I had plenty of provisions. I had provisions for five people, and because four of my housemates left, they left me all of the provisions. And so I was doing fine in those regards. And there are a few people who actually did stay. But I didn't want to take the chance.

Dave took me to just outside of Gonzales, Louisiana, where Andrea Garland and Jeffrey Holmes, my good friends, came and picked me up and took me to a Red Cross shelter where we set up tents and camped with the animals. Andrea and Jeff were big on the relief effort thing because they had evacuated, so they raised a lot of money. They were trying to come back into the city to bring supplies and things like that to people who weren't able to get out.

At first, it was weird. It was a whole different kind of chaos.

I thought I was gonna be leaving for peace and quiet, and chill out, but it was a smaller shelter, and it was also a staging area for grass-roots relief effort. You had the Veterans for Peace staging there, you had various other grassroots people staging there, bring supplies, doing this and that. You know, making runs into the city, relief runs, and so that was kind of a hectic thing. We kind of squared away a little camp off in the corner. Andrea and Jeffrey knew I needed some solitude.

Impostors started showing up. On the third night over there, some guy showed up saying he was a nurse. I got a bad vibe on him. He's wearing scrubs, and turns out, later that night, the marshals come into my camp and arrest him and take him away. To his own credit, just to be fair, he hadn't ever been convicted or anything. But he had six priors for child molestation. I mean, in situations like this, you know that impostors are pulling out the stops. If you weren't one, then all good to you. But if you were one, then fuck you.

And then Andrea and Jeffrey were in the city, and they come back and they get jacked up 'cause they were seen giving this guy, the impostor, a ride somewhere. So they were like, "Are you friends with this guy? What's up? Are you in league with him? Blah blah blah." So they just had to straighten that out and it was fine. But at that point I was a little scared. Like, what is this madness? What did I leave for? I had cops in my camp all day that day. Why are there all these cops in my evacuation camp, and there were none in my neighborhood? I don't understand this.

FATHER JEROME LeDOUX

For a week I had no electricity, had no running water at St. Augustine, so I would not flush the toilet until the last thing in the day, and the last thing in the day I took one of these plastic buckets, Tidy Cats buckets, would go down to the goldfish pond, scoop up a bucket, and do my daily flush, making sure I didn't catch one of the goldfish.

I had to do whatever I had to do before dark. After dark I just had the two big vigil lights from the church, and couldn't do too much, didn't want to read or anything. And then of course, being the vegan I am, I had a lot of tomatoes on hand. Nature supplied me with first one bunch of bananas—our banana trees bloomed and bore just at the time of the hurricane—and before I left there were two other bunches that got ripe during the ensuing week. I had my whole-grain pasta stashed away. I was living like a Mafia don. Because I still had gas, before it got dark I would do some pasta marinara. I said, "Boy, I haven't eaten this well in a long time!" Because usually I'm running around like crazy. I've cooked as late as nine and ten o'clock at night, which is not good but sometimes you get mixed up. But this time I had my leisure, I just cooked when I knew I had to cook, before dark, so I was eating well, living well, and just checking with the neighbors.

The police were frequent visitors, daily visitors. The police wanted to make sure there were no looters around, wanted to make sure I was the one who belonged there, not somebody else, not an interloper. They would come by daily—the municipal police, the state police, the National Guard, and finally we had those awesome people out of North Carolina, the 82nd Airborne. These guys, any criminals around would have to run out of town just to see them. They had combat fatigues, combat boots, they had their red beret, and right here they cradled their M-16s, and I asked one big guy, about 6'3", I asked, "Did you serve overseas?"

He said, "These younger fellows, most of them, had not served overseas. I served in Afghanistan and Iraq."

I said to myself, concerning the thugs, "You better look out, you don't fool with these people!"

By the seventh day, which was the Monday after that fateful

Monday, August 29, the police had come by every day, and they kept telling me, "You know, we think you should leave." Of course they knew who I was, kept telling me as if about to strong-arm me, "We think you should go. There's a danger of the water, the waters are polluted."

So on the seventh day I'm computing all this, thinking back and forth, and I'm realizing all the while, my relatives don't know where I am. Nobody knew because there was no communication going out and nothing coming in so I'm thinking it's about time to let people know I'm okay. And furthermore these police wanted me out of here, so on the seventh day I decided to leave.

On the morning of the eighth day I began to get my things together in the house, the things I wanted to take with me, the rest I would just lock up. And by this time I figured maybe the police would have things in hand, although they really did not.

I would have survived very well where I was. All I needed was the tomatoes and the olive oil, the pasta, the apples, stuff like that, the water. But anyway, I figured out what I wanted to take with me, and by late morning I began to put items into the trunk of my car, and then by midafternoon I was almost ready to load up the heavy stuff like the computer and stuff like that. Right around three o'clock, I was taking my last look around at everything, making sure the power was off everywhere—the church, the rectory, the hall—and double-checked everything. About 4:30 I spoke to the caretaker and his brother, and fired the car up. Of course there's no water out there at all, wind damage, a little bit, made a right on Decatur, just moving along slowly straight up Governor Nicholls, then right, and carefully and making sure that the police could see who I was. I made sure I had my collar on.

The police were omnipresent but not in places like the Lower Nine. Well, they still had water—the east, the Lower Nine, the Upper Nine, Lakeview, all these places still had water. I could see, as you went toward Claiborne, you had some issues with water, and the Superdome would have been over that way and a little to the south, so I kept on Decatur across Canal. I can remember on the left was the Morial Convention Center, and there were lawn chairs, just these folding chairs everywhere. You had to imagine thousands of people having been there for many, many days, for a whole week, and by this time they were all in the Dome or evacuated, so I just saw litter and litter and more of it.

I was very angry. See, at any given moment, you had a staging area possible on the West Bank. There was no water there. How many buses do we have in the United States? How many hundreds? Let's say the presidential family and retinue just happened to be in the area, and got trapped into such an environment. I don't know how different it would have been but I bet the whole hacienda and the whole ranch that it would not have been even close to the same. They would've gone beyond hell and high water, literally, to change things. The military would be out. They have sea planes, they have all kinds of hovercraft and seacraft, amphibious craft. Everyone would have been gone from New Orleans.

When I got to La Place, I got down and made my telephone calls, told my relatives where I was.[12] They all breathed a sigh of relief; many of them thought I was gone. Many of my friends thought I was gone. They thought I was on the second floor of the rectory surrounded by eight or ten feet of water, had to be plucked out by the coast guard or somebody, National Guard in helicopters, but I allayed their fears.

I went to Baton Rouge, just holed up in Baton Rouge, did not really bother with church authorities. I guess I should have been more in touch but they sounded so discombobulated, and I said, I think what I need is a break, which is what I took.

---

[12] La Place is a suburb of New Orleans, located to the west of the city.

I didn't even think of celebrating Mass anywhere. On Sunday, I put a sport shirt on, and I went to the church almost at the farthest point from where I was. And every Sunday, I would just go over and just sit back and just enjoyed being a plain, lay person and listening to the Sunday sermon, throwing a few dollars in.

I had this time and it's God-given time in a way. I've been doing a book on the history of St. Augustine Church in Tremé, so I figured, "I'll go in for the kill." I said, "I will finish this," and I finished the book. There was only one problem. After I finished the book, somebody wrote a last chapter to the book. Archbishop Hughes decided there has to be one last chapter to the book, so he wrote it.

RENEE MARTIN

When I left the Houston Astrodome, it was Tuesday, September 6. I had left by myself because other days, everybody was walking and trying to get apartments and stuff like that, and it's very hard when it's two, three hundred people, and they're only giving out maybe a hundred apartments. So I went by myself and caught the bus and wind up down here at West Oaks Nursing Home in Houston. I went there and I told them I was down from New Orleans, and do they have any job openings. And the girl said, "I believe they do have a opening in housekeeping."

I said, "Well, I have my CNA [Clinical Nursing Assistant] license, and I'm hoping to do something with that."

She said, "Well, I don't think they have any openings right now in that. We can give you a call."

I'm like, "Ma'am, I will take the housekeeping right now because I live in the Astrodome."

She was like, "Wait a minute, let me call a supervisor."

And she did, and she came, the supervisor came. She said, "Can you be here at six in the morning?"

I said, "Better than that, I'll just stay here till six in the morning. I don't have nowhere to go." So they talked to the administrator and she offered me to stay at her place, and then other people's coming in, and everybody wanted to see who I was. Everybody wanted to take me to their house. Even the owners of the facility, they came. They wanted to meet the lady from New Orleans. It was something.

But what had happened is that the administrator and the accountant, she said, "Well, she needs a place, an apartment, that she can get to work," which was true because they had hired me. Her name is Darcy. She's real cool. And the accountant, her name is Jenny. So they had some apartments right across the street from my job. They gave me a check to go pay for this apartment, and I got it the same day. I went in there, and I took a bath. Ohhh, I went to sleep that night. I slept so good. I actually slept.

It had carpet, and nobody was there but me. I didn't have to worry about getting raped or getting beat up while I'm asleep. Nobody's stealing from me. And I slept so good. And I got up that morning, I washed up and I put the same clothes back on. I went across the street to my job. They had bought me two uniforms. Two uniforms, and they brought me to Wal-Mart to buy some tennis shoes. So it feels nice.

They helped me way before I got assistance from FEMA. I didn't really have to get anything because my job. They paid my rental deposit, and then they helped me with my washer, dryer, dishes, pots, glasses, everything. Before I got my bed, they gave me a mattress, so I could get on the mattress and sleep. It felt so good. They're like family at my job, the people I work with. They've been real good. I came right from the Astrodome, went right in there and got a job. And from there, they helped me with everything else. And the dietician—her name is Mary—she used to see me every day. And then I was eating too. Oooooh. I was wearing a size three, and I'm wearing a size seven now.

They call me Katrina. "Hey, Katrina!" At work, they call me Katrina. It never bothers me. I would rather talk about it because I don't like to hold stuff in. I talk about it, but when I talk about it, we start cryin'. I'm like, "I didn't want to make you cry."

"But it's so sad," they say.

That's why they call me Katrina. Katrina at work. But it's okay.

I had started working on September 7. I used to cry, "I don't know where none of my family are. I'm all by myself." You know, you feel lonely when no one around. And then at times I was sad because when you wake up, and you in one place, and you wake up and you somewhere else, and you look at the reason why you're somewhere else is because of a catastrophe or whatever, it's like a nightmare. And you don't know where nobody at. It's hard. And if you gotta go to hell, you want somebody to be with you. You don't wanna go through all of that by yourself, but I had to. I didn't have nobody to cling to.

I had gone on the Internet at the Astrodome. The Red Cross put me on there, my name and stuff like that. And then when I moved out and got my job, I went over again and put more information like my name, my address, and phone number.

My birthday's on September 10. The nurses gave me a birthday party—I'd never had a birthday party before—and the hospital gave me that day off. When I got home, the phone rang. It was my sister. It was my older sister, and she said she was at the Drury Inn. And I'm like, I don't know where that is. And she said, "I was comin' to get you from the Astrodome 'cause I had heard you were in the Astrodome."

I said, "I was, but I'm not in there now. I'm in an apartment. My job's here."

She's like, "You got a job? You got an apartment?"

I said, "Yeah."

She said, "How'd you get a job and an apartment in the middle of all of this?"

I said, "Well, I do," I said, "but I'm off today. You can come get me?"

She said, "Yeah, but I have to get the address."

And she said she was gonna look for it, the directions, off the computer. She called me back, she said, "Come here. You're right down the street from me."

I said, "Is that true?" and I come to find out she was off Highway 6, right on the other side of I-10. And she came and got me. And when she came and got me, she had my mom, my grandson, my daughter, my nieces. And she had cake and ice cream. So they gave me a little party.

They opened the door, everybody like, "Surprise! Happy Birthday!" I just stood there, and I just cried. I was happy too at the same time. After we ate ice cream and cake, we had went to the Drury Inn on Highway 6. It was the whole family, and on my birthday.

And I'll never forget that birthday. I remember all those dates. Katrina was August 29, and the Superdome was September 4. Getting my job, September 7. And my birthday, and reuniting with my family, September 10.

RHONDA SYLVESTER

On Tuesday, about four days after we got to Houston and checked into a hotel, we looked for an apartment. They had everybody tellin' you you could get these rent-free apartments, no deposit.

My sister's son used to work for Budget Rent-a-Car in New Orleans, so they accommodated him. We had one car when we got out here. Everybody was lookin' for an apartment. I didn't have no money. I was waitin' on my paycheck to come in—we was supposed to get paid the week of the storm—so we didn't have no money.

We had found these apartments. They wanted $199 to move in. In the process of me goin' to move in, a man from Lazy Brook Baptist

Church in Houston called me on the phone, and I'll never forget his name: Abraham. He said, "Rhonda, I have an apartment complex that wanna give you and your relatives apartments free of rent for three months."

So I came over and come see the apartment. I filled out all the papers and the lady, she told me, "Well, you can move in Saturday."

She said I'm'a have the apartment so we moved in. They were so nice. They had gave us three beds. One full-size bed and two queen-size beds. Oh it's nice and quiet. It's a two-bedroom apartment, one-and-a-half bath, living room, kitchen, and a dining room, which is real nice and it's comfortable.

If we needed to go places, the church people used to come and get us and bring us to places. They welcome us in. They welcome us. And I didn't deal with different organizations; I just stuck with the church down there 'cause if I deal with other organizations that means I was gonna be knockin' somebody else. That organization could help somebody else. I just dealt with the church. Whatever they gave us, I accepted that down there. They used to give us ten dollars' worth of quarters a week to wash our laundry. Detergent, bleach. They really blessed us. Clothes unlimited for the kids.

It didn't matter to them what color we was. Believe it or not, we was the only black-American, African family that come close to them. It ain't that they didn't want to help nobody else. Nobody else didn't reach out to them. We reached out to them and they accepted us for who we was, and they're a very loving, Christian family there. Very supportive. And you can go to 'em for any problem, anything. You can go there and talk to them if you need to get on the computer, if you need to take care of business, they're 100 percent behind you. And they didn't even much know us. They didn't even much know our background; they didn't know nothing about us. But they accepted us. And that was, I believe, that was love. That was true love.

ABDULRAHMAN ZEITOUN

Monday, Labor Day, I went to do a favor for my client. He wants me to check on his house. And also, he had a cat loose where he lived. He said he couldn't find it. I got in my canoe and did my rounds. I go to the place and look over there. And I did go a different direction. I went to Napoleon, from like Fontainebleu all the way. The guy I brought from Tulane, Nasser, he used to live at Napoleon and Galvez, and we tried to see if he could get in to get some of his stuff. No luck. The water was up to the ceiling.

On Tuesday morning, I looked in on my other house to see what was there. I was with the same guy, Nasser. And also I have a cousin who lives in the area. On my way over there, it happened I meet a military boat and he saw me and asked me what I'm doing here. I said, "Checking. Trying to help."

He said, "Who do you work with?"

I said, "I work with anybody."

He had a reporter with him in the boat. I continued. I come to Canal Street, I crossed Canal. From Canal, I go to Jefferson Davis. I take left on Jefferson Davis, and I go all the way past Orleans in the canoe. I think probably a couple of miles. Sometimes you have to carry the canoe because we have overpass, like Jefferson Davis/Tulane area. You have to carry the canoe over the bridge. I never felt tired. When you have a idea in your head that you wanna do it, then you don't think about it.

I got to my house on Claiborne and when I got there the phone rang and it was my wife. I talked to her a few minutes. Then this guy Ronnie just stopped by to use the phone. After that, I go to the bathroom and I opened the water, I see water running. I jump in the shower right away. I take shower, and when I come out I tell Nasser, "Go ahead. Cleanse yourself because maybe the water will go off."

And he jumped in the shower too. And I go outside to use the phone again. I'm in the dining room making phone calls, and I hear Nasser talking to someone outside. Usually no one's there, and it was unusual to hear someone talking.

I said, "Who are you talking to?"

The military was asking him if we need any water. And I hear him say, "No we don't need any. We have enough." And these guys come in and jumped into the house. And I see the military walking in.

I hear, "Do you need any water?"

"No. Thank you, we have."

At this point, it was Nasser and the other guy, Ronnie.

The military boat continued coming closer. The boat's coming closer, and these guys, five, six military people, inside on the porch. They walked straight to the house, started looking around and came back. He said, "What you guys doing here?"

I said, "This is my house."

He said, "Give me ID." I got my ID and I gave it to him. Never looked at it, said, "Get in the boat."

Three of us in the house, and my tenant, Todd Gambino, it happened he's passing by. He has bad luck I think. It happens he's passing by. He sees the military, he wants to see what happened. He tries to tell them it's his house, he lives there.

He come and said, "It's my house. I live here," and said, "I'll give you proof. It's inside the house." They not let him go inside.

They said, "Get in the boat."

I start arguing with him. "Why?" I said.

One of them, a female soldier, she talking to someone. She told the guy, she said, "Bring him in." I don't know what she told the guys.

I said, "What's wrong?"

She said, "You talk to my boss."

If you know you'll get arrested, you try to get out of it. I don't have no reason to. If I know that, I would jump in the water. It doesn't matter what. I never let them arrest me because I know I never done anything to deserve this. And I had a chance to leave if I want to. I not see worse to get endangered for no reason, because I know I'm clean. I came to my house to talk to someone. The worst, tell us, "Leave the city."

We listened. They said, "Get in the boat," we go in the boat. And they brought us to St. Charles and Napoleon. We have impression to talk to someone there. Soon as we got there, we had a few guys jump on us and handcuff us with plastic ties. It doesn't matter how loose they are, it's just not comfortable. And also, we have a few reporters there start taking pictures. We got a van, like a military van. Nobody except our four guys. Me, Todd, and Nasser, and we have other guy—the lucky man, he stopped to use a phone, never saw him in my life.

We talked with one guy. He's not the one arrest us, the one who's there on St. Charles. He said, "We're from Indiana"—this is what he tell me—"we're doing our job."

I said, "Okay." He brought us to this bus station, processed us, took our fingerprints, and keep us for a long time. This was in common with the Taliban.

When they brought us to the bus station, we see something like overreacting. Like these guys have a catch, it feels like. A very high security. When I first see it, it reminded me of Guantánamo Bay. Exactly look like Guantánamo Bay. Nothing different. The way you have to sit, you have to sit open your legs. You can't relax. You can't sit on this chair, you have to sit a different way. And the one guy's watching us, every move. And I see something not normal.

We thought we would be a few hours or something. We stayed there three days. One of the guys called, "You guys are Taliban. You guys are terrorists."

And also we got a few government officials come in to us, get information, like Homeland Security guys. This guy works for air-ports, my tenant, and he usually got maps with him. My wife gives me the same thing, she gives me Mapquest maps. They tell you directions to different locations so it's easier to go there. This guy, he had job work for airports to deliver missing luggages. This is why he had a few of them. He have them with him, and have a mark where the luggage is going. And this guy starts asking, "What is this for?" The thing nothing to do with looting or stolen things. The way he asking about, you know, something else.

Nasser had the money he worked with for the time he been here. He has a briefcase. I never asked him what he have in there. Just his money, and he's going to take with him. Not my business what he has. And this maybe why he refused to go from any place when he had a couple option to—he want to be a safer place to leave. Anyway, the lady, when she takes the personal things when you go in jail, she opened the money, and she says, "This money not from here."

This why we are under questioning. Accusing us of something to do with loot.

They brought us in the cage. The cell we have, the first one's a larger one, close to the station, and the further you go under, smaller it get. They sometimes bring sandwiches, some other times bring military MREs. The sandwiches mostly come with ham. I'm not allowed to eat the meat. In my religion, we can't eat ham.

I had shorts and a T-shirt. You can't sit on the ground, you get greasy. Or you can't lay down, concrete. Also, the worst thing about it, we have a train I think using like generator, with a very loud noise next to us. I mean, you can't imagine how loud. It's like you're inside an engine. This thing running 24 hours, never stopped.

All four of us, they keep us separate. And the other cells have maybe fifty, sixty persons. We're all by ourselves. I mean, we asked each one of them what he's here for. All of them just like a joke. One of 'em walking down the street, they grabbed him. One guy he's moving his furniture from place to the other, he got grabbed. I talked to one guy. He got hit by police. The police hit him. He goes to file a complaint against the police, he got arrested.

The guards is very ugly people there. These people train to deal with the criminals, and you're there with him, count you like one of them. You there, you criminal. Doesn't matter who you are. I see things you can't believe it. We have one person, he's not stable, mentally retarded, inside the jail, next to us. And, like, he's hyper. He can't listen to someone. And they sprayed him with pepper a few times. I mean, this guy, he's not normal, and they're very ugly with him.

In the bus station, my foot started swelling. It started bother me to walk on it. It's swollen, like black spot on my foot. I talked to one of the security there in the jail. I said, "Look, I have something in my foot." I said, "Give me a needle or something I can take it out. I can do it."

He saw it, and he said, "Okay, I'll talk to the nurse."

And I said, "Okay."

And a few hours passed, I see him again, he said, "Okay, she will call you later." It passed all day and nobody. I feel like it wouldn't stop bothering me. And I feel like nobody care. I saw doctor passing by. Somebody called because with the crowd, too many people there, some kind of problem there. I see him go with the guy. On his way back, I tried to talk to him. When I called him back he said, "I'm not doctor," and he keep walking.

I said, "It's fine." When the lunch come and I see the glass come with the lunch, military lunch, I break it in half, I cut my foot with it. Take the splinter out. After that, better. I walk better.

Really, I never believed it could go this far. All I believe is some-body going talk to us, and at least, just let us go somewhere else. I mean, to leave the city, okay. They say, "You're under a disaster, you have to leave," we'll leave. I never believed this what going happen.

When the guy looked at my ID and he said, "Go on the boat." I see this guy, he have something in his mind.

We're asking the jail security people who work for jail, each one of them said "terrorist," other guy said "Taliban." We see that we're under special watch. Different from the others. This why keep us separate.

No phone calls allowed. I asked each one of them. I had to beg to any one of them. Just call my wife tell her I'm here, just to know that I'm okay. They said, "We can't do it." Ladies, men, anybody.

Three days, we don't know what we're at the bus station for.

Finally, on Friday they load us on the bus and take off. Each two guys together on the bus. Brought us to Baton Rouge.

They took us to Hunt Correctional Center. We got there and then they take us out and start process again. Take information, what you eat, whatever. Take information, allergic to any foods, what you can't eat. I mean, they ask the very nice question. All these questions just put on the paper, don't mean anything in there.

I expected at least let us use the phone. We're in, like, a established place. I know, like, New Orleans, first you get in phone, anybody, you have the right to use phone. Hunt like military base, really. It's not jail. Just military base in the middle of nowhere. All surrounded with wire. I mean a huge jail. This jail designed for criminals, for somebody already he got time. This place not designed for people to visit, to stay there a couple days.

First day, they brought us to one section. I mean, this jail designed in stages. First you be there to train you, then they start moving you to better. The worst place have small rooms. This room designed for one person, each room designed for one person. We've got four people in each room. Each room have one bed. And they give us small mattress. One guy on the bed, and three sleep on the floor. We switched. I have a bathroom in there. You go use the bathroom there's somebody there between your foot. It's very ugly. Although much better from the bus station.

They ask you what kind of food you can't eat, and I can't eat pork. In the morning we have a cup of coffee, and most the food have some kind of some type of ham in it. Sometimes hot dog in the morning. And we have grits in the morning most time. And lunch we have colored water like juice.

We stayed over a week in same place. You can't get out. Each cell have iron gates, and also, from where your room to the shower, have iron gate too. And when you go to shower, take shower, you'll be locked in too. No see light. We never see the light. I never seen a place like it in my life. I mean, I see it on TV and movie or whatever.

Everybody says the phone doesn't work. All I need is to call my wife, just let her know I'm there. I begged everybody. I tried to talk to everybody. "The phone doesn't work," they say.

FATHER VIEN THE NGUYEN

So I evacuated from New Orleans on September 2. I assigned my assistant, Father Luke, to take care of the people in Houston and San Antonio, and my other assistant was taking care of the people in Austin and Dallas, while I drove in between. That's how we kept in touch with our people.

In general, the Vietnamese communities responded well. They were offering rooms in their houses for the people to stay. And so there were some really touching stories. At first, the Vietnamese evacuees gathered at a Vietnamese shopping center called Hong Kong 4 in Houston. Houston Vietnamese were just driving up and holding up fingers to indicate how many they could take in their homes.

And so they just jam in the car and just take off. That's how we responded and that's why you couldn't find a Vietnamese in a shelter because the communities pick them up. It was a very touching story when I arrived.

I was traveling with a *Wall Street Journal* reporter at that point.

This was around September 11. It was then that I was informed that one of the parishioners was missing, an older lady.

So I went to Austin just to see if she was there. I also passed by San Antonio and I couldn't find her. And then from Austin, I went all the way to Arkansas, Fort Chaffee, to check it out to see if I could find her. She wasn't around. I was told that there was some Vietnamese in Little Rock, so I went to Little Rock and I couldn't find her and I went to Hot Springs. She was nowhere to be found.

They told me there was some other communities in Pine Bluff. I went to Pine Bluff, couldn't find her. There was another camp but I was told that there were no Vietnamese there. So I didn't go there but it was at that point Hurricane Rita was heading in. I was going to drive back to Houston to fly to Atlanta for a meeting but Rita was coming into Houston so I had to cancel the flight and just drove directly from Pine Bluff up to Little Rock over to Atlanta.

From Atlanta I drove back to New Orleans. I was coming in from Atlanta and while on the way to Atlanta I called her family and said I couldn't find her anywhere. I remember the man saying maybe she's still at home, so I asked for the address again and I said I'm on my way to Atlanta but on the way, I will swing down to check that out. I remember coming in near Mississippi when I was able to get in touch with a priest who works with the sheriff department in St. Bernard and I told him that I needed him to come in with me to break down her door and go in. We contacted the police and arranged for them to meet me at nine a.m. the next day.

So at nine a.m., I arrived with a priest and some people who had already made contact with me in order to bring people in from other parts of the country to do clean up. I think it's called group work camp. So I went with them and when I arrived the police had just walked into the house and he came out and he said, "We found her." That's when I walked in and sure enough she was there. She had died. She was lying on a hammock.

WEEKS AFTER THE STORM

- *Water levels begin to recede in many areas.*

- *FEMA continues to distribute $2,000 to each household of Hurricane victims. Over one million people apply for relief.*

DANIEL FINNIGAN

I was at a Red Cross shelter near Gonzales for two weeks. Then I left and went and camped in the Spring Bayou for a few nights, and then Hurricane Rita came. So I had to run away again. I was in tents. But they were getting sixty-mile-per-hour winds, and you can't do that in a little Wal-Mart pup tent.

I went and I hooked up with my friend Dave Brinks in Natchez, Mississippi. He put me up. He had rented a house there. He's a New Orleans resident, lifelong. Good friend of mine. That was the first night I'd actually slept in a structure with power and AC, so I slept good and felt great the next day. I was there for three days, I think. And then we came back to the city.

We drove in. We had passes because Dave is a business owner in the French Quarter, and they were letting business owners in at that time. So we got in that way. The decision to come back just came from when Rita was coming in. It was like, "Man, I was safer back at my house." I was done sleeping on the dirt, or in a tent. I was just done. It'd been three weeks, and I was just ready to come home, I guess.

The only problem I'm really facing now is trying to reconcile with myself everything that happened and how I handled it. Did I do what I could do, you know? Should I have helped more instead of worrying so much about being robbed? Mind you, the threat was there. Weird things did happen, and scary things did happen, but should I have not been so scared? I did help some, but later on, you wonder if you should have done more. That's really the only thing that's bothering me now. I got food, I got water, I have everything that I need. I haven't had electricity since the storm. I'm used to it. That doesn't bother me.

It's weird seeing people come back because when I first came back, there was still only a couple of people. I cried a little bit just because I was walking around and there was nobody. You could stand in the middle of the street and scream, and nobody would hear you. And I did, just because you could. It was bizarre.

There were the few, like maybe three, holdouts that stayed through the whole thing, never evacuated at all. And it was the same people as when I left. That was a sad thing, seeing it like that. Now it's kind of a strange thing seeing people come back, people coming and getting into their houses and taking their refrigerators out. There's all this activity.

The neighborhood is starting to come alive again. And that's kind of sad in a way, too, because you kind of got used to it how it was. I could see how you could almost go crazy if you were to live in that kind of environment for a long time. It would almost be like, you would never be ready for society again. So it's good that it's happening now so that none of us get like that. It's just a strange thing. I had to use the brakes on my bicycle yesterday for the first time. That kind of pissed me off. Like, damn! They're back! But I want 'em back. I want everybody back. Of course you do. But it's just the transition.

DAN BRIGHT

After I was transferred from Hunt, they were just holding us in

Rapides Parish Prison in Alexandria. They didn't know what none of us was in jail for, they was just holdin' us. Only thing they had was a record of whoever been in jail before. They didn't have any current charges, so now the lawyers had to come in. We had to tell 'em our charges. What they did with the misdemeanors, they was kinda letting us go, but they had to find out if we were really charged with misdemeanors, so now they have to go through this process. And this took maybe like two weeks, just sittin' there. I read. Anything I get my hand on I try to read. The numbers I'm calling wasn't going through because all the phones was shut down.

This attorney, Phyllis Mann, she came with a human rights group, and that kinda like backed the guards off us. Phyllis never looked at me but she was reading my file and she saw my name, and not too many lawyers in this state don't know my name. They don't know me but they know my name. When she looked up she say, "You don't remember me."

And then I looked in her face and I remember I had met her before and that she was a human rights lawyer. I'm telling her to get word to my lawyers Ben Cohen or Clive Smith or Barry Gerharz, let them know where I'm at. She called Ben, and Ben went to work from there.

Once again I'm put out front. I'm the leader of the inmates now, in fact, because they had to go through me to talk to Phyllis, or Ben, or one of those guys. So the corrections officer found that out, and they really didn't like me then. And you talkin' about some big old country boys: six-five, three hundred pounds. And every time the lawyers would come to see us, the officers would say I was on the yard, or I had a clinic appointment. They was lying, I was right there on the tier. And I would be the last one to go in. I was painted the bad guy.

When we finally went to court, this little hick court, kangaroo court, they had shotguns, pistols in the courtroom. Ain't nowhere in this country you going to go to a courtroom and see twenty guards in the courtroom. Not the hallway. In the *room* with guns, shotguns. And I'm like, "What the hell is going on here, man?"

I'm just ready to get outta here. I'm ready for this nightmare to be over with, and I'm ready to go. This is what happened. I was blessed to have these lawyers who move faster and gave them this ultimatum. What Ben did, he filed a writ of habeas corpus to produce our bodies in court 'cause you know, misdemeanors don't carry no more than thirty days for the charges I had. So now you holdin' me over these thirty days. Either give me a bond or cut me loose. So they cut all the misdemeanors loose and brought us to these shelters.

I stayed at the shelter for a few hours. When we went to the Red Cross, that's when I really was eatin'. I spent a few hours there. Then my pops came got me. They got me a room in a hotel, and that's the first time I could get comfortable, take me a nice hot shower, and relax in the hotel room. We stayed there maybe like two weeks and we came back. FEMA paid for it. Very good two weeks.

My family was in Dallas, and after we left the hotel, they rented a house on Tulane and Mississippi in New Orleans. I couldn't go there because it's already overcrowded. And I wouldn't feel right living with my mother. I'm a grown man.

I don't know where I'm'a be. I might be in a shelter again. I might be on the streets because I don't have the finances to even rent me a place. And FEMA is givin' me all kinds of runaround. I don't know if they mad at me because I got off death row. I don't know but it's like they tellin' me they can't give me nothing more because I wasn't head of the household. So I'm in all kinds of bad situations. But I'm not going do nothing where I'm gonna wind up back in prison, that's for sure. I have to find a way to make money, and I'm not going to go through any illegal channels to make any money. Right now I'm gutting houses out with a friend.

Basically, at first, we talked to our family members. We both have big families, so we clean their houses out. We have masks, we have all the proper tools and equipment, but you don't get used to that smell. The smell will make you sick. And not only the bodies, but these houses being locked up, and the mold and the water eatin' all that stuff up. And then you got the iceboxes and the deep freezers. And the icebox smells worse than a body.

But in New Orleans, insurance people just don't want to pay people for their houses. So I'm on hold. I have the houses but people can't pay me because the insurance people don't want to pay them. So that's why, when I ask about money, I must really need it. And the work is out here, but I say this again, the corrupt officials, they playing on a larger scale with the contractors. They're getting kickbacks and giving the contracts to who they want to give to. And I'm not one of those big fishes where I can get a big contract. I have to wait and get the scraps, the crumbs, gutting houses out. It's just New Orleans.

Anyway, most of our work is being done in New Orleans East. That's basically the Ninth Ward. My mom, my mother's house, it was a brick room, so it can be rebuilt. It's still on its foundations. It's just the inside. I seen it, it just needs cleanin' out. It's a big brick home. It did survive. The only damage they had was the roof where my pop had to break out the roof to get out. He stood on a roof three days.

He's a stubborn old man. He's not gon' leave and he's like the rest of 'em. He thought this wasn't really gon' happen. And my pop said the levee didn't break accidentally. My pop said he heard a blast and when he first looked out the window, out the door, it was just a little wind and rain. My pops, he's an electrician, so at first he thought that that bang was one of those electricity buckets on the poles. When he heard the bang, he didn't pay no attention, he thought that the electricity bucket go out. And he was sitting in his lawn chair, and he looked on the ground and saw the water risin' up.

So my pop, he gets up and he sees water, but it ain't but ankle high, so he go looks out the door and there the water is coverin' the entire house and he hear the door rattlin' like the water trying to push in there, so he turns around and runs.

As he runnin' to the attic the water busted in. He took a two-by-four that he had up there already and busted the roof open and stood up there. It was up to where he was at. His feet was in the water while he was on the roof. And my pops, he's like an asthmatic; he needs this pump. He didn't have no pump, he didn't have nothing. He left all that. My pops, he had all his stuff was sittin' on the table.

They blew a levee so the majority of the water won't come up-town. It's the Florida levee. You gotta remember, the Ninth Ward's like the lowest income, the poor. So that's what pops said happened, and he stood on that roof for three days.

He can't swim, so he stuck there. He gotta wait for them people to come and get him. He saw guys in boats, but the boats were full, so they couldn't get him. He had to sit right there on the ledge, by the chimney port, the chimney of the house. A guy in a boat came and got them after like three days.

ABDULRAHMAN ZEITOUN

Second week at Hunt, they take us to better section, less security, and give us two hours a day outside. Then when we heard that a judge come from New Orleans, we call to see the judge.

Someone like public defense come from New Orleans with the judge. Before we go to talk to judge, he come to us. The public defender said, "Look, we don't want you to say anything inside. We're here to defend you. Although this court not to prosecute you. He will say what you're charged, and how much your bond is. No reason to talk to judge." I mean, he not want us to say anything, or try to explain, just to listen.

When we go inside, it's like a big room with a couple tables, a couple chairs. It's inside the jail. One of the guys tell us we're charged for looting, and possession of stolen property. And the judge say $150,000 bail. I mean, I feel like a joke. I mean, I know it's not fair. Something is not right. Nobody will listen to you. It doesn't matter who I am, or what I've done. There's nobody who will listen to me. The public defense, the trial guy said, "This guy has his own business, and he's never been charged before. Drop it to seventy-five." And the judge said okay.

That's it. They bring us back to jail. I mean, you can't make phone calls, you can't contact anybody. Doesn't matter. And even if you could do that, who would have $75,000 at this time? I think this judge come up with this kind of number to keep us in there. I mean, he knows no one can come up with $75,000, so it doesn't matter what the reason is.

I can't believe this happening in this country. This thing might happen somewhere else, not here. I mean, we're talking about going to free other people, other countries. We have problems here. How we going to go free other people's country when we have these kinds of problems?

No one ever let us use the phone. "The phone doesn't work," and I see people using the phone. I was never in touch with my wife. From first I got arrested and sent to the bus station, I tried to tell everybody, "Just give my wife a call." I tried everybody to do it. "We can't do it, we can't do it, we can't do it."

Nobody agreed to do it except when I met with the Homeland Security person, I beg him to give a call to my wife because nobody knows where I am. I don't know how he found her, but turns out he's the one who called my wife.

I think it's third week at Hunt that my wife found me and brought a lawyer. And this make me more angry because he come to my jail empty-handed. I mean, he tell me what I know already and he say, you have bond for $75,000 to get out. I said, "I know that."

He said, "What you wanna do?"

I said, "Really, what I have to, to get out."

He said, "You have to pay to get out. You have to come up with $75,000 to get out."

I said, "I'm not coming up with $75,000. I don't have it, first. Are you sure all you can do? You can't reduce it?"

He said, "I have to fight for it."

"So go ahead and do it." I mean, he knows he's supposed to. Why's he asking me?

He asked me, "What if it doesn't work?"

I said, "Check if you can pull property."

He said, "I'll see what I can do," and he left. I see, like, he don't wanna do anything, or that's all he can do.

One week, nothing. I lost hope. He's supposed to visit me the next Wednesday. Wednesday come, nothing happened, and I never hear anything. I wait to go to court because the judge, he says I have to go to court every Wednesday. And then Wednesday passed.

Friday, it's normal. No idea, nothing's going on. Well, they called my name, I thought I was going to go talk to the lawyer or somebody. I found out I was released. They say, "Go get your stuff out," and we got a prison ID. I was held for twenty-three days before I got out.

My wife had posted $75,000 bond. They really make it very difficult to get me out. There was no way to come up with $75,000 in cash. Nothing's open. They don't accept any personal property. If you own a house, you can't put your house against your bond. You have to have something business. And we're lucky we have the office. Only way I got out, my wife, she finds the office papers in a collapsed office.

When I got out, my wife was waiting for me outside with my cousin. After that, I got to his house—he had a temporary house in Baton Rouge—and we stayed one day. Next day, we come to New Orleans to find my papers. When they released me I didn't have anything. All I had was my wallet and my clothes. Before I transferred to Baton Rouge, I asked them. They said they were going to send it there. And my things were not there. Not mine, not Nasser's, not the other guys'. All left in New Orleans.

FATHER VIEN THE NGUYEN

I think the uniqueness of our story is the return.

On September 28, on my way from Atlanta to New Orleans I heard Mayor Nagin declare over the radio that we could return to New Orleans East to "look and leave" on October 5. I called my assistants and told them the date of the return, so they were to prepare and get themselves back here. We all converged on the West Bank at a Vietnamese community center. I had spoken with the pastor there, and asked him to allow us to use it for a month. We set up our office there. During the day, we all came to our community in New Orleans East, and we made arrangements for people to cook lunch, supper. We went back to the West Bank to sleep at night. And after about three or four days, some of the men decided that they felt it was okay for them to stay in our church. So they decided they'd stay right behind the stage in the computer room.

And there were actually about thirty, forty people who gradually came and stayed. They were just coming in. My family was on the West Bank. Their home wasn't badly damaged so I could have stayed there, but I couldn't leave my people.

My assistants helped families to clean out their homes. I traveled around to purchase supplies, materials for people to clean. Then we were also bringing drinking water over. I was hauling washing water from the West Bank, and I told the parishioners, we have all of that here, and when they need it just come and use it.

The first Mass was the Sunday after we returned. So we returned on a Wednesday, and that Sunday we had the first Mass. We used two plywood boards and spray-painted the time of Mass on Sunday, ten a.m. And so just by word of mouth, some three hundred people showed up. It was an extremely touching moment. We didn't know how many people would show up.

One of my assistants expected not more than one hundred people, and so we prepared food for them for after Mass. When we realized we were running out of food, we found two boxes of instant noodles, and so we just boiled the water and threw that in and each person had a bowl. And I remember one young lady's comment was, that was the best bowl of noodles that she had had in her life.

And we were eating on the stage, and so we discussed it and said, "Okay, so we will have Mass every Sunday at ten a.m." And then people were calling in because they couldn't believe that we had Mass. The next Sunday it was eight hundred people.

I heard that the archbishop was going to Chalmette the weekend after, so I invited him to come here to celebrate a Sunday Mass, and we call it the Resurrection of New Orleans East Mass. Each Sunday we invite all of the people in New Orleans East, all the priests I had spoken with, and the priests here as well, and they agreed to that. And so the Sunday the archbishop came, there must have been a little more than two thousand people here.

This was probably the second Sunday of November. I remember it was the week after All Saints' Day. So after the Mass with the archbishop and it being reported on TV and in the paper, people knowing that there would be a Mass here every Sunday, they made it a point to be here every Sunday. It was about fifteen, sixteen hundred people and it held steady.

And so when Entergy needed a list of one hundred households to justify diverting power to us, we got five hundred. We just typed up the list and just brought it to their office. Actually, Entergy was very good about that. The man whom I met, Rod West, I think he's the vice president of Entergy in this area. I brought him the list and pictures of Mass. Around a week and a half later, we have electricity. You can't ask for more than that. In comparison to the rest of the city that was allowed to return, we were the last to have electricity. But in New Orleans East, we are the first and we are the only one that has electricity at this point.

Our councilwoman, Cynthia Willard-Lewis, she had been with us every step of the way. We came back on Wednesday. She came out and saw us the following Tuesday, and then she was back helping us to get all kinds of things. She helped us to get cleaned up. She was standing with us all throughout this time.

You keep in mind now, in all of my experience, from the time I was evacuated from here, everything was well and good. My struggle was with the city government. When I went to see FEMA, they immediately agreed to give me two hundred trailers to help my people return more than two months ago. It's the mayor who refused to sign it.

Right after the meeting with FEMA person I went over to see the auxiliary bishop, informing him what was going on so that he would also push and so we waited and waited and waited, and of course the archbishop did push. A whole week later, nothing moved.

In December there was a city council meeting, and so I sent my assistant and one of the staff to go raise the issue at that meeting. I think at that point the "ship hit the sand." The city was blaming FEMA. Well, FEMA came right back and said, "We have seven thousand trailers ready, and the permit's at the mayor's office desk, and he hasn't signed it yet."

We were asking for the permits so that FEMA can put trailers on our land. We are not asking them for permission. This is our homes. We have the right to live in our homes where we choose. That's the beauty of it, isn't it? Other countries—dictatorial, Communist—they tell people where to live and not to live. We are different from that. At our own peril we are here. At our own joy we are here. The mayor said there was some controversies with city council. There was no controversy with city council because our councilwoman was the one who requested his office to sign it.

Well then, Senator Mary Landrieu was coming down here. She wished to come by and visit. She had stopped by before and I had invited her to the first Mass, and she couldn't make it, so she said she would come at another time. So her office called and said she would like to come to the Mass, and the question was, "Can Hillary Clinton come with her?" And we said, "That's fine. What time?"

And so they arrived, I believe, the weekend before Christmas. And so by Monday, the mayor called me again, and he said he may have some good news. He said he'd come by later on that afternoon. He came by and took a look at the place and he said, "I will sign it today."

SONYA HERNANDEZ

We were in Camp Gruber in Oklahoma for about a month. There were eleven of us. There were a lot of people there; the camp was full of people. And what happened is, they gave us a bed to sleep in in a barracks, and they set us up. At first, it was okay. You could go get food in the morning and the afternoon. And then they started cracking down to the point you had to have an ID to get food, and if you came a minute too late you couldn't eat.

Then they started telling people they had to leave. We left right before they started making it mandatory for people to leave. They had some people from CAP, Community Action Plan, that came. They came and took us to some apartment.

We were there for about two months, three months. CAP said they were gonna pay the bills until FEMA kicked in, but they never paid anything. CAP ended up getting us almost evicted so we had to move. We moved to a house. We're still in Tulsa. Everybody's living there. It's a six-bedroom house.

ANTHONY LETCHER

After we got out of New Orleans, we lived out of a microwave for about two months in Dallas, but that was cool because it's half the battle when you're doing it with family. We got a big family. Damn near all of them right there in Dallas, too. Got some out there in California. Family first, and in a time like this you gotta stick with your family. That's why I'm not in Washington, D.C., that's why I'm not in the Windy City. FEMA was going to send me wherever I wanted to go, but family first. I really wanted to go to Washington, D.C., but family comes first. Anyway, I'm cool. I'm chilling right now, brother man.

Like I said, man, my family all right. The only thing I really miss right now is my kids. We're kinda like scattered apart from my babies. I see everybody with their families, their children. I never had a father, but I love my kids, man.

Motherfucker means to be there, but it's so rough. Mainly financially. I feel like if a motherfucker had some money, a motherfucker'd be straight. I don't care if you live over there in Cairo, Egypt. If I got some money, I'll come see you. You ain't got no money, you can't make no move. It's rough, man. Gotta keep your head above water though. Survival of the fittest, bro.

If I can get twenty more years out of this body, I want it. I'm gonna squeeze every piece of life I can squeeze out of it. I know how important that is now. I do. I ain't never in my life thought about smelling flowers. I smelled the flowers. I know what life is now. I know how motherfuckers take it for granted too. Never know until it is all gone, twinkle of an eye, bro. Twinkle of an eye, it can all be gone, just like that. You'll be like your boy in *Ghost* then, Patrick Swayze. Trying to find your way home, you heard me?

Just before this flood came up, I wanted to leave this motherfucker. I was so disgusted with New Orleans. That's how I felt 'bout here before the flood came. I was disgusted with New Orleans. Disgusted with it. But how they say? You never miss a good thing till it's gone. You never miss a good thing, baby. Check this here out. A motherfucker missing his home. Man, he missin' his home. And all my family missin' home, bro. That's all everybody talk about in my whole family. "Lord have mercy. I wanna go home. When they gonna get this built? When they gonna get this built?"

Man, y'all better sit your ass down. They ain't gonna get that shit built, man, for about three years. That's the thing. They sayin' they're gonna build this shit up in a year. That's how people think. People here are so messed up right now.

Look how the city looks. Look. This shit kills me. Look at Mayor Nagin sayin' like it's all good. Dude's phony, man.

"We're gonna get the French Quarter started. We're going to get the CBD [Central Business District] started. We're gonna make business right. We're gonna bring jobs."

Oh man, what a joke. You're on national television, talkin' 'bout gettin' the casinos started. Man, nobody got no money. So who's he telling that to? Tourists. It's all about the money, baby. It's all about the Benjamins.

It's just so strange. People focusing so much on the casinos. I can understand about the economy, and tryin' to get some money generating because that's what it's about. But people just hate to hear that. People want you to be concerned about them and about their well-being. You got a lot of people out there that don't even know what's gonna happen next. They don't.

"Come on back. Eat the gumbo."

New Orleans is politically ran by fucked-up-ass-mentality police officers that don't respect you as a civilian. And I ain't sayin' that because my life been fucked-up.

Motherfuckers just as human as me, but they got a badge. They're in Wal-Mart stealing. Pathetic. Out of all places, Wal-Mart.

Police. They supposed to be in the bank or something. Goddamn. You know what I'm saying? You got on a blue uniform, you can just about go anywhere you want. If I was a police, and I wanted to steal, it wouldn't be Wal-Mart. That's my point.

And look what they're showing on TV. All these people like they're rescuing people and all this here. Look at them on television talking about the heroes. Man, what heroes? Tell me, what heroes? Tell me this here, how can a police superintendent retire after the flood? I saw it on TV, so I'm not fibbin' on him or nothin'. I heard it on the news. If it's not true, the news's lying. And he's getting a two-million-dollar deal to write a book. A book on what? Was he here three, four days into the flood when nobody had nothing, scraping for something to eat, trying to get water? Trying to survive from dehydration? Was he here? Was he grinding? I'm talkin' about the police superintendent. Was he out there getting a four-hundred-pound woman outta a house in eighteen feet of water? Was he doin' it? Was he there? How can he get a two-million-dollar deal to write a book about the tragedy of Katrina in New Orleans?

They wasn't in it when it was the grind, bro. I'm the one should be getting paid. I'm the one drinking that motherfucking water, haulin' them people out, trying to get them out of the water. We was in it. We was in that water, man, knee-deep, you heard me? I was coming for the wrong things, and I still didn't end up making no money, man. I ended up helping a lot of people and that was cool.

KERMIT RUFFINS

After we left Baton Rouge, we went to Houston. Up in Houston, man, we met two cats, musicians you would not believe. These guys fell in love with me. These guys own about thirty bars around Houston. They saw me and they say, "Hey, we want to do a bar with you, split the percentage with you. We own all these clubs and we'll let you in on every other club we open up, and do you want in?"

And now Kermit Ruffins's Barbecue House is opening up any day now, and they're totally doing it. All I have to do is play there once a week and just hang at the bar every night and give up a couple of recipes.

I'm known for cooking my butt off. We had Bobby Flay out in New Orleans, with my truck parked here with a big barbecue grill on the back, two weeks before the storm, filming a show for the Food Network. I'm always tailgating on the back of my truck. I always tell everybody, "I'm a master chef and I play music on the side."

I wanted those guys to come and do the same thing in New Orleans in about a year. The same club and start a small chain. That's why I say some of the best stuff came from the hurricane, as far as just overall the attention of the shows, the gigs playing in churches and lots of benefits. I was lucky enough to get on the circuit right away, and to tour nonstop. All of the musicians up in Houston—and there were lots of them—were looking up to me.

Every time I think about the music, I always think about way, way back and what it was like and why and who and all that stuff. I always try to imagine way back then when almost every club had a piano and a piano player, and I'm always imagining that, up to the day, about how those guys made it all possible for us today, and what they did and how they did it. The church and the classical and all that kind of coming together. And I always think about stuff like that. The old stuff. I always think about how it happened.

I realize my responsibility now, especially after Katrina. I'm like, "Hey man, you the only one that's doing this and everybody's watching and you better be swingin' and well rested and ready to do this every time you hit the stage. That should be the greatest time of your life." And I'm always thinking of how the old-timers did it and how they played it and what they felt about it and whether they had grim feelings or whether they had real happy feelings. All that stuff. Just the total spiritual aspect of the whole New Orleans scene.

It's just so incredible to me when I realize what I'm doing and what was going on before the storm. Now it's kind of like double that or triple that. I was real eager to have the world hear this music. It was killing me inside not to have the world hear this music. And whenever big-timers and big-time producers or just people in general would ask me, "What can we do to make the music more accessible to the world?"

I say, "Man, put us on MTV and BET once a week. Live from New Orleans." I'm the host of the show, or somebody else is the host— Quentin Davis. We need to be on TV every day at least. And it took Katrina to do that. Everybody's looking at us, which is kind of the best thing to happen to New Orleans music, as far as world recognition, in a long, long, long, long time. And it's sad that the storm came up, but I would have to say, to the average musician, the storm was the best thing that happened to them. It's sad it takes tragedies to enlighten people.

I mean, the people that got it the hardest was elderly people and the kids. Anybody like me that travels a lot, and they have a strong love for the music and people in general, really had it easy, 'cause we're used to living in hotels. But the back side of it, every time I think about one of these elderly people, it just makes you so sick. I mean, it makes me so sad. It makes me feel so powerless.

I did pretty good. I mean, the first floor of my house probably got a little water. It wasn't too bad at all. But where I grew up at on Jordan Avenue, where I spent all my time, where all of my childhood memories—that house was just leaning and falling. Two weeks after the storm I did a documentary with National Geographic, so that's how I had the opportunity to go across the canal—they weren't letting nobody cross that—and I went in the house on Jordan Avenue with my video camera and I had tears looking in that house. That neighborhood, it just killed me, man, to see that neighborhood. It was real.

RENEE MARTIN

When all this first happened, after we had moved to Houston, I had had a bad dream and in the dream it was like—remember how I had seen a man in the water in a plastic bag, but he was dead—in the dream it was me in the plastic bag. That one scared me. It was like two days after we got here I had that dream, and it scared me. And I figured that it could've been me. It could've been me 'cause a lot of people lost their lives.

We know where all our family members at, except one of my uncles, my mama's only living relative. He's the only one living out of the whole side of my mother's family. And we've been looking for him, we don't know where he is. And he lived over there way towards the Lower Ninth Ward, and we don't know if he's living or he's dead. Elton Reed. He has to be about sixty years old.

I moved to a different apartment in Houston on November 1. That's when the social worker at my job at the hospital, her and her daughter Cindy, they brought me to get a FEMA voucher so I could pay my rent. But the apartments where I was didn't take the FEMA voucher at the time.

I met a lady at the Wal-Mart down the street from my job, and I was telling her, "I don't know what I'm gonna do. I'm'a have to move." And she's like, "Why?" And I explained the situation.

She said, "Well, they have some apartments over here where I live. Let me see what I can do." The next day she said, "Can you come and meet me? It's a one-bedroom, and the manager wants to meet you. And I came. She said, "You look like a pretty nice lady, gon' keep the place up." So she gave me the apartment, and I've been here ever since. And I like it because it's peaceful, quiet. Nobody's being loud, no drugs, no fighting. It's very clean.

It's paradise. It's totally different. In my old neighborhood in New Orleans, you walk out the door, you see some group of people hanging out and doing wrong. You know, they're selling drugs, or doing drugs, or soliciting, breaking in, you know, children fighting, grown-ups fighting. All kind of drama. You know, drama. Music playing real loud.

I like it out here. My apartment is big and spacious. It's private-owned condos. It's not managed like apartments, by offices, private owners. You can buy 'em or you can rent 'em. And right now, FEMA's paying my rent for eighteen months, but afterwards, my owner's telling me, if I decide I want to stay here, I can go for owning it, where I would only pay $300-something a month instead of paying like $500 a month.

Maybe this is my big break, to come to Houston and get my stuff together. My life out here is totally different from what it was in New Orleans. I don't even find a reason to be depressed. I'm gonna stay right here because I never advanced myself so fast and so much. I'm an assistant supervisor at the hospital. I handle the schedule, and I run the laundry department. In New Orleans, when I got advanced, it was small time. And it doesn't have nothin' to do with FEMA assistance, because before the FEMA assistance stuff started kicking in, I managed to make a way. I got a car, and now I have a way to get to work. Now I don't have to depend on nobody.

If Mayor Nagin said, "Come on back to New Orleans. We're gonna pay your rent for five years," I don't wanna go. Everything's going good here. I'd rather stay out here.

My daughter's in New Orleans. She works out there. She makes more than me! You know, the jobs are out there now because they're trying to get everybody to come back. She makes twelve dollars an hour and all she doing is a cashier at a gas station. She don't wanna stay out here in Houston. She's like, "It's too big." She don't know nobody, she don't have transportation. She's twenty-one. She'll be twenty-two in April. She's young. She still hangs out with her friends, and they go out to clubs and stuff. I'm more comfortable with her staying there than here because she likes to go out with her friends and she don't have friends here. And I don't want her to get mixed up with the wrong kind of friends. But my sisters, they're out there. My family, and her dad, and his family. So I'm comfortable with her being out there.

They're in the West Bank. All of them live on the West Bank, except my mom. My mom lived in the East right there by the Ninth Ward where it was totally messed up. They're not even allowed to live there no more. They have to go tear all those houses down and they're gonna put up trailers for everybody. So she don't wanna stay on that side no more because it's too much under sea level. So everybody's moving on the West Bank.

I had gone down there for Christmas, and my sister took me for a tour. I felt like a tourist. She brought me to see New Orleans and I rode around and the houses, the ones that are still standing up are just a frame. It's just mildew, and the flooding means that everything's still left there. Cars still left there. It's no good. But on the West Bank where I lived, it flooded, but not all the way over the roof. But we didn't have no second floor at the apartment where I live at, and on the first floor, a lot of the walls are gone, the doors. It's just pieces of frame in different areas. But there's nothing left, so they closed all them. Barricaded it off. I guess they're gonna bulldoze that all. They have no other choice. They have to.

This experience taught me a lot. It lets you know that in the moment, in the blink of a eye, your life and everything you own could be swiped from right up under you. Before the storm, I was gettin' ready to move into my own apartment. I had my own side where I lived with my niece. I had had all the stuff I had bought—

the comforters, the sheets, the curtains, everything that I needed, the dishes, the food. I had took time out to buy all that. And the storm come. And when I went back to New Orleans just to go see, it was a mess.

The stuff, I guess by being wet, had mildew everywhere. And I had some personal things. Some stuff that you can't get back. Like all my grandbabies' pictures, and long friends' phone numbers. That stuff you can't find. That stuff you can't get again if you don't know where they're at. Everything I was working for, look at it, it's gone down the drain. And when I went in there, I didn't even much try to save nothin'. I was more afraid to touch somethin' because I was afraid that I was gonna get somethin'. That's why I didn't touch none of the stuff, and I just left it there and come on out.

LOOKING BACK

DANIEL FINNIGAN

For five or six days until I evacuated it was just this survival mode sort of thing. I remember at one point on the fifth day, it hadn't occurred to me until then that there were people who probably thought I was dead, or thought I could be. But what struck me was that never occurred to me until five days later. That's where your head was.

We had no idea about the things that were going on at the Convention Center and the Superdome. The first we found out about that stuff was when this guy Joe—he was part of our neighborhood group—he took in ten people from the Lower Ninth, ten roof people. They were trapped on their roofs. They got rescued and came wandering through the neighborhood like everybody else because they had nowhere to go. And he took them into his home and they stayed there for a few days. And they were great.

So guilt is a big part of the whole thing too. You feel guilty not only about looting yourself, but about keeping other people from doing it. In the first days to keep people from doing it, and then in the later days you go and do it yourself. You feel a little bit like a chump for not having known.

Everybody here did what they had to do, and tried to do things the best way they could. It's so hard to really express the headspace that you were in when all this was happening. You got no sleep—maybe a half hour to an hour a night—so sleep deprivation was playing a role. The big-time stress piled upon stress piled upon stress played a role. I would just ask anybody to judge our actions bearing in mind that surreal headspace that we were in. It's very easy to judge actions based on your own headspace and how you are right in the moment, while you're sipping coffee in a safe place. But it doesn't really make for a true observation unless you can at least try to place yourself in a completely chaotic situation and imagine what you would do.

There were bad things that happened and there were good things that happened all over the city. Shame on the bad and good for the good. That's all. But when the supposed gangsters are the ones rescuing people instead of our own army, I'd say more power to the gangsters and less power to Bush. That's all.

FATHER VIEN THE NGUYEN

We are the first ones to return in all of the affected areas, and at this point more than half my people have returned. The attendance in my church is three thousand.

On February 14, Mayor Ray Nagin, Waste Management Incorporated, and Louisiana's Department of Environmental Quality made the decision to open a landfill one mile from where we are, one mile from the edge of my community.

It was very ironic. We were the first community in all of New Orleans to come forth with a development plan. They're still talking about development plans at this point. Out of our own pockets, we brought in thirty-three experts from all over the country and two architects from Vietnam to design the redevelopment of our area. We unveiled it on the third of February, and on the fourteenth of February, our Valentine's gift was a waste dump.

Our concerns are many. One is environmental, the disintegration of the wetlands. Furthermore, the waste dump is separated from Bayou Savage—the largest urban wildlife refuge in the continental U.S.—by the Maxent Canal. That's eighty feet wide. The canal is directly connected to the lagoon that surrounds our community. There's a lot of gardening in our community. The old people do a lot of gardening and they use that water to water their garden, and we consume the vegetables from those gardens.

Their plan was to go into the collapsed homes, extract as much as possible, and then they just collapse the houses, put them on trucks, just dump them in there. Practically anything could be dumped down there. These are homes that were built long before the 1970s. You're talking about lead-based paint. You're talking about asbestos tiles, floors, roofing, that type of thing. They were going to dump everything down there, directly into the ground.

The pit that they're dumping into is thirty feet deep, and they were going to fill it up and pile it up to eighty-five to one hundred and five feet tall and then cap it with three feet of dirt. That would be one of the highest structures in New Orleans East. That would be our skyline, our mountain. You have the Sierras, we have the waste dump. And then that's where it's most vulnerable to storm surges as well as hurricane wind, so where will all of that go when we get another storm?

And it's not just on this issue anymore. As we entered into this battle, we found out that the illegal dumping throughout New Orleans East is just rampant. I'm talking about places that are two, three, five miles from where we are. I have no idea why New Orleans East has always been seen as a dumping ground for New Orleans. Probably because we don't have as many people in the area as downtown New Orleans and elsewhere.

But we're not going anywhere. You see, for my parishioners, the question whenever I saw them was, "Can you do something to make our return quicker? Can you get them to reopen?"

People's lives revolved around the church. That is more important than any structure that we have. We were also looking ahead. We were working on the plans to build the church, and the retirement community and a cultural center. All of that was in place, and we've been working on it for the last year and a half. So now we see this as the opportunity to forge ahead.

It's altered only in the sense that it's been sped up because our elderly need to have a place to stay, to retire. On top of that, we have the lady in the low-income housing area, Versailles Arms, who died in there. If she were in a retirement community of our jurisdiction that would have never happened, because I sent people into that area twice to look for anyone left after the hurricane, to help them evacuate.

Of course, the thing that really hit all of us was, "What if?" I passed by that house twice. I know that had I been by, had I stopped in to look for her, she would not have died. Had the people that I sent immediately after the flood known she was there, she would not have died. So for the family as well, it's the question of "What if?" It's a lot of sense of guilt, of pain.

And that's why, for me, the retirement community has that sense of urgency now. If anything else happens in the future in terms of emergency, if our elderly live within a place where we have control, we can evacuate, we can take care of them in case of emergency.

In times of emergency, gathering around the priests is a natural phenomenon. Priests migrated their people from North to South Vietnam in 1954. The majority of the people who live in this area migrated from North to South Vietnam in 1954, going with their priests. And so because of that, there is the natural gravitation toward priests. That's the natural growth.

I talked to a lady—right after Mass she went in to see me in the sacristy. She said, "These last four months I wasted my time going to Mass because it brought me no fruitfulness."

And I knew exactly what she was talking about. She went to Mass in Georgia for the last four months, but she didn't feel like she was really at Mass. She was just there to fulfill the obligation and that community wasn't hers.

FATHER JEROME LeDOUX

Our first Mass back at St. Augustine was on October 9. That's the first Sunday I was back. October 9 was the birthday of the church, St. Augustine, 163rd birthday. We celebrated with maybe three dozen people. The following Sunday we had double that, then after that we would hit above one hundred and stayed comfortably above one hundred, and then we reached a point where we were close to two hundred, and we kept moving up.

The church went places it had never been before, at least certainly not in recent years. We began to average three hundred on Sunday, then four hundred, then five hundred. The collection, which was always on the low side, well, we were all smiles when we brought in about $2,000. Well, $2,000 became just "not special." We hit a high point that $5,000 became normal. And then we were hovering between $5,000 and $7,000. And every now and again we hit $8,000.

I've never seen myself as anybody but one of the neighborhood guys. I've always been just a friendly neighbor who tried to help whomever. I just walked, walked Tremé, talked to the people. And never saw myself as anything special until I realized what the people had formed in their minds. I didn't realize that until just the last year. They had formed in their minds that I had become a part of Tremé. I was the face of St. Augustine Church; I was their friend in the community. And they knew that if they needed anybody to fight for them, I was there. And it just hadn't occurred to me, but apparently over the years, gradually, the people said, well, he's always there. He doesn't run away from anything, not even a hurricane.

But I was a bit stunned, I guess, a bit shocked, that that many people rose up as one person to oppose the archbishop's decision to close St. Augustine after the storm on March 15.[13] I hadn't foreseen, and of course the archbishop had no clue either. He got a little rolled back on his heels. He had terrible advisers. All these people rose up as one voice, around Tremé, around New Orleans, the state, the country, and around the world. There were 4,000 emails from Germany alone to the archbishop.

When all of this hit the archbishop, he realized he had misjudged the whole thing. And he just made some very ill-advised conclusions and moves. First of all, when a whole people is down after a hurricane, after all we'd been saying about the post-traumatic stress syndrome, that is not the time to afflict the people with radical change.

The black people of St. Augustine rose up as one. The Catholics then the non-Catholics, rose up. "We're not Catholic, but St. Augustine is ours." "This is Tremé. It belongs to us!" All of a sudden you walked into the church on a Sunday, and you were used to seeing a half-filled church, maybe a third-filled church. All of a sudden the church was full, and it was half-black, and half-white, and most of the whites there were there because they wanted to be there. And many of them were more radical than the blacks in opposing the archbishop. Some of them went down to his house with letters in their hands and presented them.

Newspapers like *Gambit,* the *Tribune.* These newspapers took on the archbishop. They were angry, really angry. The *Tribune* was not pleased, and the story in the *National Catholic Reporter* just ripped the archbishop up. And of course he reads all that stuff, especially

---

[13] For more on St. Augustine's post-Katrina struggles, please see page 307.

from the *National Catholic Reporter*. That hits the whole country and other parts of the world. And the archbishop knew what kind of publicity he was getting. Notoriety is a better word, very negative notoriety.

I kept thinking: the oldest black Catholic parish in the United States—will it be taken down like this? I wrote the archbishop a steamy letter about this, and I said, "You are making a terrible decision at this critical juncture in history." And of course, it will go down in infamy because he did it. Even though he recanted, he did it. And that is a terrible mark historically. I even told God, "What do you want of me? Tell me what you want. Do you want me to offer up some sacrifice? You tell me and I'll do it, just spare this parish."

There is a very strong commonality between what's happening to these traumatized people after the storm and traumatized black men from way back when. I'm just old enough to remember all the bad things. See, I go all the way back to 1930. I remember in the newspapers they'd have an entire front page picture of a man hanging. Black man lynched, whole front page.

The archbishop goes back on his heels. So in the privacy of his little counsel, where his advisers are, he makes it clear that he should rescind all that he has done. But they said, "Archbishop, you cannot rescind everything you have said and done against the church otherwise the Catholics in Metairie and Kenner"—understand, the white Catholics, extreme right-wing—"they will view this as weakness."

Eventually the archbishop was so hard-put—the pressure just got worse, it never let up—finally they cried for mediation. They said, "We'll give you eighteen months to prove yourselves." One of the benchmarks was, "Show us one hundred more members in those eighteen months." We did that in two months.

It's called racial insensitivity, gross racial insensitivity. You're talking about the oldest, longest running, most necessary focal point for a large community. The purpose of church is very plain, very simple. The purpose of church is community. That's what we're all about. You can't always be full of joy, but you can always help other people when they're not full of joy—you can lift them up. Why would you take it out from under them?

Why afflict these people who are grievously afflicted? Critically afflicted, some of them. Some are dying, because of the trauma. And the trauma affects our health on many fronts—this whole psycho-somatic thing. I had a double funeral. A mother and her daughter survived the hurricane—the mother was seriously old, early nine-ties—but the aftermath, just the stress, killed both of them. And these people want to afflict the black community? Leave us alone, at least for a while.

RHONDA SYLVESTER

At the beginning when we got here in Houston, they was real nice here. If it wouldn't've been for Lazy Brook, we wouldn't have noth-in'. But now everybody else is harsh. It was a front from the begin-ning. It's just like some places that you go, they must think that we wanted this to happen to us. We didn't want this to happen to us. And some places you go, people, when you say you're from New Orleans, their whole attitude changes about you.

They label us bad. They judgin' people from other people's stan-dards. That's what I think. They scandalize the name real bad—where we come from, not my name individually. It kinda hurt when they say "the evacuees." Everything happens because "the evacuees" here. We didn't have a part in the crime that was takin' place here. We didn't do what they say took place here. The crime was high before we come here. At first they gave us a good impression but at the end they didn't.

You go somewhere and you be talkin', and they don't know where you from. They were talkin' to you, and you say, "I'm from

New Orleans," their whole expression change. "Well, I know you got that FEMA money." I don't have no FEMA money.

I'm having a hard time here. You know, I hold on dearly because I have two grandkids, and my son and my daughter-in-law, and none of us have no income. No Medicaid, no Medicare. They cut us off because they said it was going before the legislators to see who was still eligible for it. They cut us off after two months and we have two babies that need shots.

After the storm, the older baby, all he did was cry after the storm. Today, still, he cries a lot. I don't know why he cries a lot, but like I said we had took him to the doctor to see if anything was wrong with him. Nothing was wrong with him. He just cries all the time. I guess he's tryin' to sense what's going on. My son and my daughter-in-law can take responsibility for their own lives, but when you have kids involved you have to go to the extra length to stick to these kids and that's what we're doin', trying to maintain. Eventually, somethin'll break. Somethin'll give.

I worked through a lot of temp works, but since I've been here they've been calling me for jobs in New Orleans, but I don't have no-where to stay out there in Louisiana. I tell them if I had somewhere to stay, I'd come. After the hurricane first hit, they had a job for me for seventeen dollars an hour, but I didn't have anywhere to stay out there. All my family was relocated. You got to have transportation and somewhere to stay and I don't have that because we don't have nothing left. We lost everything.

I'm going to Workforce. It's some kind of school that you can enroll in. It's called Hazard Class. What it is, they teach you about hazards so you go down and go to New Orleans. It's a forty-hour class and they have a GED program, but I don't know how it works yet. What they say is, they give you a hazard license within forty hours. It's free. That's what they said. I won't know till I get there. They say everything's free but when you get somewhere it costs.

About two months ago, I was tryin' to get in a GED school out here. Don't you know, it costs to get a GED out here, to go to school? You could get the home course but you would have to pay. You have to pay. And if you go to a little school, it's so much you have to pay out here. It's nothing really free out here. Everything costs.

I feel so many things that they did to people wasn't fair. I'm speakin' of FEMA. It wasn't fair what they did to some people because the people who they did give money to, some of them people never had a house, never had a job, never owned no property or anything. And that's the ones who got everything. People who worked, had things before the storm, they can't get anything. We didn't get nothin'. We haven't got anything from FEMA. The only thing we got was from Red Cross.

So now I'm struggling to start over again in another state, where it's pretty hard for me right now 'cause of my past. In this state, your past'll hurt you. They don't care what your present is, how you're striving to better yourself. They look at your past. They judge you by your past, so it's been quite hard here for me.

The little I did accomplish, I lost it. Just in a moment, in the blink of an eye I lost it. And you know, you feel good about yourself when you change your life and do something. That's why I felt good about myself: 'cause I was doin' somethin' with myself. I was getting my life back in order, the mess I had made of it. So I was gettin' it back in order.

But see, I'm not gonna give up, I'm'a keep going 'cause see, some things'll set you back, but I'm not gonna let that set me back. It will take time but you can't depend on nobody to do it for you. You have to do it for yourself if you plan on getting ahead. In ten years, I'm seein' myself as ownin' a house. I see myself as prosperin'. I see myself as being a great, successful, black business owner. I believe that in my heart. I want to go to school for catering. Culinary arts. I love to cook. I love Cajun food. I'm not really a baker, but I can cook.

RENEE MARTIN

I don't really have the kind of relationship that you think you should have, mom and daughter. I try to have it with my daughter because that's my daughter and I know what I didn't have, what I'm still lacking of, and I want her to have it. So I try to give her the same thing I wish I had from my mom. And it works out pretty good. She was very happy.

Being placed here in Houston, it's like a whole new start in life. Different people, different place, different atmosphere. Everything is new to me, and I like it. There's nothing that reminds too much of my past. I can't go across the street and say, "Oh, I remember this store. So-and-so did this and that to me at the store." I look up and see another store. There's nothing to remind me about being in front of that store.

So everything is new and different and better to me. I like every-thing down here. I can say thank God for Katrina. If it wasn't for Katrina, I probably wouldn't be here. I always felt like I wanted to move on to something better and different, but never had a chance. So it took Katrina to bring me here to Houston, Texas. It was the hands of God lifting me up and taking me and moving me too. So I thank God for that. Katrina wasn't bad all the way.

I changed a lot. I done changed from being not motivated and severely depressed to past all of that. I'm happy every day. Some-times, if I can think of the saddest moment, it's still not sad enough to make me just, you know, cry, just drown myself in tears. It's given me a reason to go on, be stronger. I thank God for where I'm at. I thank God every day. Even when everything that I have comes to me, and come into my life, no problem; I have to say, "Thank you Jesus."

In New Orleans, I was afraid of living alone. That's why I always lived with my family, because I always was afraid somebody was gonna do me something, break in my house, rape me, rob me, kill me. But here, no. I'm not worried. I look on the TV, on the news, and I see incidents every day in Houston. But it's really not nothing for me to wanna worry about.

After the storm, people in New Orleans need a very nice place to live. They need a place to live where they can be very comfortable. They need jobs. They need clothes, food, and transportation. That doesn't mean, you know, provide a motor vehicle, but since the storm, a lot of people may have physical problems, mental problems, and they need to come together, have group sessions. They need group sessions for a lot of displaced Katrina victims, where they can come together and reunite with each other, and talk about issues.

Children need a stable environment. That's the main focus. They done been through a lot. The main focus should be on kids, dealing with mental issues that they have to go through. A lot of them, they're here, and they don't quite understand why because they're not old enough to even understand why. They just see why, hear why, but they hear from their parents' voices, and sometimes what their parents saying is a lot of negative, so they get in their mind that's the way of looking at it. I've had some of them say, "What you think about your mayor?" "He needs to be shot," stuff like that.

But I'm like, he's only one man, you know? He's not God. If you were placed in front of all these people, work with all these people, it's hard. And you can only do so much. And you can't really blame Bush, either. You've got Bush and you've got the mayor, you've got these people here in New Orleans, you've got a two-hundred-foot breach, you've got a water pump that wasn't on, you've got Katrina storm twelve hours over us. It's hard for one man to make a decision on all of that. It is.

But I can say it could've been dealt with better before the storm. The evacuation could've been dealt with better. The mayor could've provided cabs, you know. He could've provided public service transportation, schoolbus transportation, charters, trains, planes, boats, ships. You got all these means and ways to get these people out before the storm, but you didn't think about doing that. It took a catastrophe, and then this transportation forced on these people to get 'em out because everybody had no other choice. Because everybody lookin' at, "It cost too much to move these people to just to go here." But what it cost you to have all these people lose their lives, when you could've moved them at no cost. When a man comes to you, to rescue him costs him nothing. You can't just put a person's whole life at jeopardy, at risk, because you don't have the money. It's just not right.

It might be important to America just to know what lies under the Katrina storm, what really goes on in the world, especially in New Orleans. Salary's low pay. It's hard to get by in New Orleans, especially on minimum wage. I know a lot of people that don't have education. And it's hard. You have to be really determined to come out of that rut, if you really want to, like I did. I didn't even have my high school diploma, but I did not wanna live getting government assistance all my life.

Some people get caught up in a circle and a cycle, and repeat their parents' lives. When I was a teacher, we used to have this can. We would draw eyes on the can, and it was the "Eye can do anything I wanna do" can. And you'd write down a wish and put it inside the can. And it's just like, motivation. I used to do that when I was teaching because a lot of students, they didn't have no self-esteem. They needed something to motivate them. They don't know which way to go, where to go, what to do. All they know is they have this dream. They have this big wish, but don't know where to go to start with it.

DAN BRIGHT

New Orleans is where my history lies. It's like, you can't go nowhere and see another Bourbon Street. And that's why I'm so tied to New

Orleans. And I figure, if I'm not doing anything illegal, why would I keep havin' to run and hide? So, that's the thing with me and New Orleans.

I've stayed in San Francisco. I've stayed in Richmond. I've stayed in Houston and Dallas. New Orleans has its own flavor. This is where I'm born and raised. It's just the officials, man, the corruption. It's not everybody. It's just a few corrupt officials.

I'm surprised that this guy didn't evacuate this prison, the sheriff. He was supposed to evacuate. The mayor gave a mandatory evacuation. That includes the sheriff too. He was supposed to evacuate the prisoners. He didn't do it. Sheriff Gussman, this guy didn't come. He didn't come to Central Lockup and say, "We're going to get you all out, and everything will be all right." He didn't give no motivational speech. He didn't do anything. You know what he said when they asked him about it? "They belongs in there."

I'm surprised that it wasn't handled more professional. I'm surprised that y'all would let this happen on a larger scale. Everybody's watching and y'all still doing the same nonsense that y'all been doing. What you figure? If you keep us in there, that you's gon' still make money? If we go to another correctional facility, they get the money from the federal government. That what you worryin' about?

Now, now you have to worry about the lawsuit, the repercussion, because by right, what you did was wrong. Now you have all these lawsuits comin' at you. This sheriff, I seen this guy with my own eyes, on CNN, and he stood right there and lied and said he went in there personally, him and his officers went in there and got everybody out. We never seen this guy. This guy ain't never step foot on that bridge. He never step foot in the parish jail, and he damn sure never step foot on Hunt field and told us what was going on. This guy just looked at us like we was cattle. So he's lying, and I would love to see him and talk to him, debate with him.

ABDULRAHMAN ZEITOUN

When we got arrested, they took us to Napoleon–St. Charles. We're put in the van. I told the guys, "Look, we have animals in the house. Any way I can give you the address? Someone go there to take them out?"

He said, "Yes, we'll go take care of it."

And I asked him, "You want the address?"

He said, "No, I know where it is."

When I finally come back home, I found the animals. All of them died. Some of them in the house, some of them up on the roof.

I know always what we say back home, we say, "Each house have a drain." I mean, each house have nice people there, and have dirty people there, black sheep in the family. Somehow I run into wrong hands. I mean the one who arrested me from the beginning. The one he got to my house. The one he got me, he feel he got something.

First, I think he saw my name, and when he see us together, he overreact. He think like, "I catch something." Like, he feel like he get good catch. I think he thought he catch a group of terrorists. I think that's the first thing that come to his mind. He saw what he's seen on TV, what he's seen on the news and he got, like, some kind of match and there's a bunch of money there, and all these Arab men, these guys together. This is it.

I mean, what happened on 9/11 is not something simple. Really, you have to explain to people, it's not normal people. This is against anyone's religion. All religions, first thing say, "No kill." Any kill happen, anywhere, against religion. All kinds of religion.

But I'm innocent. We were charged with looting and possession of stolen property. The house on Claiborne, the guy downstairs, Todd, has most of his furniture and he brought everything from downstairs how much he can—electronic stuff—upstairs and he left it in the room. I think they thought all this stuff in the house was stolen. He have triple TVs, triple computers. Anyway, this what he means by possession of stolen property. They didn't give us any time to talk. Just get in the boat.

We got dismissed case last week. It was very difficult to get through my case. Three or four lawyers tried because they don't have information. Doesn't have any access to my case. Really, any way it turned out, I know who I am. I feel like I'm strong enough for anybody else. I believed and hoped it will be okay. Because what happened, I know who I am, and I know what I've done. And I know I never done anything to deserve that. It's not easy to just continue to be yourself, when you feel like you tried to everything to be straight, and they take you down anyway.

But this happens anywhere. Inside your house, you have five brothers, not all of them like you. I mean, this happened. I can't blame somebody because somebody did mistake. I got in wrong hands, with the wrong guy. The timing. I feel that we're in wrong time.

PATRICIA THOMPSON

Katrina was truly a disaster, but for me Katrina was a blessing 'cause Katrina turned my life around. I've been wanting to leave New Orleans. You're not treated right in New Orleans, you're not treated fair. New Orleans is the city that forgot to care, and the city that care had forgotten about. You hear about the Big Easy, you hear about Carnival. But man, we go through hell in New Orleans.

Me, all six of my kids, my sisters, every family member—we're talking about at least twelve, maybe fifteen households, everybody has left New Orleans. This is our chance to get out.

Katrina made me aware that racism is alive and well. I have been taught to undo racism, but Katrina only was the proof in the pudding that racism is alive and well. Eighty percent of New Orleans rides public transportation. That lets you know that these people don't have cars. I lived there, but I'm sure the mayor, the governor, and the president knows it as well. First of all, we shouldn't have got a mandatory evacuation order less than twenty-four hours before the storm made landfall. The meteorologist and everybody was saying how bad that storm was going to be. Preparations should have been made to get us out of there.

That's what let me know that the race card was being played. Because when just about everybody that could get out had gotten out, the city was primarily black. They tried to keep us there. They were waiting for a few more of us to die. I will die believing that and I'm not telling you something anybody told me. I lived maybe five or six blocks from a very well-to-do neighborhood. I'm in the ghetto, but five or six blocks down it's a very prestigious white neighborhood, St. Charles. There wasn't a drop of water in St. Charles.

In the beginning I faulted Ray Nagin for a lot of this stuff, but I'm willing to bet you that Mr. Nagin learned something through all of this too. I used to see Mr. Nagin around the city a lot and it was all good. "I'm Ray Nagin, I'm the mayor." Of course they're gonna show you respect. But when it got down to where the rubber meets the road, he was just one of them black folk just like us. That's why he had to get on the radio and talk bad and everything to get some help. But I thank God for one thing. Mr. Bush, he's got a soul and he's gotta pay. I wouldn't want to be him for nothing in the world. He's got a soul. It ain't the right kind, but he's got one to be accountable for. This man knew well what we were in for.

Like I told you, Katrina was not when our problems started. Katrina was more like when our problems very much subsided in New Orleans, and we were able to get out of there.

Still, we've been through several things since we've been up here in Texas. When we got to College Station, we were treated like royalty. I don't know if they thought it would help the economy to have us here, or what. But there is a distinct difference in how we were treated in September and the way we're being treated now.

The place I live is called Hickory Park, and I think me and my daughter are the only blacks in this place. My grandson made eighteen the Friday before Thanksgiving, and my granddaughter made eighteen Thanksgiving Day, so we had family over here. It's their birthdays so we're just enjoying each other. We did have music on, but trust me, it was not what these people tried to make it to be. The children were on their best behavior, everything was beautiful. The police came to my door twice.

And it wasn't because of the music, it was because they just seen too many black faces. This is what I'm talking about. Texas is beginning to show her true colors.

When we first got here, a lot of folk were sitting back waiting on FEMA. I wasn't waiting on FEMA, and I'm glad I didn't because FEMA didn't give me nothing. I started working at a place called A&M Consolidated High School, but I was only working four hours a day. I really thought I liked that job until I saw the division at that place. There's blacks, whites, Mexicans, and nobody seems to like each other or even wanna respect each other. People are constantly doing things to cause one another to lose their jobs.

The thing about it is, I'm gonna be totally honest with you, and I mean this literally. They couldn't give me $100 an hour to work at a high school in New Orleans because the kids are totally out of control. But up here, I love working with the kids. I resigned from the high school in April because of my coworkers but now I'm a child-care provider at Kindercare. They keep you on your toes. So this is my second job out here and I'm gonna stick with these babies as long as I can. But this is not the last job I'll have out here. I'm gonna climb as high as I can climb.

On a positive note, since I've been out here I have been blessed to become part of a new church called New Jerusalem. It's under the pastorship of a lady named Marie Nutall, and I get so much positive energy on Sunday because this woman is pulling souls from all four corners of the globe. In this church, you see Mexicans, you see blacks, you see whites, you see different cultures.

My church and my pastor, oh God, I can't even begin to make you realize how much they mean to me. When I needed a truck to go back to New Orleans, to try to get the stuff that I had left, I had been part of that church less than a month. That church sent me back. My pastor is who I speak with when I'm feeling overwhelmed about what happened in New Orleans. No matter what time of day or night, she's there. It makes it bearable.

KALAMU YA SALAAM

In the summer of 2004, Hurricane Ivan came near the city. Five thousand people were in the Superdome. There were a lot of problems, and the city said, "It will never happen again. We will be prepared next time." The following year, Hurricane Katrina comes and they're woefully unprepared. If you took a picture of what was going on at the Convention Center—basically the scenes of crowds of people without anything—and said it was Haiti, nobody would doubt it.

The civic government had the responsibility to deal with that. The city government had had an indication of what would happen when you have a large number of people in that facility, and they were still not prepared. That's a failure of leadership. And it wasn't that anybody could've prepared for the extent of the damage that was done by Katrina, but certainly, given the example of what happened with Hurricane Ivan, there should have been some preparation that was done.

There was a meltdown, and Mayor Nagin was not capable—mentally and physically capable—of providing leadership. I'm not talking about whether he was present or not present. He was here most of the time. I'm not talking about what his public posture was, what he said in radio interviews and anything else like that. I'm saying, you've got a crisis, a communications breakdown first. Secondly, you have limited resources to work with. You have to make decisions, and there's nothing forthcoming from higher authorities, nothing significant forthcoming from higher authorities. What decisions do you make? How and when?

As far as Bush goes, the first week it was clear that there was nobody home. What has he done the first week in terms of the things that have gone on in Lebanon? It's a pattern. It's a pattern of inaction on his part because he doesn't know what to do. If you look at it, you see that that's how he functions. What did he do on the day of 9/11? My father used to say, "Do something. Even if it's wrong, do something. Don't just stand there."

In New Orleans, no one was in charge. In many of the stores that were "looted," weapons were taken. None of the authorized people or civil authorities could exert full civic control over an area, and the police were receiving so much fire in some places they basically had to lock down and wait out the night because they couldn't control the night. There were fires up and down the river on the wharves, major fires going on. Firemen couldn't put them out. People away from here don't have an idea of the immensity of the situation. Not only was it flooded, you've got these fires, you've got the police under fire, and you don't have any back-up forces. There's no coordination.

The troops did not come into the city until Friday afternoon. I figured out what the problem was. They waited until they had enough troops so they could come in and apply the whole "shock and awe" routine and take the city back. They needed thirty thousand armed troops with weapons at the ready. They didn't feel they could do it with two or three thousand. And they couldn't get what they felt was significant firepower here until Friday.

Within two days after the troops arrived, the Superdome and the Convention Center were all cleared out. People were forced out by gunpoint. People think that the rescue mission was not a military mission, but this was a military operation. People with guns telling you what to do, when to do it, where to stand, what not to do. Everywhere.

* * *

When I first came back into the city, I was not living here on a permanent basis, I was coming in and out. I would write reports, from time to time—about things I was doing when I would come into the city and this, that, and the other.

I remember driving through New Orleans East, and I had to stop driving, come out of there. It was making me cry. Part of it for me, personally, is that I have a history of being anti-petit bourgeois, so when I am moved to feel empathy and extreme sympathy for the professional class, it must be because of some really extreme circumstance 'cause in general, those are the people who are more inclined than not to aspire to be part of the system, and to, in the long run, go along with the system, both in terms of thinking and in terms of behavior. But I could not drive through New Orleans East and see what I saw without feeling empathy, active empathy.

In the aftermath of the storm, people are not here for the most part, so I mean as far as people are concerned, the whole city is shut down. The Sewage and Water Board is not taking any more new customers. The reason they're not taking any new customers is because they don't have the infrastructure to serve new customers. So by attrition, they are reducing the base of services that the city has to offer, because they just do not have the resources.

It's the same way with education. There's certain resources that were already in place, and they don't have the room to take any more students. Our school, Douglas, accommodates eight hundred, nine hundred students. There's no more room after that, all right? And of course people who were here first, who were already enrolled here, if they come back and they apply, they get first chance. Let's just say 60 percent of those students came back—we're roughly talking about two, two hundred fifty slots that will be available. If two thousand other students come back, where are they gonna go?

Let's say you are a schoolteacher with a master's degree, six years of experience teaching, some experience doing some other things. You now find yourself in Albuquerque, New Mexico, you have a mortgage note on your house that's flooded, you've got a couple of kids in school, you've got to deal with a vehicle. There's no way that you could sit for a whole year and do nothing but wait to get back to New Orleans.

So the black professionals have virtually been wiped out of the city of New Orleans, and now having to survive somewhere in the United States for almost a year without being in New Orleans. Come September, they're supposed to come back on faith? What are they supposed to do? We're talking about professional plans. What are they supposed to do? And my supposition is that they will stay, or go where they can find employment consistent with their education, where they can find opportunities for their children, where they can find housing, medical care—you know, support services.

Recently, a reporter from the *Boston Globe* who referred to me as, what, "morbidly pessimistic" or something like that, he asked me, "Well, what do you think New Orleans is gonna look like?"

I said, "Well, look out your window."

He said, "What?"

I said, "Look out your window. That's what New Orleans is gonna look like, except maybe the buildings probably won't be as tall, but other than that, that's pretty much it."

My brother Keith is a cardiologist. He had a clinic on Poland

Avenue. Poland Avenue is two blocks from the Industrial Canal, literally blocks from the canal on the Canal Street side. He had about a million dollars' worth of equipment in his building. He was completely flooded out. He cannot start that practice back up. Keith is widely recruited, but he would be working as a staff physician, he would not have his own practice. What is he gonna do?

He's made a practical decision, and that practical decision is that he's not going to reopen his practice right now. He can't. That whole *Field of Dreams* bullshit just doesn't work in New Orleans, which is if you open it, they will come. Ain't no buses, ain't no place to live, you know.

My little saying about this is: people who had nothing lost everything, people who had everything lost everything. So who's hurting? People who had everything, who had resources, when they lost everything, they moved someplace else. Never again, never again will New Orleans be 70 percent black. It won't happen again.

All the buzzwords are talking about the rebuilding of New Orleans. Nobody's talking about repopulating New Orleans, 'cause that's the last thing they wanna do. And I said, "I don't see any rebuilding going on. I see repair in areas where the damage was light." But have you seen any major rebuilding in the areas where there was severe damage? There is none, and there's certainly no repopulation of the city going on.

I know that there are many white people who are very, very happy about the population shift, and everything like that that's going on. It's to be expected. People in power are always happy when they win. That's just the way it is.

I see the loss being that there's no more lived tradition. In New Orleans we had a lived tradition that was passed on, adult to child, on an active, daily basis. I'm an example of that. Somebody looks at me and says, well, if you want to know about New Orleans, why don't you ask this guy. You didn't have to go to school to learn how to second-line, you grew up in it and so forth.[14] That's gone. It's just not gonna be here.

And so, what we're seeing now is a disruption of the African pattern, the traditional, passing it on to youth and then the youth taking that and doing whatever they do with it. That's the disruption of that, and that effectively means the end of this type of culture. That's what it means.

If I am not available to teach the young people, the young people are not available to me to teach them, then there's a disruption, and you may never see a set of writers that come along and have a firm grasp of the culture as a lived tradition that they're a part of. But rather you have people who are researchers, who even though they're black, they're outside of the culture and looking at it as a thing that existed apart from them.

And I'm saying if you have an absence of mentors, the young people are going to follow the ways of the dominant society. So now, kids'll go to school, they'll all come out soundin' the same. The traditional jazz model is that everybody had to find their own voice, and you worked, you struggled so that you had your identifiable sound. The basis of the European model is that you have a standard that you try to attain. So you end up being very technically proficient, but relatively anonymous in terms of what you sound like.

My hope is that these young people are gonna carry on something somewhere. It may not happen here, but they're gonna do something. So I don't feel like I've lost everything. I don't feel professionally frustrated. I have a way of getting work out there and I have an ability to produce the work. If anything, I am able to do more than I was able to do before the storm, so there is no sense of mourning and grief and sadness in me because my professional life,

---

[14] The second-line is the group of spectators and admirers that follows the main body of a parade or funeral procession through the streets.

serving my community, using the skills I have, I'm able to do it more, at a higher level, and more effectively than ever before. There are critical questions I'm not cheerful and optimistic about the current conditions or anything, but I am functioning.

Double displacement is the main issue. People were displaced by the hurricane, moved out of the city. They wanted to come back. So, this double displacement works in this way: when you get back into the city, you find out where you are and who you are is not where you were and who you were. So you're initially displaced from the city, and then when you get back into the city, you're displaced from what your memory and assumptions are about what the city is.

Well we have a phrase: you got what you wanted, but you don't want what you got. We wanted to be back here, but this is not what we wanted. And it seems ungrateful to say, "This is not what I want" when there are so many people who can't get back into the city, but the fact is this is not home. I'm not back home.

JACKIE HARRIS

I thought I'd be in New York for three days and I was there ten weeks after I left New Orleans. I was able to get an apartment—a friend has an apartment on Fifth Avenue and I'm subletting from her.

Out of every terrible thing, some good comes out of it. What Katrina has done is provided opportunities for New Orleans artists to travel all over the world. And I'll tell you what it's going to do, because in many instances New Orleans artists have been exploited and not been paid fairly, and now that they are playing all over, people are paying them a fair market wage. They are finally receiving the recognition they deserve and they are being paid what they are worth. It gave them an opportunity to express themselves, to feel free. Let me say this: if you don't have power you can't seize power. And so the whole exploitation thing in New Orleans is going to change. I also think that Katrina may change wages for people. I just hope some good can come out of this devastation because it's certainly a lot of suffering.

The thing is, these musical efforts may cause people not to come back because the city can't keep giving this lip service to these musicians about loving them and wanting them, and then not allowing them an opportunity to make a living. And also, there have to be some housing incentives for musicians and people who are perpetuators of the culture. And so, New Orleans music, it seems is bubbling all over the world after Katrina. Musicians are performing all over this year—maybe for the next two years. But then after that, if the city doesn't create some sort of mechanism to get them back, then there might be some atrophy of the culture and of the music.

We now really understand what we are, what New Orleans is to the world of culture. And I knew that. I felt it. I think we needed the world to say to us who we are. During my tenure in the Mayor Morial administration, I thought it was very important that the city use artists as cultural ambassadors in every opportunity it can. The music commission—which I am a part of—is part of the office of economic development, so therefore I tried to educate the business community about the importance of culture and music. Music is as much a component of economic development as bricks and mortar and factories.

Music in New Orleans is not just entertainment or a hobby. It's a way of life. Young people in New Orleans are exposed to music in the womb. You look at young parents attending concerts, you look at parents participating in second-line parades, you look at kids listening to music at an early age, kids playing music in the streets at eight, nine, and ten years old. You know music in New Orleans is a necessity. We need music in New Orleans as bad as we need water and food. I can't spend more than a day or two of not hearing some music, some New Orleans music.

New Orleans music will make you just want to jump up. When

I hear that music, man, I wanna move. Even if you don't jump up and dance, you pat your feet, you're bobbin' your head, you're clapping your hands. You're thinking about joy. That's what it is. It's a release. It's an expression. I mean, we use this music to celebrate life. We use it to celebrate death. We use it to celebrate good times, bad times, football games, parties, mourning situations. I mean, it's a necessity of life for us. Is it because of our human experience? Maybe it's because we're totally surrounded by water and we live very close to the land. Maybe it's because we're a gumbo of all of these cultural offerings. Maybe it's because the African-American experience has been an experience of oppression.

I had been in New York for a week, I guess, maybe a few days, and Wynton Marsalis asked if I would work on the Higher Ground benefit concert and really work on identifying New Orleans artists. I started consulting on what kind of music would be played, what works well with others, instrumentation we'd use on some of the songs, that sort of thing.

Two days before Wynton's Higher Ground concert, Paul Simon did something at Sony Studios in New York and they asked me to put together a brass band for that. And there were some students at Juilliard that knew the music. There were some musicians that had studied in New Orleans living in New York. And when they used this brass band to play behind Paul Simon's "Come and Take Me to the Mardi Gras," it was almost uncontrollable tears for me, but it was a little part of healing.

Then Higher Ground was two days later, and it was all these New Orleans artists, we were all backstage. And we had all been e-mailing back and forward, trying to make sure that everyone was all right, because this is a close knit group of people. We all care about each other, and we love each other. And you know, in New Orleans, we've got our own way of talking—we speak a different language here. So you know, most common to all of us is when we ask about our families it's about five words as one syllable, and it all goes together and it's, "Howyamamathen?" And so, I asked about how everybody was doing and that was really healing.

SONYA HERNANDEZ

You know what? I'm positive sure that the police was not prepared for the major storm like that. It was like, I don't know if Ray Nagin don't listen to the meteorologists, or the weather people don't say what was happening, but I can tell you that the New Orleans authorities was not prepared to handle a major storm like that.

I was in Miami for Hurricane Andrew 1992, and we stayed home. I remember my brother was living with us. I got the five kids but they were small, and my brother. He actually made a hole through the walls so he could walk from his apartment to my apartment inside. Soon as the storm was over, the National Guard was there. People was already there, bringing water, bringing people out to the emergency places. Actually, they was all around with a lot of trucks.

By the way Ray Nagin talked, I was having all my faith in him. I was telling my kids, "Don't worry. He knows what he's doing." And then I found out that Ray Nagin was in Baton Rouge while we was struggling in the Superdome. I feel like we was left out. I feel like they really wanted to get rid of the black people in New Orleans, but they never got the chance 'cause the black population is too big. Katrina was like a good excuse for them to remove us 'cause they already was trying to do it.

Like in my neighborhood, the black community was getting good. There is trees. It was not no more crack houses 'cause we as neighbors, we was not permitting that. Like when this house got burned and we as neighbors we was making sure that the house was covered with plywood and stuff. That way the kids don't be inside. And stuff like that. We cleaned the neighborhood.

When all the people start seeing that all sides was getting livable and nice, they don't feel comfortable with that. Not everybody, but some people, they feel like when they got money, they feel like they're the only one who can have the money. So when they start seeing that my little part of the town started getting nice, they start getting upset.

Everything is about money.

What they wanna do with New Orleans is what they've been planning for a long time. They want New Orleans for the white people. So for them, this was an opportunity to move everybody out of the city. That's what they did. New Orleans is not the only city of Louisiana. They could've do like they did in Miami: FEMA buy about five thousand trailers and they put the trailers somewhere else in another part of Miami. They don't move the people.

They don't want that type of people in New Orleans 'cause they're planning something else. They think that by removing all the African-American community, they can bring all type of people to the idea of New Orleans. People with money, especially. I think they not want to have people that they have to give no food stamps or nothing like that. They don't worry about the culture. They're worrying about money. They do understand, they just don't wanna do. That's what it is.

They draw us away from New Orleans and then Ray Nagin, he's calling the millionaires, the people with money, to make casinos and things. How're you going to tell me that the lights and the water is not restored where we was living, and they got light and water in French Quarter? How that works? They got lights on Uptown, on the part of where the people with money live. What about the people who got their own houses in the poor neighborhood? People like me, we was renting, but it was a lot of people that got their own place. They just don't want to live in no rich neighborhood. They want to live with their people, and they buy the property in there. What about them?

It's sad because it was so warm in between us as a community that money was not a matter in there.

My son was killed in a car accident in 2004. He was driving from La Place 'cause he got his mama, his baby mama, she live in La Place. This man, an airline driver, this drunk guy, runned the stop sign, and my son was trying to avoid the guy. When he got to the opposite lane they hit my son on the passenger side, but they smooshed the car all the way to the driver's side.

Reverend Tilly, he got his funeral home on St. Claude and Port by the railroad tracks. My son got killed and it caught us in a real bad time. Mr. Tilly, Reverend Tilly, sent somebody to my house and he sent his son to let us know that it was not a matter of money. We was supposed to pay about $3,000-something, but he say, "I know you guys don't make that money, so just give me $1,700."

Everybody was very concerned. I can tell you my neighbor next door bring $40. The other one on the corner bring $100. The other one bring food. My neighbor across the street bring a case of beer. The other one bring a case of Kool-Aid. It was like the neighborhood funeral.

Right now, where we live in Tulsa, people in there are so deep into theyself. Everybody got kids and everything, but you don't see people like in New Orleans you see people talking and all the older couples sitting on their porch. You don't see that in there. Actually in Tulsa, when it's around seven p.m., you don't see nobody in the street. Sometimes you not even see cars in there.

Where I'm living it's like people be treating us like we're aliens, and I do not feel comfortable with the way my kids being treated. I try to approach my neighbors 'cause since I was little my mother showed me the courtesy. Say, "Good morning." Or I see you: "How you doing? How you feel today?" If you pass by anybody, even a stranger, they will tell you, "Good morning. How you doing today?" Sometimes I get upset when I say hello and people in Tulsa turn their face like they're not interested to say, "Good morning." And that was not happening in New Orleans.

My husband say he's not going back, but soon he's going to start feeling strange. He's fifty-nine years old, so he won't let out his emotions, but being with him for twenty-five years I can tell you he feels. He miss his house. He miss his animals. He miss his people.

ANTHONY LETCHER

Everybody talkin' 'bout "back home." Even us poor people who've been renting, I wanna come home to what I know. They say a lion's gotta come back to his lair. He can go travel clean across Africa, man, but he's the king. He gon' come back to the place that he know.

I just talked to my Aunt Joanie today in Abbeyville and she was tellin' me go in her house, go look by her house and see if she can get the family graduation pictures. That's all she's thinkin' about, them pictures. I guess that's probably all she could think about. She ain't got no more house. I mean, it's torn up 'cause it's right there in the Ninth Ward too. It was on Clouet Street, right by Carver School. So all that's gone. All that's tore up. Everything through there; I mean everything.

Everybody in the Ninth Ward, down in that Desire project, where a brother used to rock at, that's where all the water was. Back there where I live at, it's through, it's finished. You got a lot of people back there, man, already really didn't have nothin', you know? People back there scufflin' to keep the little bit they got. All they got now, as far as the black poor people are concerned back there, is uncertainty. And mildew, they got plenty of that out there. They ain't got nothing but poor black people out there, gettin' the stuff out their houses, breathing in toxins. That's real. That's real, man.

But I want to come home. Look, nobody wants to be in Dallas. I can't lie, I don't like Dallas. I wish I could just snap my fingers and make this all go back the way it was. I'd take it like that. I would take it like it was. A lot of people want to come home. People don't like where they're at. There's a lot of uncertainty.

Everything is brand-new. You don't know it, it's hard to get around. You don't know your way here, so you wanna come back to something that you know. Where you can get on your feet at. Where I know Miss Evelyn down the street, and Miss Elizabeth down on the other end. In my neighborhood, they had a lot of older people, and they got this old lady named Miss Elizabeth, and she's like a family member. She's blind, and old as she is, she's still goin' on, still kickin' it. This lady is totally blind, and I go in there and I say, "Hey Miss Elizabeth."

She say, "Oh Lord, who is that?"

I say, "You don't know who this is?"

"Oh, that's TT's boy. That's Anthony. That's Mr. Ever-Letcher." That's what she calls me, Ever-Letcher. Say, "Boy, how you doin'?"

So I say, "Nothin', Miss Elizabeth," say, "I'm doin' all right."

So man, we'll sit there and talk about everything. This is a lady who don't know what Alzheimer's is, who don't know what getting old is. She remembers everything back from when. She's blind, she's old, and you can sit up there with her and talk about everything. Have you ever been around an old person like that? That's old, blind, body's riddled, can't move on her own, but in her head knows everything. She don't even ask you a question twice. This lady is still in her right frame of mind. And I used to go in there with her and sing a couple of church songs for her and stuff. She liked that.

They got her out though. She's still living. They got her out the house before the storm hit, so that was a blessing.

I don't think New Orleans will ever be back like it was. I think what it could be is new improved, people maybe with a lot more positive attitude, a more positive outlook on things. I don't know. I think this is a political thing. I don't think they're looking for what is best for anyone. That is my opinion. They're not looking for what is best for long term. So if the people don't have a positive mentality, it can never be done.

What they got to do is lead themselves and do the right thing. I mean, that's not hard to understand. You don't need a leader to do the right thing. After all this tragedy, why should you need a leader? Pretty soon, you'll have a large sum of money. I mean, two thousand dollars is enough to pay your rent and the security and get started. They go and they buy an eight-hundred-dollar wardrobe. But don't let that overweigh the good. Don't let the bad overweigh the good. There are a lot of people out there who want to do the right thing.

You know, there a lot of people out there that are not idiots. And most of the people doing that, buying clothes, is a lot of younger people, who really don't have a sense of what has really happened. They're kids.

But a lot of people talkin' about how they don't want no money. "Just fix my house up." Seriously, I have heard several people say that. And they're saying that they don't want no money. Get them a house, fix it up. Spend my money like that.

That's a pretty good deal. I think they should give everybody the opportunity to be a owner or something. They're talkin' bout, puttin' two hundred billion in this. Two hundred billion back into this here? Man, I'm dumbfounded. I mean, literally. I can't even count that far. We couldn't even count that.

You can give me a little slice of that. I could really use two thousand dollars. I am still waiting on mine but actually man, for the first time in my life, I'm not even stressing. I am on a dialysis machine, but I ain't even stressing about it. I'm sitting here with a newfound attitude, and New Orleans's fucked up. Ain't this a trip? It takes tragedy to make a man realize the good things in life, you know? It is sad, bro, that it takes all this here.

It's been kinda hectic and shit, but we've been lookin' out. Under the circumstance? This is what you really call "pillar to post." "Pillar to post" means here, and there, and everywhere, and goddamn, man. Pillar to post, man. This is really living pillar to post.

A NOTE ABOUT METHODOLOGY

The narratives in this collection were made possible by a wide network of interviewers, transcribers, researchers, and interns who donated their time and energy to the cause.

In the late summer of 2005, Voice of Witness's series editors, Dave Eggers and Lola Vollen, put out an open call for volunteers interested in collecting stories from survivors of Hurricane Katrina. The response was overwhelming. Hundreds of concerned students, teachers, writers, editors, and photographers were eager to help. Volunteers in New Orleans, Houston, Austin, and Atlanta began conducting interviews with hurricane survivors and sending their tapes back to the Voice of Witness office in San Francisco.

A majority of the interviews were conducted by Stacy Parker Aab, a writer in Houston, and Lola Vollen, who traveled the Gulf Coast interviewing displaced New Orleanians. Many of these initial interviews took place at the Disaster Recovery Center in Houston, or at the homes of the interviewees. Each person was then reinterviewed by a Voice of Witness editor. The interviews ranged in length from two to eight hours.

A small group of dedicated and meticulous interns and volunteers transcribed each interview, and the transcripts were returned to the interviewee. The editors then shaped each transcript into a clear, chronological narrative. In most cases, this process involved paring a raw transcript—on average, the transcripts were about 30,000 words—down to a narrative of about 10,000 words. In no cases were any changes made to the context or meaning of the narrators' words. The edited versions were then sent to the narrators for approval.

The editors of Voice of Witness are dedicated to presenting the stories of the interviewees as accurately as possible; the only way to ensure this, we feel, is to involve the interviewees throughout the process. The changes requested by the narrators were generally limited to those involving factuality and grammar. In addition to receiving the approval of the narrators, the stories in *Voices from the Storm* were fact-checked against news reports, primary source documents, and weather reports. Many of the materials used in the fact-checking process can be found in the appendices of this book.

For more information about methodology, and to view the transcripts of many of the interviews, visit:

www.voiceofwitness.org

APPENDICES

NEW ORLEANS AT A GLANCE

The following information was gathered from the U.S. Census Bureau's 2005 American Community Survey and the 2000 U.S. Census.

Age and Ethnicity of the New Orleans Population

	New Orleans	United States
Total	437,186	299,658,802
Median Age	35.2 Years	36.4 Years
Age 65 and older	11.7%	12.4%
Black	67.5%	12.1%
White	28.0%	74.7%
Hispanic	3.1%	14.5%
Asian	2.4%	4.3%
American Indian	0.2%	0.8%
Other	1.7%	7.9%

Education and Income of the New Orleans Population

	New Orleans	United States
High school graduates	74.7%	80.4%
Unemployment rate	13.2%	6.9%
Median household income	$30,711	$46,242
Families below poverty line	21.8%	10.2%
Home renters	53.5%	34.1%
Households without a vehicle	27.3%	10.3%

PATH OF HURRICANE KATRINA

Below is the National Hurricane Center's storm track of Hurricane Katrina.

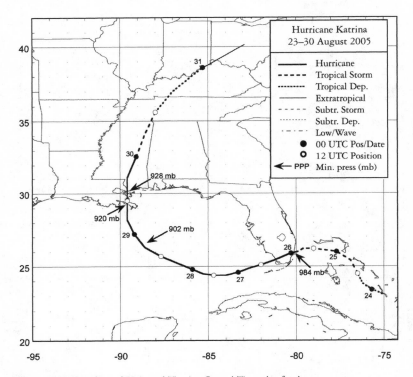

Note: UTC (Coordinated Universal Time) = Central Time plus five hours.

Source: National Hurricane Center

SAFFIR-SIMPSON SCALE

The Saffir-Simpson Hurricane Scale assigns a 1–5 rating to hurricanes, based on the hurricane's present intensity. It is used to estimate the potential property damage and flooding from a hurricane landfall. Wind speed is the determining factor in the scale.

Category 1 Hurricane:

Winds 74–95 mph (64–82 kt or 119–153 km/hr).

Storm surge generally four to five feet above normal. No real damage to building structures. Damage primarily to unanchored mobile homes, shrubbery, and trees. Some damage to poorly constructed signs. Also, some coastal road flooding and minor pier damage.

Category 2 Hurricane:

Winds 96–110 mph (83–95 kt or 154–177 km/hr).

Storm surge generally six to eight feet above normal. Some roofing material, door, and window damage. Considerable damage to shrubbery and trees with some trees blown down. Considerable damage to mobile homes, poorly constructed signs, and piers. Coastal and low-lying escape routes flood two to four hours before arrival of the hurricane center. Small craft in unprotected anchorages break moorings.

Category 3 Hurricane:

Winds 111–130 mph (96–113 kt or 178–209 km/hr).

Storm surge generally nine to twelve feet above normal. Some structural damage to small residences and utility buildings with a minor amount of curtain wall failures. Damage to shrubbery and trees with foliage blown off trees and large trees blown down. Mobile homes and poorly constructed signs are destroyed. Low-lying escape routes are cut by rising water three to five hours before arrival of the center of the hurricane. Flooding near the coast destroys smaller structures with larger structures damaged by battering from floating debris. Terrain continuously lower than five feet above sea level may be flooded inland for eight miles or more. Evacuation of low-lying residences with several blocks of the shoreline may be required.

Category 4 Hurricane:

Winds 131–155 mph (114–135 kt or 210–249 km/hr).

Storm surge generally thirteen to eighteen feet above normal. More extensive curtain wall failures with some complete roof-structure failures on small residences. Shrubs, trees, and all signs are blown down. Complete destruction of mobile homes. Extensive damage to doors and windows. Low-lying escape routes may be cut by rising water three to five hours before arrival of the center of the hurricane. Major damage to lower floors of structures near the shore. Terrain lower than ten feet above sea level may be flooded, requiring massive evacuation of residential areas as far inland as six miles.

Category 5 Hurricane:

Winds greater than 155 mph (135 kt or 249 km/hr).

Storm surge generally greater than eighteen feet above normal. Complete roof failure on many residences and industrial buildings. Some complete building failures with small utility buildings blown over or away. All shrubs, trees, and signs blown down. Complete destruction of mobile homes. Severe and extensive window and door damage. Low-lying escape routes are cut by rising water three to five hours before arrival of the center of the hurricane. Major damage to lower floors of all structures located less than fifteen feet above sea level and within five hundred yards of the shoreline. Massive evacuation of residential areas on low ground within five to ten miles of the shoreline may be required.

Category	Wind Speed	Examples
1	74–95 mph	Lili (2002), Gaston (2004)
2	96–110 mph	Frances (2004), Isabel (2003)
3	111–130 mph	Betsy (1965), Katrina (2005)
4	131–155 mph	Charley (2004), Dennis (2005)
5	155+ mph	Andrew (1992), Camille (1969)

U.S. HURRICANE STATISTICS

The following graphs are derived from data compiled in "The Federal Response to Hurricane Katrina: Lessons Learned," a 217-page document compiled by various White House and military officials.

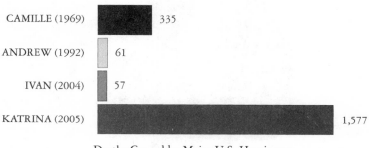

Deaths Caused by Major U.S. Hurricanes

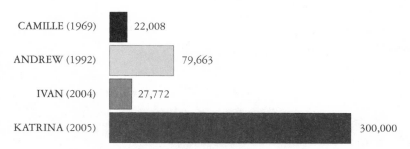

Estimated Number of Homes Lost to Major U.S. Hurricanes

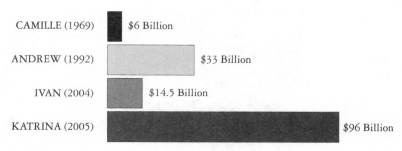

Estimated Damages (in U.S. Dollars) of Major U.S. Hurricanes

Ethnicities of Deceased Identified
at St. Gabriel and Carville Morgues

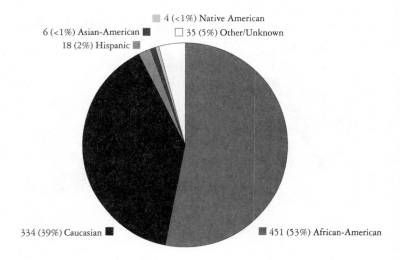

4 (<1%) Native American

6 (<1%) Asian-American

35 (5%) Other/Unknown

18 (2%) Hispanic

334 (39%) Caucasian

451 (53%) African-American

Ages of Deceased Identified
at St. Gabriel and Carville Morgues

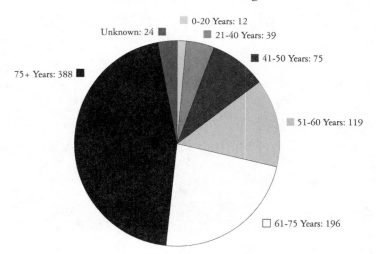

0-20 Years: 12

Unknown: 24

21-40 Years: 39

41-50 Years: 75

75+ Years: 388

51-60 Years: 119

61-75 Years: 196

NHC/NWS WARNINGS

As Katrina made its way through the Gulf of Mexico, the National Hurricane Center and National Weather Service posted continuous updates. The following are excerpted from bulletins issued between August 25 and August 29, 2005.

Thursday, August 25—7:00 p.m. EDT

```
BULLETIN
HURRICANE KATRINA INTERMEDIATE ADVISORY NUMBER 9A
NWS TPC/NATIONAL HURRICANE CENTER MIAMI FL
7 PM EDT THU AUG 25 2005
```

...EYE OF KATRINA CURRENTLY MAKING LANDFALL BETWEEN HALLANDALE BEACH AND NORTH MIAMI BEACH WITH 80 MPH WINDS...PORT EVERGLADES JUST REPORTED GUSTS TO 92 MPH WINDS...

A HURRICANE WARNING REMAINS IN EFFECT FOR THE SOUTHEAST FLORIDA
COAST FROM JUPITER INLET SOUTHWARD TO FLORIDA CITY...INCLUDING LAKE OKEECHOBEE. PREPARATIONS TO PROTECT LIFE AND PROPERTY SHOULD HAVE BEEN COMPLETED.

A TROPICAL STORM WARNING HAS BEEN ISSUED FOR ALL OF THE FLORIDA KEYS AND FLORIDA BAY FROM KEY WEST NORTHWARD. A TROPICAL STORM WARNING IS ALSO IN EFFECT ALONG THE GULF COAST OF FLORIDA FROM LONGBOAT KEY SOUTH AND EASTWARD TO SOUTH OF FLORIDA CITY. A TROPICAL STORM WARNING REMAINS IN EFFECT ALONG THE FLORIDA EAST COAST FROM NORTH OF JUPITER INLET TO VERO BEACH.

FOR STORM INFORMATION SPECIFIC TO YOUR AREA...INCLUDING POSSIBLE INLAND WATCHES AND WARNINGS...PLEASE MONITOR PRODUCTS ISSUED BY YOUR LOCAL WEATHER OFFICE.

KATRINA IS MOVING TOWARD THE WEST NEAR 6 MPH AND THIS GENERAL MOTION IS EXPECTED TO CONTINUE DURING THE NEXT 24 HOURS. ON THIS TRACK... THE CENTER SHOULD MOVE FARTHER INLAND ALONG SOUTH FLORIDA TONIGHT AND FRIDAY.

LATEST REPORT FROM A NOAA RECONNAISSANCE AIRCRAFT AND THE MIAMI NOAA DOPPLER RADAR INDICATE MAXIMUM SUSTAINED WINDS ARE 80 MPH... WITH HIGHER GUSTS. KATRINA IS A CATEGORY ONE HURRICANE ON THE SAFFIR-SIMPSON SCALE. STRONGER WINDS...ESPECIALLY IN GUSTS...ARE LIKELY ON HIGH RISING BUILDINGS. A GRADUAL WEAKENING IS EXPECTED AS KATRINA CONTINUES TO MOVE INLAND ACROSS SOUTH FLORIDA AND THE EVERGLADES TONIGHT AND FRIDAY.

Friday, August 26—9:00 a.m. EDT

BULLETIN
HURRICANE KATRINA INTERMEDIATE ADVISORY NUMBER 11B
NWS TPC/NATIONAL HURRICANE CENTER MIAMI FL
9 AM EDT FRI AUG 26 2005

...KATRINA GETTING BETTER ORGANIZED OVER THE EASTERN GULF OF
MEXICO AS IT MOVES SLOWLY AWAY FROM SOUTH FLORIDA...
...FLOODING STILL A THREAT FOR EXTREME SOUTHERN FLORIDA...

A TROPICAL STORM WARNING REMAINS IN EFFECT FOR ALL OF THE FLORIDA
KEYS AND FLORIDA BAY FROM DRY TORTUGAS NORTHWARD... ALONG THE
EAST COAST OF FLORIDA FROM FLORIDA CITY NORTHWARD TO DEERFIELD
BEACH...AND ALONG THE GULF COAST OF FLORIDA FROM SOUTH OF FLORIDA
CITY WESTWARD AND NORTHWARD TO LONGBOAT KEY. A TROPICAL STORM
WARNING MEANS THAT TROPICAL STORM CONDITIONS ARE EXPECTED WITHIN
THE WARNING AREA WITHIN THE NEXT 24 HOURS.

AT 9 AM EDT...1300Z...THE CENTER OF HURRICANE KATRINA WAS
LOCATED NEAR LATITUDE 25.2 NORTH... LONGITUDE 82.0 WEST OR ABOUT
45 MILES NORTH-NORTHWEST OF KEY WEST FLORIDA AND ABOUT 65 MILES
SOUTH-SOUTHWEST OF NAPLES FLORIDA.

KATRINA IS MOVING ERRATICALLY TOWARD THE WEST NEAR 6 MPH AND
THIS MOTION IS EXPECTED TO CONTINUE FOR THE NEXT 24 HOURS...
WITH A SLIGHT INCREASE IN FORWARD SPEED.

INFORMATION FROM NOAA DOPPLER RADARS INDICATE MAXIMUM
SUSTAINED
WINDS ARE NEAR 75 MPH... WITH HIGHER GUSTS. KATRINA IS A
CATEGORY ONE HURRICANE ON THE SAFFIR-SIMPSON SCALE. SOME
STRENGTHENING IS FORECAST DURING THE NEXT 24 HOURS. AN AIR FORCE
RESERVE UNIT RECONNAISSANCE AIRCRAFT IS SCHEDULED TO INVESTIGATE
KATRINA LATER THIS MORNING.

Saturday, August 27—2:00 a.m. EDT

BULLETIN
HURRICANE KATRINA INTERMEDIATE ADVISORY NUMBER 15A
NWS TPC/NATIONAL HURRICANE CENTER MIAMI FL
2 AM EDT SAT AUG 27 2005

...KATRINA CONTINUES TO STRENGTHEN... STILL MOVING TOWARD THE
WEST-SOUTHWEST...

A TROPICAL STORM WARNING REMAINS IN EFFECT FOR FLORIDA BAY AND
FOR THE FLORIDA KEYS FROM KEY LARGO SOUTHWARD AND WESTWARD TO
KEY WEST INCLUDING THE DRY TORTUGAS.

FOR STORM INFORMATION SPECIFIC TO YOUR AREA...INCLUDING POSSIBLE
INLAND WATCHES AND WARNINGS...PLEASE MONITOR PRODUCTS ISSUED

BY YOUR LOCAL WEATHER OFFICE.
AT 2 AM EDT...0600Z...THE EYE OF HURRICANE KATRINA WAS LOCATED
BY RADAR NEAR LATITUDE 24.4 NORTH... LONGITUDE 84.0 WEST OR ABOUT
450 MILES SOUTHEAST OF THE MOUTH OF THE MISSISSIPPI RIVER AND
ABOUT 135 MILES WEST OF KEY WEST FLORIDA.

KATRINA IS MOVING TOWARD THE WEST-SOUTHWEST NEAR 8 MPH. A
GRADUAL TURN TO THE WEST AND WEST-NORTHWEST IS EXPECTED DURING
THE NEXT 24 HOURS.

MAXIMUM SUSTAINED WINDS HAVE INCREASED TO NEAR 110 MPH WITH
HIGHER GUSTS. KATRINA IS A CATEGORY TWO HURRICANE ON THE
SAFFIR-SIMPSON SCALE. KATRINA IS EXPECTED TO BECOME A MAJOR
HURRICANE TODAY.

KATRINA IS EXPECTED TO PRODUCE RAINFALL AMOUNTS OF 5 TO 10 INCHES
OVER NORTHWESTERN CUBA AND 1 TO 3 INCHES OF RAINFALL IS EXPECTED
OVER THE YUCATAN PENINSULA. RAINFALL IS EXPECTED TO SLOWLY
DIMINISH ACROSS THE LOWER FLORIDA KEYS... ALTHOUGH AN ADDITIONAL
1 TO 2 INCHES OF RAIN IS POSSIBLE IN SOME OF THE HEAVIER RAIN
BANDS.

Saturday, August 27—7:00 p.m. EDT

BULLETIN
HURRICANE KATRINA INTERMEDIATE ADVISORY NUMBER 18A
NWS TPC/NATIONAL HURRICANE CENTER MIAMI FL
7 PM CDT SAT AUG 27 2005

...DANGEROUS HURRICANE KATRINA BEGINS TO MOVE TOWARD THE WEST-
NORTHWEST...

A HURRICANE WATCH IS IN EFFECT ALONG THE NORTHERN GULF COAST
FROM
INTRACOASTAL CITY TO THE ALABAMA-FLORIDA BORDER.

A HURRICANE WARNING WILL LIKELY BE REQUIRED FOR PORTIONS OF
THE
NORTHERN GULF COAST LATER TONIGHT. INTERESTS IN THIS AREA
SHOULD
MONITOR THE PROGRESS OF KATRINA.

AT 7 PM CDT...0000Z...THE CENTER OF HURRICANE KATRINA WAS
LOCATED NEAR LATITUDE 24.8 NORTH...LONGITUDE 85.9 WEST OR ABOUT
360 MILES SOUTHEAST OF THE MOUTH OF THE MISSISSIPPI RIVER.

KATRINA HAS BEGUN TO MOVE TOWARD THE WEST-NORTHWEST NEAR 7
MPH.
THIS GENERAL MOTION SHOULD CONTINUE TONIGHT AND SUNDAY.

MAXIMUM SUSTAINED WINDS ARE NEAR 115 MPH...WITH HIGHER GUSTS.
KATRINA IS A CATEGORY THREE HURRICANE ON THE SAFFIR-SIMPSON

SCALE. STRENGTHENING IS FORECAST DURING THE NEXT 24 HOURS...
AND
KATRINA COULD BECOME A CATEGORY FOUR HURRICANE LATER TONIGHT
OR
SUNDAY.
DATA FROM BUOYS INDICATE THAT 12-FOOT WAVES ARE ALREADY
APPROACHING PORTIONS OF THE NORTHERN GULF COAST. STORM SURGE
FLOODING ALONG THE SOUTHWESTERN COAST OF FLORIDA SHOULD SUBSIDE
TONIGHT.

Sunday, August 28—10:00 a.m. EDT

BULLETIN
HURRICANE KATRINA ADVISORY NUMBER 23
NWS TPC/NATIONAL HURRICANE CENTER MIAMI FL
10 AM CDT SUN AUG 28 2005

...POTENTIALLY CATASTROPHIC HURRICANE KATRINA...EVEN STRONGER...
HEADED FOR THE NORTHERN GULF COAST...

A HURRICANE WARNING IS IN EFFECT FOR THE NORTH CENTRAL GULF
COAST FROM MORGAN CITY LOUISIANA EASTWARD TO THE ALABAMA/FLORIDA
BORDER...INCLUDING THE CITY OF NEW ORLEANS AND LAKE PONTCHARTRAIN.
A HURRICANE WARNING MEANS THAT HURRICANE CONDITIONS ARE EXPECTED
WITHIN THE WARNING AREA WITHIN THE NEXT 24 HOURS. PREPARATIONS
TO PROTECT LIFE AND PROPERTY SHOULD BE RUSHED TO COMPLETION.

AT 10 AM CDT...1500Z...THE CENTER OF HURRICANE KATRINA WAS
LOCATED NEAR LATITUDE 26.0 NORTH... LONGITUDE 88.1 WEST OR ABOUT
225 MILES SOUTH-SOUTHEAST OF THE MOUTH OF THE MISSISSIPPI
RIVER.

KATRINA IS MOVING TOWARD THE WEST-NORTHWEST NEAR 12 MPH...AND A
TURN TOWARD THE NORTHWEST AND NORTH-NORTHWEST IS EXPECTED OVER
THE NEXT 24 HOURS.

REPORTS FROM AN AIR FORCE HURRICANE HUNTER AIRCRAFT INDICATE
THAT THE MAXIMUM SUSTAINED WINDS HAVE INCREASED TO NEAR 175
MPH...WITH HIGHER GUSTS. KATRINA IS A POTENTIALLY CATASTROPHIC
CATEGORY FIVE HURRICANE ON THE SAFFIR-SIMPSON SCALE. SOME
FLUCTUATIONS IN STRENGTH ARE LIKELY DURING THE NEXT 24 HOURS.

HURRICANE FORCE WINDS EXTEND OUTWARD UP TO 105 MILES FROM THE
CENTER...AND TROPICAL STORM FORCE WINDS EXTEND OUTWARD UP TO 205
MILES.

COASTAL STORM SURGE FLOODING OF 18 TO 22 FEET ABOVE NORMAL
TIDE
LEVELS...LOCALLY AS HIGH AS 28 FEET ALONG WITH LARGE AND
DANGEROUS BATTERING WAVES...CAN BE EXPECTED NEAR AND TO THE EAST
OF WHERE THE CENTER MAKES LANDFALL.

RAINFALL TOTALS OF 5 TO 10 INCHES...WITH ISOLATED MAXIMUM
AMOUNTS OF 15 INCHES...ARE POSSIBLE ALONG THE PATH OF KATRINA
ACROSS THE GULF COAST AND THE TENNESSEE VALLEY. RAINFALL TOTALS
OF 4 TO 8 INCHES ARE POSSIBLE ACROSS THE OHIO VALLEY INTO THE
EASTERN GREAT LAKES REGION TUESDAY AND WEDNESDAY.

ISOLATED TORNADOES WILL BE POSSIBLE BEGINNING THIS EVENING
OVER
SOUTHERN PORTIONS OF LOUISIANA...MISSISSIPPI...AND ALABAMA...AND
OVER THE FLORIDA PANHANDLE.

Sunday, August 28—4:13 p.m. EDT
Urgent Message from the National Weather Service

URGENT - WEATHER MESSAGE
NATIONAL WEATHER SERVICE NEW ORLEANS LA
413 PM CDT SUN AUG 28 2005

...EXTREMELY DANGEROUS HURRICANE KATRINA CONTINUES TO APPROACH
THE MISSISSIPPI RIVER DELTA...DEVASTATING DAMAGE EXPECTED...

MOST OF THE AREA WILL BE UNINHABITABLE FOR WEEKS...PERHAPS
LONGER. AT LEAST ONE HALF OF WELL CONSTRUCTED HOMES WILL HAVE
ROOF AND WALL FAILURE. ALL GABLED ROOFS WILL FAIL...LEAVING
THOSE HOMES SEVERELY DAMAGED OR DESTROYED.

THE MAJORITY OF INDUSTRIAL BUILDINGS WILL BECOME NON FUNCTIONAL.
PARTIAL TO COMPLETE WALL AND ROOF FAILURE IS EXPECTED. ALL WOOD
FRAMED LOW RISING APARTMENT BUILDINGS WILL BE DESTROYED.CONCRETE
BLOCK LOW RISE APARTMENTS WILL SUSTAIN MAJOR DAMAGE...INCLUDING
SOME WALL AND ROOF FAILURE.

HIGH RISE OFFICE AND APARTMENT BUILDINGS WILL SWAY DANGEROUSLY
...A FEW TO THE POINT OF TOTAL COLLAPSE. ALL WINDOWS WILL BLOW
OUT.

AIRBORNE DEBRIS WILL BE WIDESPREAD...AND MAY INCLUDE HEAVY ITEMS
SUCH AS HOUSEHOLD APPLIANCES AND EVEN LIGHT VEHICLES. SPORT
UTILITY VEHICLES AND LIGHT TRUCKS WILL BE MOVED. THE BLOWN DEBRIS
WILL CREATE ADDITIONAL DESTRUCTION. PERSONS...PETS...AND
LIVESTOCK EXPOSED TO THE WINDS WILL FACE CERTAIN DEATH IF
STRUCK.

POWER OUTAGES WILL LAST FOR WEEKS...AS MOST POWER POLES WILL BE
DOWN AND TRANSFORMERS DESTROYED. WATER SHORTAGES WILL MAKE HUMAN
SUFFERING INCREDIBLE BY MODERN STANDARDS.

THE VAST MAJORITY OF NATIVE TREES WILL BE SNAPPED OR UPROOTED.
ONLY THE HEARTIEST WILL REMAIN STANDING...BUT BE TOTALLY
DEFOLIATED. FEW CROPS WILL REMAIN. LIVESTOCK LEFT EXPOSED TO THE
WINDS WILL BE KILLED.

AN INLAND HURRICANE WIND WATCH IS ISSUED WHEN SUSTAINED WINDS NEAR HURRICANE FORCE...OR FREQUENT GUSTS AT OR ABOVE HURRICANE FORCE...ARE POSSIBLE WITHIN THE NEXT 24 TO 36 HOURS.

HURRICANE KATRINA CONTINUES TO APPROACH THE AREA. TROPICAL STORM
FORCE WINDS ARE CURRENTLY MOVING INTO THE COASTAL MARSHES AND WILL PERSIST FOR THE NEXT 26 TO 28 HOURS. HURRICANE FORCE WINDS WILL ONSET AROUND MIDNIGHT NEAR THE COAST AND BY 3 AM CLOSER TO THE NEW ORLEANS METRO AREA AND PERSIST FOR 9 TO 15 HOURS. MAXIMUM WIND GUSTS AROUND 175 MPH ARE LIKELY IN THE WARNED AREA BY DAYBREAK MONDAY.

DO NOT VENTURE OUTDOORS ONCE TROPICAL STORM FORCE WINDS ONSET!

Monday, August 29—4:00 a.m. EDT

BULLETIN
HURRICANE KATRINA ADVISORY NUMBER 26
NWS TPC/NATIONAL HURRICANE CENTER MIAMI FL
4 AM CDT MON AUG 29 2005

...EXTREMELY DANGEROUS CATEGORY FOUR HURRICANE KATRINA MOVING
    NORTHWARD TOWARD SOUTHEASTERN LOUISIANA AND THE NORTHERN GULF
    COAST...
...TROPICAL STORM-FORCE WINDS LASHING THE GULF COAST FROM
    SOUTHEASTERN LOUISIANA TO THE ALABAMA-FLORIDA BORDER...

A HURRICANE WARNING IS IN EFFECT FOR THE NORTH CENTRAL GULF COAST
FROM MORGAN CITY LOUISIANA EASTWARD TO THE ALABAMA/FLORIDA BORDER...INCLUDING THE CITY OF NEW ORLEANS AND LAKE PONTCHARTRAIN.
PREPARATIONS TO PROTECT LIFE AND PROPERTY SHOULD BE COMPLETED THIS EVENING.

A TROPICAL STORM WARNING AND A HURRICANE WATCH ARE IN EFFECT FROM
EAST OF THE ALABAMA/FLORIDA BORDER TO DESTIN FLORIDA...AND FROM
WEST OF MORGAN CITY TO INTRACOASTAL CITY LOUISIANA.

AT 4 AM CDT...0900Z...THE CENTER OF HURRICANE KATRINA WAS LOCATED NEAR LATITUDE 28.8 NORTH... LONGITUDE 89.6 WEST OR ABOUT 90 MILES SOUTH-SOUTHEAST OF NEW ORLEANS LOUISIANA AND ABOUT 120 MILES SOUTH-SOUTHWEST OF BILOXI MISSISSIPPI.

KATRINA IS MOVING TOWARD THE NORTH NEAR 15 MPH... AND THIS MOTION IS FORECAST TO CONTINUE TODAY. A GRADUAL TURN TOWARD THE NORTH-NORTHEAST AT A SLIGHTLY FASTER FORWARD SPEED IS EXPECTED LATER TONIGHT AND ON TUESDAY. ON THE FORECAST TRACK...KATRINA

WILL MOVE ONSHORE THE SOUTHEASTERN LOUISIANA COAST JUST EAST OF GRAND ISLE THIS MORNING... AND REACH THE LOUISIANA-MISSISSIPPI BORDER AREA THIS AFTERNOON. CONDITIONS WILL CONTINUE TO STEADILY DETERIORATE OVER CENTRAL AND SOUTHEASTERN LOUISIANA...SOUTHERN MISSISSIPPI...AND SOUTHERN ALABAMA THROUGHOUT THE DAY.

MAXIMUM SUSTAINED WINDS ARE NEAR 150 MPH...240 KM/HR...WITH HIGHER GUSTS. KATRINA IS A STRONG CATEGORY FOUR HURRICANE ON THE
SAFFIR-SIMPSON SCALE. SOME FLUCTUATIONS IN STRENGTH ARE LIKELY PRIOR TO LANDFALL...BUT KATRINA IS EXPECTED TO MAKE LANDFALL AS
A CATEGORY FOUR HURRICANE. WINDS AFFECTING THE UPPER FLOORS OF HIGH-RISE BUILDINGS WILL BE SIGNIFICANTLY STRONGER THAN THOSE NEAR GROUND LEVEL.

KATRINA REMAINS A VERY LARGE HURRICANE. HURRICANE FORCE WINDS EXTEND OUTWARD UP TO 105 MILES FROM THE CENTER...AND TROPICAL STORM FORCE WINDS EXTEND OUTWARD UP TO 230 MILES. RECENTLY...A SUSTAINED WIND OF 53 MPH WITH GUST TO 91 MPH WAS REPORTED AT GRAND ISLE LOUISIANA ...AND A WIND GUST TO 71 MPH WAS REPORTED IN NEW ORLEANS.

COASTAL STORM SURGE FLOODING OF 18 TO 22 FEET ABOVE NORMAL TIDE
LEVELS...LOCALLY AS HIGH AS 28 FEET...ALONG WITH LARGE AND DANGEROUS BATTERING WAVES...CAN BE EXPECTED NEAR AND TO THE EAST OF WHERE THE CENTER MAKES LANDFALL. SOME LEVEES IN THE GREATER NEW ORLEANS AREA COULD BE OVERTOPPED. SIGNIFICANT STORM SURGE FLOODING WILL OCCUR ELSEWHERE ALONG THE CENTRAL AND NORTHEASTERN GULF OF MEXICO COAST. NOAA BUOY 42040 LOCATED ABOUT 50 MILES EAST OF THE MOUTH OF THE MISSISSIPPI RIVER RECENTLY REPORTED WAVES HEIGHTS OF AT LEAST 46 FEET.

THE TORNADO THREAT AHEAD OF KATRINA CONTINUES TO INCREASE AND SCATTERED TORNADOES WILL BE POSSIBLE TODAY OVER SOUTHEASTERN LOUISIANA... SOUTHERN MISSISSIPPI...SOUTHERN ALABAMA...AND OVER THE FLORIDA PANHANDLE.

TRANSCRIPT FROM TESTIMONY
OF MARTY J. BAHAMONDE

Marty Bahamonde, an official from FEMA's Office of Public Affairs, was the first FEMA official on the ground in New Orleans during Hurricane Katrina. Bahamonde testified before the Senate Committee on Homeland Security and Governmental Affairs on Thursday, October 20, 2005.

Good Morning. I appreciate the opportunity to appear before you today.

I am Marty Bahamonde. I work for the Federal Emergency Management Agency (FEMA) as a public affairs officer for FEMA's Boston office and worked in FEMA's headquarters in Washington, D.C. I worked in New Orleans prior to and immediately following Hurricane Katrina and have spent that past six weeks working at the joint field office in Baton Rouge. I was the only FEMA employee deployed to New Orleans prior to the storm. I am here today to tell you what I experienced during the five days before and after Hurricane Katrina in New Orleans and specifically at the Superdome.

Let me briefly explain why I was there.

Since 2003, I have often been tasked by the undersecretary of FEMA Mike Brown and his staff to do advance work for the undersecretary in preparation for or response to large disasters. My assignments included Hurricane Isabel in 2003, Hurricane Charley in 2004, Hurricane Dennis this past June, and others. My responsibilities varied, but always included providing accurate and important information to FEMA's front office and Undersecretary Mike Brown. On Friday, August 26, I was tasked by FEMA's front office to work advance wherever Hurricane Katrina was going to hit, which by Saturday appeared to be New Orleans.

I arrived in New Orleans Saturday night, August 27. Through the generosity of the New Orleans Emergency Operation Center (EOC), I was able to work in their office, and they provided me with shelter during the hurricane. The city EOC is located in City Hall, almost directly across from the Superdome.

On Sunday, August 28, I met the city staff at the EOC, got to know people and their roles at the EOC, and developed my own plans for my advance work, which included coordinating with the coast guard to arrange a flyover after the hurricane passed. On Sunday, Katrina intensified to a Category 5 storm. I sensed a great deal of worry among everyone. I was worried too. My contact at FEMA headquarters told me to leave New Orleans because it would be too dangerous. But like the thousands of other people left in New Orleans, the traffic jams leaving the city that morning prevented me from leaving.

The Superdome had been opened as a special-needs shelter, but on Sunday, as thousands of residents were unable to evacuate, the Superdome became a shelter of last resort for anyone left in the city. By noon, thousands began arriving and by midday, lines wrapped around the building. It was also at that time that I realized that the size of the crowd was a big concern at the EOC. Terry Ebbert, the city's homeland security director, made an announcement in the EOC that struck me. He asked the maintenance staff to gather up all of the toilet paper in city hall and any other commodities they could find and immediately take them over to the Superdome. I specifically note this because it told me that supplies at the Dome might be a serious issue.

I was between the Superdome and the EOC throughout the day on Sunday. I took pictures of the crowds and sent them back to FEMA headquarters. On Sunday evening, I was at the Superdome to do media interviews and afterwards I met with the National Guard inside the Superdome to discuss a range of things including the expected arrival of a FEMA Disaster Medical Assistance Team (DMAT) from Houston. The National Guard also told me that they expected 360,000 "meals ready to eat"— "MREs"—and fifteen trucks of water to arrive that night. As the storm intensified outside, a series of critical events began to unfold. Instead of 360,000 MREs, only 40,000 arrived. Instead of fifteen trucks of water, only five arrived, and the medical team did not arrive either.

Later that night, after most of the 12,000 evacuees entered the Superdome, I returned to the EOC around midnight to ride out the storm. By early Monday morning, with the storm upon us, reports from throughout the city were moderately optimistic; some low-level flooding, no levee breaks, and limited wind damage. But by 8 a.m.—the nearest point of eye passage—the situation worsened; I could clearly see and reported back to FEMA headquarters that the Hyatt hotel and other tall buildings in downtown had suffered incredible window damage, and I could see the roof peeling off the Superdome. I received several calls from FEMA headquarters seeking confirmation of the situation on the ground.

At approximately 11 a.m., the worst possible news came into the EOC. I stood there and listened to the first report of the levee break at the 17th

Street Canal. I do not know who made the report but they were very specific about the location of the break and the size. And then they added it was "very bad." I continued to provide regular updates to FEMA headquarters throughout the day as the situation unfolded.

At approximately 5 p.m., I rushed over to the Superdome because I had been notified that a coast guard helicopter was able to take me for a short fly-over so that I could assess the situation in the city and plan for Undersecretary Brown's visit the next day. My initial flyover lasted about ten minutes and even in that short time I was able to see that approximately 80 percent of the city was underwater, and I confirmed the 17th Street Canal levee break. I was struck by how accurate the 11 a.m. call was about the levee.

About fifteen minutes later, I went back up on a second coast guard helicopter for approximately forty-five minutes, and during this flight, I was able to get a real understanding of the impact of Katrina on New Orleans and the surrounding area.

Upon landing, I immediately made three telephone calls. The first was to Undersecretary Mike Brown at approximately 7 p.m. The second was to FEMA's front office, and the third was to FEMA Public Affairs. That third call was to set up a conference call with FEMA Operations in headquarters, the Emergency Response Team–National (ERT-N) team in Baton Rouge, the Regional Response Coordination Center (RRCC) in Denton, Texas, and with FEMA's front office, so I could make as many people aware of the situation that faced FEMA and the city of New Orleans.

In each report and on the conference call, I explained what I saw and then provided my analysis of what I believed to be the most critical issues we were facing:

- Ground transportation into the city was virtually non-existent because of the massive flooding. Any ground transportation must come from west of the city because the I-10 bridge to Slidell on the east side of the city was completely destroyed and there was no access from the north because of flooded roads. I also stated that the situation would only worsen in the next day or so because of the massive amounts of water being deposited into the city via the levee break. I described the levee break as being really bad.
- Search-and-rescue missions were critical as thousands of people stood on roofs or balconies in flooded neighborhoods.

- Supplying commodities would be a challenge as more and more people were headed to the Superdome to escape the floodwaters and food and water supplies were already very short at the Superdome. I told them that the Superdome population was at almost 20,000 people.
- Medical care at the Superdome was critical because the staff there had run out of oxygen for special-needs patients and more and more people needed medical attention.
- Housing an entire city worth of people would be a major issue as approximately 80 percent of the city was underwater to varying degrees and many areas were completely destroyed.
- Environmental issues would be major as I reported that an oil tanker had run aground and was leaking fuel.

I believed at the time and still do today that I was confirming the worst-case scenario that everyone had always talked about regarding New Orleans.

I then had a meeting with New Orleans mayor Nagin and his staff of approximately twenty-five people, and I told them of the situation so that they would know what they faced in the hours and days ahead. It was a very emotional meeting for everyone. Following that meeting, Terry Ebbert pulled me aside and said, "You have done this before. What do we need to do now?" I told him that he needed to make a list of the city's priorities, actions, and commodities, so that they could move forward with an organized plan. I also told him that they needed to let the state know so that FEMA could be tasked to help. He said, "Consider it done."

On Tuesday, August 30, I woke early to discover that water was rising around the Superdome and that by 6 a.m., two to three feet of water was in the streets around City Hall and the Superdome, and it was continuing to rise. I called Bill Lokey, the federal coordinating officer in Baton Rouge, immediately and told him of the rising waters and once again tried to express the seriousness of the situation. He told me he would have an operational team deployed to the Superdome later that day to relieve me.

About an hour later I was informed that Undersecretary Brown, Governor Blanco, senators Landrieu and Vitter and others were planning on flying to the Superdome later that morning. At approximately 8 a.m., I went to find Mayor Nagin, who was at the Hyatt hotel, to inform him of the visit and asked him to meet with the group. So I put on tennis shoes and shorts and walked through what was now waist-deep water over to the Hyatt, and told the mayor of the visit. I then walked through the water again to get to the Superdome.

At the Superdome, I spoke with the National Guard to get the latest conditions and it was obvious that the Superdome conditions were in rapid decline and that there was a critical need for food and water. I communicated this to Undersecretary Brown when he arrived later that morning. I told him that the Superdome conditions were deplorable, and that we desperately needed food and water.

During the subsequent meeting with the mayor and the incoming group, Mayor Nagin pulled out his list of priorities and proceeded to tell everyone what he needed for his city and the residents.

By early Tuesday morning a FEMA medical team arrived at the Superdome and by early afternoon a four-member Emergency Response Team–Advance (ERT-A) arrived. For the next three days I worked and lived at the Superdome with the ERT-A team and with the FEMA medical team. Each day it was a battle to find enough food and water and get it to the Superdome. It was a struggle, meal-to-meal, because as one was served, it was clear to everyone that there was not enough food or water for the next meal. But because of some truly heroic efforts from FEMA staff, the coast guard, and the National Guard, enough food was always found and brought to the Superdome so that at least two meals were served each day.

While we battled food and water issues, rescue missions continued, more and more people arrived at the Superdome, and the medical conditions of many at the Superdome were in rapid decline. Many people were near death. Working in absolutely deplorable conditions, the FEMA New Mexico DMAT Team saved lives. They worked with helicopter Medivacs to evacuate the most critically ill.

I would like to say that what has been lost in all of the discussions and criticisms of what did or did not happen in New Orleans is that real heroes existed there, and the FEMA New Mexico medical team did truly amazing things to save lives and make a difference. They worked 24 hours a day to treat patients and it can be said that without their work, more people certainly would have died. I am honored that I can call them coworkers because they are the best of what FEMA has to offer.

It is well known what happened over the next several days—most of it real, some of it hyped and exaggerated by the media, but all of it tragic. I am most haunted by what the Superdome became. It was a shelter of last resort that cascaded into a cesspool of human waste and filth. Imagine no toilet facilities for 25,000 people for five days. People were forced to live outside in 95-degree heat because of the horrid smell and conditions inside. Hallways and corridors were used as toilets, trash was everywhere, and amongst it all, children, thousands of them. It was sad, it was inhumane, and it was so wrong.

By Thursday, plans to evacuate the Superdome were underway, but there were critical missions to still carry out at the Dome. But early Thursday, the National Guard approached the FEMA staff and told us that there was intelligence that a riot was being planned for noon and that they did not want to be responsible for our safety so they recommended that we leave. Phil Parr, who was the senior FEMA official on the ground, made the decision to evacuate all FEMA assets from the Dome including the medical team. I strongly voiced my concerns about abandoning the mission and the critical need to continue with medical care and the coordination of food and water into the Dome. I pointed out that overnight, approximately 150 heavily armed forces arrived at the Superdome by helicopter, raising the security level. I called Mike Brown to tell him that we were leaving. I contacted FEMA's front office to let them know that we were leaving. Within an hour, all FEMA personnel were ordered onto trucks and driven out of the Dome. Our leaving meant that FEMA lost visibility of the situation and operational control at the Superdome. I do not believe that it was the right decision for us to leave.

I have worked for FEMA for twelve years and have been a full-time employee since 2002. I have spent most of that time in the field, not behind a desk. I have responded to numerous hurricanes, earthquakes, floods, tornadoes, and fires. At the personal request of Undersecretary Brown, I deployed to Bam, Iran, in 2003 in support of the medical team that worked miracles in a city that was totally destroyed and resulted in more than 30,000 deaths. I have seen the worst mother nature can hand out, and I saw it in New Orleans and at the Superdome.

My purpose before you today is to help you understand what happened in New Orleans and when it happened, as I know it from my own perspective. I hope that what you learn from me and the many others that will come later is a better understanding of emergency management and response. From this I hope that we are able to effect change, so that no other child, no other senior citizen, no other special-needs patient, no other parent, and no other community in this country will have to experience the horrors and tragedy that happened in New Orleans and the entire Gulf Coast.

I will now answer any questions that you may have.

PRE-STORM CONFERENCE CALL

The following are excerpts from the transcript of a video conference between various state and federal officials on August 28, 2005. Portions of the call have been edited out for clarity.

Participants:

Mike Brown, Undersecretrary of FEMA
President George W. Bush
Michael Chertoff, Secretary of Homeland Security
Colonel Bill Doriant, Operations Officer, Louisiana Office of Homeland Security
Michael Jackson, Deputy Secretary of Homeland Security
Max Mayfield, Director of National Hurricane Center
Colonel Jeff Smith, Acting Director of Louisiana Office of Homeland Security

AUGUST 28, 2005

MIKE BROWN: Everyone, let's go ahead and get started. It's noon, and we have a lot of business to cover today.

Before we get started, I wanted to very briefly introduce Michael Jackson, deputy secretary of Homeland Security, and my good friend from the old days. So, Michael, welcome to our little operation here.

MR. JACKSON: Hi.

MIKE BROWN: Let's get started immediately. National Hurricane Center, do you want to give us an update?

NATIONAL HURRICANE CENTER: For those following along on the website, we have made some last minute adjustments, so please refresh the website at fema.gov/hlt. We have both the Mobile Bay and New Orleans official storm-surge slosh model best track runs posted on this website, and we will continue to post them as they are made available as the storm comes closer to the coast. With that, we'll turn it over to Max Mayfield.

MR. MAX MAYFIELD: Okay. Good afternoon. I don't have any good news here at all today. This is, as everybody knows by now, a very dangerous hurricane, and the center is about 225 miles south-southeast of the mouth of the Mississippi River.

Putting the visual loop up here, Slide 100 here, just so you can see the size. You know, if there was ever a time to remind people not to focus on that skinny black line, this is it. This is a very, very large hurricane, and you can even see some of these outer rain bands have already moved across the southeast Louisiana coast and are moving into the New Orleans area right now. That band will dissipate, and additional bands will start coming in later this afternoon.

Let's go to Slide 200, the infrared satellite loop. And I show this to really emphasize the eye. Right now, this is a Category 5 hurricane, very similar to Hurricane Andrew in the maximum intensity, but there is a big, big difference. This hurricane is much larger than Andrew ever was.

And for the folks in Louisiana, in Mississippi, and Alabama, and the Florida Panhandle, when we're talking about the intensity—in fact, especially the folks in Louisiana, if you remember Lili, Lili had been a Category 4 hurricane in the central Gulf of Mexico. It had a very, very small pinhole eye, and those small eyes usually don't maintain themselves very long.

Lily weakened down to a Category 1 hurricane by the time it made landfall. This one is not going to do that. When you have a large-diameter eye like this, and as strong as this one is, I really don't expect to see any significant weakening. So I think the wisest thing to do here is to plan on a Category 5 hurricane.

* * *

MR. MAX MAYFIELD: I want to say that—and I know I'm preaching to the choir here—that this hurricane in particular is not just a coast event. The strong winds, the heavy rains, and the tornadoes will spread well inland, along this path that you see here. Having said that, I also want to make absolutely clear to everyone that the greatest potential for large loss of life is still in the coastal areas from the storm surge.

So let's go to Slide 500, where it says the storm surge forecast. This is the actual forecast based on the last forecast that came out about an hour ago that has the center coming over here, passing just east of the city of New Orleans, and covering the eastern side of the lake.

On the west side of the track, this is very, very complicated. You know, there's a very complex system of levees there in the New Orleans area. Some of the valleys that we see—and I'm sure that all of these areas are already going underwater out near the mouth of the Mississippi River. The colors that you see here show inundation over the land areas.

One of the valleys here in Lake Pontchartrain, we've got on our forecast track, if it maintains its intensity, about twelve-and-a-half feet of storm surge in the lake. The big question is going to be: will that top some of the levees? And the current track and the forecast we have now suggests that there will be minimal flooding in the city of New Orleans itself, but we've always said that the storm surge model is only accurate within about 20 percent.

If that track were to deviate just a little bit to the west, it would—it makes all the difference the world. I do expect there will be some of the levees over-topped even out here in the western portions here where the airport is. We've got valleys of ten feet that can't overtop some of those levees.

The problem that we're going to have here—remember, the winds go counterclockwise around the center of the hurricane. So if the really strong winds clip Lake Pontchartrain, that's going to pile some of that water from Lake Pontchartrain over on the south side of the lake. I don't think any model can tell you with any confidence right now whether the levees will be topped or not, but that's obviously a very, very grave concern.

* * *

MIKE BROWN: Thank you very much. At this time, I'd like to go to Crawford, Texas. Ladies and gentlemen, I'd like to introduce the president of the United States.

PRESIDENT BUSH: Yes, Mike, thank you very much. I appreciate so very much the warnings that Max and his team have given to the good folks in Louisiana and Mississippi and Alabama. Appreciate your briefing that you gave me early this morning about what the federal government is prepared to do to help the state and local folks deal with this really serious storm. I do want to thank the good folks in the offices of Louisiana and Alabama and Mississippi for listening to these warnings and preparing your citizens for this, this huge storm. I want to assure the folks at the state level that we are fully prepared to not only help you during the storm, but we will move in whatever resources and assets we have at our disposal after the storm to help you deal with the loss of property. And we pray for no loss of life, of course.

Unfortunately, we've had experience at this in recent years, and the FEMA folks have done great work in the past, and I'm confident, Mike, that you and your team will do all you can to help the good folks in these affected states. Again, I want to thank Governor Blanco, and Governor Riley, and Governor Barber, Governor Bush of Florida, for heeding these warnings, and doing all you can possibly do with your state folks and local folks to prepare the citizenry for this storm. In the meantime, I know the nation will be praying for the good folks in the affected areas, and we just hope for the very best. Mike, thanks for letting me speak to the people, I know, who are working long hours. Again, I want to thank everybody involved in this effort. I appreciate the long hours you're keeping. I expect you to keep more long hours until we've done everything we can in our power to help the folks in the affected areas. Thank you, sir.

MIKE BROWN: Mr. President, thank you. We appreciate your support of FEMA and those kind words very much. Thank you, sir.

PRESIDENT BUSH: Okay.

MIKE BROWN: Okay. We'll move on now to the states. Louisiana?

COLONEL SMITH: Good morning, Mike. This is Colonel Jeff Smith here in Louisiana. We certainly appreciate those comments from the president, because I can tell you that our governor is very concerned about the potential loss of life here with our citizens, and she is very appreciative of the federal resources that have come into the state and the willingness to give us everything you've got, because, again, we're very concerned with this.

I'm going to turn the briefing over for a moment to our operations officer, just to kind of give you a quick laydown of things. This is Colonel Bill Doriant.

COLONEL DORIANT: The Emergency Operations Center is at a Level 1, which is the highest state of readiness. We've got currently eleven parishes with evacuations, and climbing. Eight are mandatory, including a first-ever mandatory for New Orleans. We've got thirty-eight parish declarations of emergency; also the state declaration and the presidential declaration of emergency.

Evacuations are underway currently. We're planning for a catastrophic event, which we have been planning for, thanks to the help of FEMA, when we did the Hurricane Pam exercises. So we're way ahead of the game there.

Our priorities right now are sheltering, and then planning for search and rescue and commodities distribution after recovery.

That's all I have at this time.

COLONEL SMITH: I'll just tell you that the evacuation process is going much better than it did during Hurricane Ivan. Nobody anticipated that it would be easy. Nobody anticipated that there wouldn't be traffic jams. But by and large, it has gone much better than it did with Ivan. And, of course, we still have a contraflow in effect at this particular point in time, and we do still have heavy traffic coming out of New Orleans, but by and large that process is going very well.

We have established a unified command here with our federal coordinating officer. Our ERT-A [Emergency Response Team-Advance] team, ERT-N [Emergency Response Team-National] team is on the ground here. And, again, as our operations officer pointed out, we're spending a lot of time right now with the search-and-rescue, making sure that we marry the appropriate state assets and the federal assets, so we can have an effective search-and-rescue effort just as quickly as possible.

We're also taking a look at our sheltering needs, long-term sheltering needs, looking at sites to start bringing in the temporary housing. So we're not only fighting the current battle, managing expectations here with our local parishes, but we are also working with FEMA and our other federal partners to have the most effective response and recovery that we possibly can during this time.

So, again, I want to say thank you very much for all that you're doing. I think that at this point in time our coordination is as good as it can be, and we just very much appreciate the president and your commitments to resourcing our needs down here. Any questions that you have, we'd be glad to take them now, unless you want to hold that until later. That's your call, Mike.

MIKE BROWN: Any questions? Colonel, do you have any unmet needs, anything that we're not getting to you that you need or—

COLONEL SMITH: Mike, no. [Inaudible] resources that are en route, and it looks like those resources that are en route are going to be a good first shot. Naturally, once we get into this thing, you know, neck deep here, unfortunately, or deeper, I'm sure that things are going to come up that maybe some of even our best planners hadn't even thought about. So I think flexibility is going to be the key.

And just as quickly as we can cut through any potential red tape when those things do arise, you know, we just need to look at it. We appreciate your comments. I think they were to lean as far, far as you possibly can, you know, without falling, and your people here are doing that. And that's the type of attitude that we need in an event like this.

So, again, thank you very much.

Mike Brown: All right. I'll be in Baton Rouge probably about four o'clock this afternoon, so I'll see you sometime this evening.

* * *

MIKE BROWN: In fact, let me just go ahead and [missing] and tell you what my priorities are and what my concerns are. Number one, you know that the mayor has ordered the Superdome to be used as a shelter [missing] first resort. I didn't hear about any other shelters for people to go to as they left New Orleans. As you may or may not know, the Superdome is about twelve feet below sea level, so I don't know what the heck [missing]. And I also am concerned about that roof. I don't know whether that roof is designed to withstand a Cat. 5 hurricane.

So not to be [missing] kind of gross here, but I'm concerned about NDMS [National Disaster Medical System], and medical, and DMORT [Disaster Mortuary Operational Response Team] assets and their ability to respond to a catastrophe within a catastrophe. So if I could get some sort of insight into what's going on in that Superdome, I think it would be very, very helpful. While we're on [missing], I want to make sure that NDMS and the DMORTs and DMATs [Disaster Medical Assistance Team] are ready to go, as soon as, because I do believe I also heard there is no [missing] mandatory evacuations. They're not taking patients out of hospitals, taking prisoners out of prisons, and they're leaving hotels open in downtown New Orleans. So I'm very concerned about that. So let's just keep that in mind.

My gut tells me—I told you guys—my gut was that this [missing] is a bad one and a big one. And you heard Max's comments. I still feel that way today.

Now, the good thing about this is we've got a great team around here that knows what they're doing, and they [missing] to do it. I want to emphasize what I said yesterday, get to the edge of that envelope. And, in fact, if you feel like you [missing], go ahead and do it. I'll figure out some way to justify it, some way [missing] tell Congress or whoever else it is that wants to yell at me, just let them yell at me, [missing] not to worry about—in fact, I don't want any of these processes in our way.

* * *

SECRETARY CHERTOFF: [inaudible] Yes. Hi, this is Secretary Chertoff. And, again, as it relates to the entire department, if there's anything that you need from coast guard or any other components that you're not getting, please let us know. We'll do that for you, okay.

MIKE BROWN: I appreciate it. [missing] Having been through many of these, the coast guard and ICE and all of the others have been incredibly good to us. And I hope we never have to call you and tell you that I can't get help from the coast guard or somebody. Thank you for those comments.

SECRETARY CHERTOFF: Secondly, are there any DOD [Department of Defense] assets that might be available? Have we reached out to them, and have we, I guess, made any kind of arrangement in case we need some additional help from them?

MIKE BROWN: We have DOD assets over here at the EOC [Emergency Operations Center]. They are fully engaged, and we are having those discussions with them now.

SECRETARY CHERTOFF: Good job.

REPORT TO THE WHITE HOUSE

At 10:30 p.m. on Monday, August 29, the Department of Homeland Security issued this report of Marty Bahamonde's observations in New Orleans. The White House would receive this report just after midnight.

HSOC SPOT REP

SPOT REP #: 013
Date/Time (EDT): 08/29/05 @ 2230
Reference: New Orleans Helicopter Overflight
Source of Information: FEMA Teleconference—observations from Marty Bahamonde, FEMA Public Affairs. Participants include Patrick Rhode, Mike Lowder, Bill Locke, Mike Pawlowski and Mary Anne Lyle
Type of Incident: Hurricane Katrina

Update

Summary: Marty Bahamonde of FEMA Public Affairs made two aerial over-flights of the New Orleans area the afternoon of Monday, August 29, 2005. As additional information becomes available it will be reported.

He concluded the two immediate major problems would be

1. Access to the city because roads are flooded to the north and east.
2. Housing

His observations include the following:

- The I-10 Twin Span bridges to the east of the city to Slidell are compromised in both directions for a stretch of five to seven miles. On the east side, bridge sections are gone. On the west side, bridge sections are buckled and askew.
- There is no way to enter New Orleans from the east. Highway 11 appears generally intact but is underwater where it enters the city and will require some repair, but appears to be a quick fix.
- The western I-10/I-610 junction connecting Jefferson and Orleans Parish is underwater.
- Entrance from the north is not possible because as roads get into the city, they are underwater.

- I-10 to the west appears to have several underwater sections.
- The Airline Highway by the airport is above water.
- There is a quarter-mile breach in the levee near the 17th Street Canal about 200 yards from Lake Pontchartrain, allowing water to flow into the city.
- The levee in Metairie is intact.
- Only one of the main pumps is reported to still be working but cannot keep up with the demand and its longevity is doubtful.
- In the neighborhoods there are many small fires where natural-gas lines have broken.
- Flooding is greatest in the north and east in New Orleans, Metairie, and north towards Slidell—an estimated two-thirds to 75 percent of the city is under water.
- The flights did not go all the way north to Slidell so conditions there are not reported.
- Some homes were seen with water to the first floor and others completely under water.
- Hundreds of people were observed on the balconies and roofs of a major apartment complex in the city. The location has been provided to city officials.
- Downtown there is less flooding. Most buildings have windows blown out but otherwise appear structurally sound.
- West and south of the city appear dry.
- Lake Front Airport by Lake Pontchartrain is under water.
- There is an oil tanker grounded in the Industrial Canal—two tugs were observed working with the ship.
- The coast guard reported two other tankers aground but they were not observed.
- The coast guard is flying rescue missions for people stuck on roofs. They reported seeing about 150 people but also said that as they lifted people out, they saw others breaking through the roofs of adjacent homes.
- The coast guard will use night vision devices and continue rescue missions into the night.
- Search and rescue will need boats; in some locations, high-wheeled trucks may be usable. FEMA USR [Urban Search and Rescue] Teams are coordinating boat use with Louisiana Fish and Game officials.
- The city reports about 300 people have been rescued by boat so far. These rescue operations will continue through the night.
- Boat traffic is not restricted and movement of supplies by boat and barge is feasible.
- The Inter Harbor Canal is not visible.

- A few bodies were floating in the water and coast guard pilots also reported seeing bodies, but there are no details on locations or numbers.

Significance:
Action/Follow-Up: N/A
Miscellaneous:
Prepared By: Matthew Thompson NRCC Planning Section Analyst

MAYOR NAGIN'S LIST OF NEEDS

The following are excerpts from a list of concerns and aid requests submitted to FEMA by Mayor Ray Nagin on Monday, August 29, 2005.

Post-Hurricane Katrina Critical Needs Assessment
Refuge of Last Resort—Superdome:

Concerns:

- Poor physical conditions (lack of a/c, leaking roof, lack of power, lack of access to media reports, lack of information, lack of entertainment) are causing frustration and panic among evacuees.
- Poor physical conditions are creating a medical crisis in terms of caring for the special needs evacuees.
- Lack of access to information about the damage caused to the City by Hurricane Katrina and lack of any entertainment are causing increased frustration among evacuees and are prompting many to demand opportunity to leave the Superdome.
- Mandatory evacuation and curfew order are still in effect due to dangerous conditions in the City, thereby eliminating the option of allowing evacuees to leave the Superdome.

Needs:

- Request from FEMA, sufficient generators (in terms of size and quantity) and fuel to light the dome, provide a/c, enable big screen video feeds, and generally to improve the overall physical conditions of the facility for the 20,000 evacuees.
- Request from FEMA, sufficient portable lighting, generators, and fuel to accommodate the 20,000 evacuees.
- Request from FEMA, a temporary video- and audio-feed capacity (including, screens, speakers, projectors, etc.) to enable mass-broadcasting capability of news and entertainment for the 20,000 evacuees.
- Additional security personnel may be required as evacuees become more frustrated with the passage of time.
- Request from FEMA, assistance in providing food, water, and toiletries for evacuees, employees and volunteers.
- (Alternative Need) Access to the convention Center to use it as the refuge of last resort in lieu of the Superdome; if this option is exercised, each of the above-listed needs would also be required for the Convention Center

and, additionally, vehicles and drivers to coordinate the transport from the Superdome to the Convention Center would also be required. Advantages of using the Convention Center include no leaking roof and large open space that may help with claustrophobia of some evacuees. Doctors Stephen and Lupin are exploring feasibility of this option.

Search and Rescue—Boat Operation

Needs:
- Request FEMA search-and-rescue team;
- Request FEMA mortuary team and assistance with identifying and/or establishing a temporary morgue;
- Request information on length of time before floating bodies become serious health issue;
- Request FEMA vet-assistance team;
- Request media assistance in publicizing rescue hotline number of 504. 658.8700.

Charity Hospital

Concerns:
- Charity is overwhelmed by failing generator, flooding, and other issues and is considering shutting down;
- Must stabilize critical medical situation.
- Fatigued medical personnel (Additional medical personnel teams are expected to provide relief soon).

Needs:
- Request FEMA assistance with necessary equipment and personnel with requisite technical expertise for repair and/or replacement of pumping system and repair or replacement of generators;
- Request FEMA clean-up/sanitization team;
- Need FEMA to set up separate triage facility for special-needs evacuees.

DEFENSE DEPARTMENT BRIEFING

On September 3, 2005, Lt. General Steven Blum—chief of the National Guard Bureau—gave a briefing on the ongoing National Guard response to Katrina.

GEN. BLUM: Good morning gentlemen. I just got back late last evening from New Orleans and the stricken areas in Mississippi along the Gulf Coast, and if you want I'll give you a quick assessment of what we've seen. Dramatic changes in the last thirty-six hours. The security situation in New Orleans continues to improve. The most contentious issues were lawlessness in the streets, and particularly, a potentially very dangerous volatile situation in the Convention Center where tens of thousands of people literally occupied that on their own. We had people that were evacuated from hotels, and tourists that were lumped together with some street thugs and some gang members. It was a potentially very dangerous situation.

We waited until we had enough force in place to do an overwhelming force. Went in with police powers—1,000 National Guard military policemen under the command and control of the adjutant general of the State of Louisiana, Major General Landreneau—yesterday shortly after noon, stormed the Convention Center, for lack of a better term, and there was absolutely no opposition. Complete cooperation, and we attribute that to an excellent plan, superbly executed with great military precision. It was rather complex. It was executed absolutely flawlessly in that there was no violent resistance, no one injured, no one shot, even though there were stabbed, even though there were weapons in the area. There were no soldiers injured and we did not have to fire a shot.

Some people asked why didn't we go in sooner. Had we gone in with less force it may have been challenged, innocents may have been caught in a fight between the Guard military police and those who did not want to be processed or apprehended, and we would put innocents' lives at risk. As soon as we could mass the appropriate force, which we flew in from all over the states at the rate of 1,400 a day, they were immediately moved off the tail gates of C-130 aircraft flown by the Air National Guard, moved right to the scene, briefed, rehearsed, and then they went in and took this convention center down.

Those that were undesirable to re-enter the convention center were segregated from the people that we wanted to provide water, shelter, and food. Those people were processed to make sure they had no weapons, no illicit dugs, no alcohol, no contraband, and then they were escorted back into the building. Now there's a controlled safe and secure environment and a shelter and a haven as they await movement out of that center for onward integration to their normal lives.

It's a great success story, a terrific success story.

Q: Yesterday afternoon?

GEN. BLUM: This was yesterday afternoon, actually during the president's visit, while the president was watching the reconstruction of the levees. The sling-load bags of gravel and sand that were being flown by the Texas National Guard. UH-60 helicopters were ferrying in bags of sand, about 8,000 pounds each, 7,500 pounds each, slung load under a UH-60 Black Hawk, plugging that football-field-sized gap in the flood wall that has to be repaired before we can begin the job of draining the city.

It's amazing to watch all of this going on simultaneously, At the same time during the same period, several hundred rescues continued to occur, finding people and bringing them out of their attics or bringing them out of the second story or off the roof tops, saving lives. Some people have said the golden window is closed, we've missed our opportunity. As long as there are people that are still stranded and in want of evacuation, we will continue the evacuation process.

We claim 2,000 evacuations by Army Guard helicopters this week, which is significant. Each one of those represents lives saved. That is enormous.

So there are lots of good things going on. There is plenty of work to be done. I've only just talked about New Orleans. The same could be said all across the region. Each hour the situation improves for those we know about. There are others, I'm sure, that think that each hour their situation gets more grave because we haven't found them yet, and we haven't begun to provide any lifesaving support or subsistence to them. But I am convinced that we will continue to do this and save lives.

A great task lies ahead of us, so at the request of the governors of Mississippi and Louisiana, forty other governors have sent their National Guard soldiers and airmen to the aid through emergency mutual-assistance compacts that each governor has with every other governor in the country. They're flowing their National Guard forces in to do security work, support to civilian law enforcement, providing food, water, medicine, shelter, transportation, vital communications, and all of the other emergency support functions, not as the lead agency but in support of the lead agency, which happens to be FEMA, the lead federal agency.

Martial law has not been declared anywhere in the United States of America. That keeps continually being erroneously reported. An emergency condition exists in parts of the states and there are curfews that are being enforced by the existing civilian law enforcement agencies. The Army National Guard, having police powers given to them or provided to them by the governors of Louisiana and Mississippi, are augmenting, expanding, giving manpower and extra capabilities to these existing police forces. They're actually acting almost as a deputy would. They're deputized, essentially, by the governors of the states to use their state militias for this purpose.

There are separate agreements, because the EMAC [Emergency Management Assistance Compact] compact does not allow law enforcement support within the states. So there is a separate agreement between the governor of Mississippi and the states that sent their military policemen down there or their National Guard down there to do, for the purpose of military police work or law enforcement. These are legally binding, legally sufficient agreements that must be in place before we put National Guard military police law enforcement officers in that role out of their home state.

Q: Is that why it wasn't done earlier? They didn't have those agreements in place?

GEN. BLUM: It was not foreseen. When they put the original EMAC together it was really for disaster response. Law enforcement was not envisioned. So it has to be handled as a separate process. The governors may get together and modify their EMAC in the future so that it is all-inclusive, but this fills that gap and it makes the activity of the National Guard in this regard totally legally sufficient and supportable.

Q: Does that explain why it took several days to get to this point?

GEN. BLUM: No, there was no delay. The fortunate thing is with modern technology they faxed the agreement back and forth, the two governors signed it. It was a matter of moments. That was not the delay.

The delay was in—if you want to call it a delay. I really don't call it a delay, I'll be honest about that. When we first went in there law enforcement was not the highest priority, saving lives was. You have to remember how this thing started. Before the hurricane hit there were 5,000 National Guardsmen in Mississippi and 5,000 National Guardsmen—excuse me, let me correct the record. There were 2,500 National Guardsmen in Mississippi, and almost 4,000 National Guardsmen in Louisiana that were sheltered and taken out of the affected area so as soon as the storm passed they could immediately go into the area and start their search and lifesaving work, and stand up their command and control apparatus, and start standing up the vital functions that would be required, such as providing food, water, shelter and security for the people of the town. So, it was phased in. There was no delay.

The real issue, particularly in New Orleans, is that no one anticipated the disintegration or the erosion of the civilian police force in New Orleans. Once that assessment was made, that the normal 1,500-man police force in New Orleans was substantially degraded, which contributed obviously to less police presence and less police capability, then the requirement became obvious and that's when we started flowing military police into the theater.

Two days ago we flowed 1,400 military policemen in. Yesterday, 1,400 more. Today 1,400 more. Today there are 7,000 citizen soldiers—Army National Guard, badge-carrying military policemen and other soldiers trained in support to civil law enforcement—that are on the streets, available to the mayor, provided by the governor to the mayor to assist the New Orleans police department.

I am absolutely confident that the security situation as it has improved in the last 24 hours will improve two-fold in the next 24 hours, and soon it won't be an issue at all.

Will something ever go wrong in New Orleans? Sure. Things went wrong in New Orleans and every other populated area around in our country and around the world every day. But I think you'll see a return to normal levels very soon, perhaps in the next 24 hours.

Q: Across the disaster zone our reporters have consistently run into people over the past week, victims who have asked where's the National Guard, why aren't they here, why aren't they helping us? I know it's not your job to decide where and when aid is delivered. You have to provide these forces. But as a general who's been there and a commander with a can-do reputation, I just wanted to ask your opinion. Do you think in retrospect that more creativity, more ingenuity could have been employed early on to use the military to deliver more aid to people sooner?

GEN. BLUM: It would be easy to draw that conclusion, Jamie, but if you've ever been to Gulfport, remember the highway that runs along the coast was a four-lane superhighway. It was impassable. So where you could— If a normal infrastructure existed, no question, you could have saturated the area with more, faster. But we were putting forces in in very degraded infrastructure. Airports had reduced capability. Roads, in some cases we had only one road in because of lack of bridges, flooding, loss of infrastructure, or the structures were too unsafe to cross or we would become casualties ourselves.

So we couldn't rush to failure on this thing and we had to take a more measured approach than any of us wanted. But to call this response late to need, if you're talking about the National Guard response, that would be a low blow to some incredible individuals who were on watch before the storm, harbored during the storm, on the scene immediately after the storm cleared. Just think about, when was the storm? When did it hit? How many days ago?

Q: Early Monday.

GEN. BLUM: And today is what?

Q: Saturday.

GEN. BLUM: In that short time we're talking numbers of 40,000. This is just military. You're talking about being able to provide food, fuel, water for an unknown number of people that we have to first find and discover in lots of cases, and then immediately care for with extremely high expectations.

I think the response of the National Guard is nothing less than unbelievably sensational. It's actually better than any planner could ever expect.

When I first laid out the numbers of reinforcements that would be coming into theater and then I went down there to ensure that they arrived so that the plan was in fact being executed, I was very surprised to find that every single projection that we had made had been exceeded because of the magnificent response that we're getting from all over this nation. Puerto Rico, in the height of hurricane season, is sending 1,000 soldiers to the relief effort. Think about what that means. One of the first forces in there were coming in from Oregon, Washington, Alaska. Forty states have soldiers there. Others are lined up to come in later because they have different skill sets that we think we'll need down the road, particularly as we get some of these roads uncovered and we have to start with reconstruction and rehabilitation of the area, rather than just getting in and getting the necessities in, the essentials.

Q: I'd like to get your thoughts on two things. One, what do you see as the role of the active-duty troops that are going to be coming in? The second thing is you talked about how no one foresaw that it would become a big law-enforcement problem rather than just a typical search and rescue. Is that still the case? Are there still other points like the Convention Center that will require the military-type operations to get in there and restore order and—

GEN. BLUM: Yes, and they're not all in New Orleans. Any place where you harbor a group of people that have been damaged by the storm and dislocated from their houses, their lives have been interrupted, and they've lost in many cases everything, or have nothing on them—these kind of events bring out the best in people, and in some very limited number of folks brings out the worst in people. The governors have sent a clear message that citizens that have already suffered enough from the ravages of the storm, they will not tolerate lawlessness to make them a victim again. So there's very firm and forceful law enforcement. We have not suspended any laws. In fact they have invoked some emergency powers with curfews and all those type of measures. In some states the order has been given to shoot to kill.

The governor of Louisiana has given that order. I think the governor of Mississippi did it earlier.

So this is serious business, and that is done to ensure that the lives of innocent people that have suffered this loss are not further traumatized by lawless citizens.

We will put the force in place that is required, as much as necessary for as long as it's needed. That's the easiest way I can put it to you. Now who decides what is necessary? That has to be the legally constituted government and in this case it's the governors of the states and the president of the United States flew down there to show his commitment to each and every one of the Gulf state governors yesterday, and reinforced that he will send them anything and everything within his legal powers to ensure that they are successful in restoring order and restoring normal life and regenerating the future of these great states down in the Gulf Coast.

GOOD MORNING AMERICA INTERVIEW

Four days after being briefed by National Hurricane Center director Max Mayfield on the potential danger of levee breaches, President Bush gave this interview to Diane Sawyer on Good Morning America.

DIANE SAWYER: Mr. President, as we speak, as you say, there are people with signs saying, "Help, come get me," people still in the attic waving. Nurses are phoning in saying the situation in hospitals is getting ever more dire, that the nurses are getting sick now because of no clean water. Some of the things they have asked our correspondents to ask you is— They expected, they say to us, that the day after this hurricane that there would be a massive and visible armada of federal support. There would be boats coming in, there would be food, there would be water, and it would be there within hours. They wondered, "What's taking so long?"

PRESIDENT BUSH: Well there's a lot of food on its way, a lot of water on the way, and there's a lot of boats and choppers headed that way. It just takes a while to float 'em. For example, the Iwo Jima's coming from the east coast of the United States towards New Orleans. People've gotta know that there's a massive relief—one of the most massive federal relief efforts ever—in combination with state and local authorities. There is a lot of help coming.

DIANE SAWYER: But given the fact that everyone anticipated a hurricane five, a possible hurricane five hitting shore, are you satisfied with the pace at which this is arriving, and which it was planned to arrive?

PRESIDENT BUSH: Well I fully understand people wanting things to have happened yesterday. I understand the anxiety of people on the ground. I just can't imagine what it's like to be waving the sign that says, "Come and get me now." So there is frustration, but I want people to know that there's a lot of help coming.

I don't think anybody anticipated the breach of the levees. They did anticipate a serious storm, but these levees got breached and as a result, much of New Orleans is flooded and now we're having to deal with it, and will.

DIANE SAWYER: Couple of quick questions about the concerns. Any signs of disease outbreaks reported yet?

PRESIDENT BUSH: Not yet. But I talked to Secretary [of Health and Human Services] Leavitt who's been working with the CDC [Centers for Disease Control] to rally doctors and nurses to go down there to help, just to make sure that disease doesn't outbreak. But I think people— That's gonna be one of the real problems we're gonna have to deal with is disease.

DIANE SAWYER: What about the other nations of the world? Are they offering the kind of help you expected them to, that you want them to help? And there is a report that you're going to deploy your father again, and President Clinton again, to go out there and seek it. What is it you are expecting from them, and will you get it?

PRESIDENT BUSH: I'm not expecting much from foreign nations 'cause we haven't asked for it. I do expect a lot of sympathy, and perhaps some will send cash dollars. But this country's gonna rise up and take care of it. You know, we'd love help. But we're gonna take care of our own business as well, and there's no doubt in my mind that we'll succeed. And there's no doubt in my mind, as I sit here talking to you, that New Orleans is gonna rise up again as a great city. It's gonna take a lot of work and a lot of effort. But this is a compassionate nation. It's got a lot of resources at its disposal, and we're gonna help those people.

DIANE SAWYER: There was worry about the levees breaking, as we know, years before, and re-placing New Orleans in a situation where you have to have massive expenditures in order to protect it, do you want to see it in the same place?

PRESIDENT BUSH: I think we'll let the experts determine how New Orleans is rebuilt. I just want the people of New Orleans to know that after we've rescued 'em and stabilized the situation, there will be plans to help this great city get back on its feet.

NEW ORLEANS POLICE AFTER-ACTION SUMMARY

On October 16, 2005, at the request of Deputy Chief Steven Nicholas, Captain Timothy Bayard of the New Orleans Police Department authored this interoffice review of the department's performance in handling Hurricane Katrina. Portions have been edited out for clarity.

Department of Police
Interoffice Correspondence

To: Deputy Chief Steven Nicholas, Chief of Operations
From: Captain Timothy P. Bayard, Vice Crimes-Narcotics Section
Subject: Hurricane Katrina—2005 After Action Summary

Sir,

As per your request, I respectfully submit the following summary for your review. This document was prepared with input from the personnel assigned to the Vice Crimes-Narcotics Section.

Summary/Recommendations:

1) The Office of Emergency Preparedness needs to be revamped. If their role is to have us prepared to handle a disaster such as this they FAILED. They lacked a plan, did not provide the necessary equipment, provided no direction or leadership, did not coordinate or attempt to have commanders of filed operations coordinate with any state, or federal agency etc. We really need to take a long hard look at this section.

2) Connect with FEMA as soon as possible. They have an unlimited amount of assets, personnel, and equipment available. We must assign a Captain to FEMA as soon as they arrive. This Captain must coordinate all search, rescue, and transportation operations with the FEMA commanders.

3) Purchase flat and airboats, trailers and outboard motors. Purchase the oil and other equipment needed to make these boats fully operational for an extended period of time. Provide training on how to operate both types of boats.

4) Position modes of transportation (school and RTA buses) on high ground, with full access to, in the event that emergency personnel have to

utilize this equipment to evacuate refugees. Spare keys should be secured in the OEP. Secondly, the city should have a signed contract with bus companies throughout the metro area, in the event of an emergency such as this, to ensure that there are more than enough buses available to evacuate our citizens. Rescue and the transportation of evacuees must work as one entity. Train and issue CDL licenses to officers certifying that they can drive commercial vehicles.

5) Have MREs and water stored in a building located on high ground. If it floods around the location we can still access the food and water by boat and truck it to the evacuation centers. Store enough for 50,000 people, not including emergency personnel, for a ten-day period.

6) Fuel reserves—Unleaded and Diesel—Trucks need to be in our city, on high ground two days prior to the storm's arrival. Several hours prior to the arrival of the storm, all emergency personnel SHALL top off the fuel tanks in each and every vehicle (including spare vehicles) at the gas pumps. The trucks are reserves only to be used if our pumps are inaccessible. We cannot be without fuel.

7) Mandate that each hospital and nursing home is equipped with an emergency generator large enough to provide electricity to ensure the housing of critical care patients. Secondly ensure that each hospital and nursing home has a yet to be determined amount of fuel to ensure that the generators can operate independently for at least a ten day period. Store MREs and water in a secured area inside the hospital/home to ensure that the medical staff and patients can sustain themselves for a ten day period.

* * *

16) Based on this experience all departmental vehicles should be secured at the Convention Center or any elevated parking facility located within the warehouse district. We lost hundreds of vehicles to wind-related and water damage.

17) Emergency personnel shall report to work one day prior to the storm's arrival. Each district and unit commander shall forward to the Chief of Operations the total number of officers sick, furlough, IOD etc. as well as the number of officers that reported as instructed. This gives our Command staff an accurate depiction of our workforce. Reporting personnel shall have enough clothing, food, water, and bedding for six days. On the day prior to the storm, personnel shall move all vital equipment into

areas for immediate deployment and to locations designated as safe havens.

18) Designate a rally point for all outside law enforcement agencies to report to. A NOPD Captain shall coordinate with the lead supervisor from each and every agency represented. The personnel and assets from each agency will report to the District Commander of the area they are assigned for specific instructions.

19) Purchase a completely equipped Urban Search and Rescue Unit for our Department. With the on-the-job training and experience gained by many members of our department (Vice-Narcotics/Tactical) along with proper training we will have a fully trained and equipped unit that can deploy immediately.

20) Coordination of water rescues or any type of rescue is a must. Hasty, primary, and secondary rescues must be coordinated. Thirteen days into the storm, we knew that the entire city had been offered hasty and primary rescue opportunities. When in reality, the entire city was covered twice if not three times. This was because FEMA was launching boats, the Louisiana Wild Life and Fisheries was launching boats and the NOPD & NOFD were launching boats. This entire operation was NOT coordinated and had no centralized command center. This was a major flaw that must be corrected.

* * *

23) Recovery of Human Remains: We drove trucks, piloted boats and walked past bodies in the first fourteen days of the storm. We did not have the proper clothing, equipment, or training to attempt body recovery. We notified the communications section where human remains were and secured the bodies to unmovable objects. No one knows when these bodies were recovered or if they were even in the location initially reported. Kenyon was the contractor for the recovery phase. When they commenced operations they did an outstanding job. My concern is when did their operations commence. This needs to be part of the COORDINATED search-and-rescue operations. That means they need to engage within the first few days. Many remains floated away with the water's currents and will never be recovered. I know it would have been impossible to recover all of the remains. I feel we could have recovered more.

24) New Media: I do not know if we could have slowed them down. I granted their every request. Therefore I created the monster. Their presence in and around our Harrah's command post, at times hindered our operations.

They blocked the driveway and street, interrupted meetings and were a distraction, especially in the first two weeks when our operations were at its peak. In the first couple of hours, we need to designate and cordon off an area for media interviews and keep them in this secured area for the entire event. When available, the Superintendent, Deputy Chiefs, and personnel assigned to the department's Public Information Office can meet the media in this area.

25) We need to move our food and water supplies to an area away from our Command Post. Our officers choked the access points just as the media did. Our supplies (MRE & Water) and chow line should have been set up on the river front (Spanish Plaza) with parking in the Hilton Circle and on Poydras St.

26) Each district commander will establish relationships with the owners/managers of businesses such as Wal-Mart and Walgreens and secure these locations prior to the storm's arrival. This will curtail looting and can provide resources for emergency workers.

27) Distribute fliers notifying officers where Red Cross, Insurance Companies, FEMA, and other benefit resources are located. Many officers worked into the night and feel that they missed out on some other opportunities.

In closing, our biggest flaw is the fact that we failed to communicate. This has been our problem for the thirty plus years that I have been associated with the department. The instructions and plans that are formed at the top are not clearly communicated to the rank and file. This leads to individual commanders implementing the operation as they understand it. This causes confusion and misdirection. In the time of crisis, our leaders need to be SEEN and HEARD.

Yours in Quality Law Enforcement,

Timothy P. Bayard—Captain
Vice Crimes-Narcotics Section

ST. AUGUSTINE PARISH

Located in Tremé, St. Augustine is the oldest African-American church in New Orleans. Less than six months after Hurricane Katrina, Father Jerome LeDoux received word from the Archdiocese that St. Augustine Parish would be closed. Below is a brief timeline of the events that followed.

February 8, 2006: Archbishop Alfred Hughes informs St. Augustine's pastor, Father Jerome LeDoux, that he will close St. Augustine Parish on March 15, 2006, making its parishioners part of St. Peter Claver Parish.

February 17: St. Augustine's pastoral council requests a meeting to discuss the closing, but the Archbishop does not respond.

March 3: Sandra Gordon, president of the St. Augustine pastoral council, and Father LeDoux formally submit an appeal to the Archdiocese.

March 13: Father LeDoux receives a call from the Archbishop informing him that the appeal has been denied.

March 20: Hurricane relief workers, unaffiliated with St. Augustine, occupy the church in protest of the Archdiocese's decision. They refuse to leave until the Archbishop restores the parish.

March 21: The New Orleans City Council sends a letter to the Archbishop requesting that St. Augustine remain open as a parish.

March 31: The Reverends Jesse Jackson and Al Sharpton attend a vigil for St. Augustine, and implore the Archbishop to reconsider his decision.

April 5-6: Representatives from St. Augustine Parish and the Archdiocese meet with a mediator.

April 8: Archbishop Hughes announces that St. Augustine Parish will be given an eighteen-month reprieve to meet twelve challenges related to the church's attendance, finances, ministries, and administration. Sandra Gordon expresses her confidence that these goals will be met.

NARRATORS' LOCATIONS DURING THE STORM

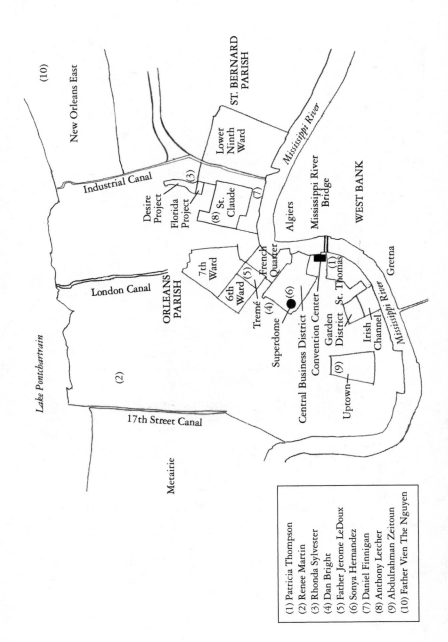

(1) Patricia Thompson
(2) Renee Martin
(3) Rhonda Sylvester
(4) Dan Bright
(5) Father Jerome LeDoux
(6) Sonya Hernandez
(7) Daniel Finnigan
(8) Anthony Letcher
(9) Abdulrahman Zeitoun
(10) Father Vien The Nguyen

NARRATORS' LOCATIONS AFTER THE STORM

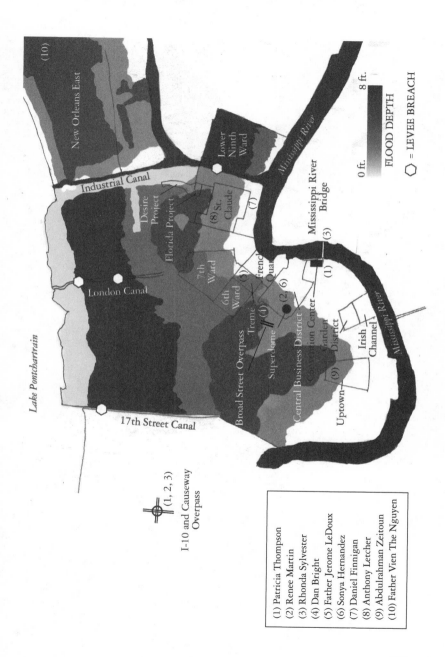

FLOOD DEPTH

8 ft.

0 ft.

⬡ = LEVEE BREACH

(1) Patricia Thompson
(2) Renee Martin
(3) Rhonda Sylvester
(4) Dan Bright
(5) Father Jerome LeDoux
(6) Sonya Hernandez
(7) Daniel Finnigan
(8) Anthony Letcher
(9) Abdulrahman Zeitoun
(10) Father Vien The Nguyen

ABOUT THE EDITORS

Lola Vollen is a physician specializing in the aftermath of large-scale human rights abuses. She has worked with survivors of systemic injustices in Somalia, South Africa, Israel, Croatia, and Kosovo. Working with Physicians for Human Rights, she developed Bosnia's mass-grave exhumation and identification program. She is the founder of the Life After Exoneration Program, which helps exonerated prisoners in the United States with their transitions after release. She is a visiting scholar at the University of California, Berkeley's Institute of International Studies, co-editor of the Voice of Witness series, and a practicing clinician.

Chris Ying is an editor and writer living in San Francisco. He is the managing editor of the Voice of Witness series.

INTERVIEW CREDITS

DAN BRIGHT
Interviews by Lola Vollen, Billy Sothern, and Colin Dabkowski

DANIEL FINNIGAN
Interviews by Andy Young and Chris Ying

PATRICIA THOMPSON
Interviews by Colin Dabkowski, Stacy Parker Aab, and Chris Ying

JACKIE HARRIS
Interviews by Colin Dabkowski

SONYA HERNANDEZ
Interviews by Lola Vollen and Chris Ying

FATHER JEROME LEDOUX
Interviews by Lola Vollen and Chris Ying

ANTHONY LETCHER
Interviews by Mary Beth Black

RENEE MARTIN
Interviews by Lola Vollen, Colin Dabkowski, and Chris Ying

KERMIT RUFFINS
Interviews by Colin Dabkowski

KALAMU YA SALAAM
Interviews by Lola Vollen

RHONDA SYVLESTER
Interviews by Lola Vollen and Stacy Parker Aab

ABDULRAHMAN ZEITOUN
Interviews by Lola Vollen and Billy Sothern

The VOICE OF WITNESS SERIES

The Voice of Witness series allows those most affected by contemporary social injustice to speak for themselves. Using oral history as a foundation, the series illustrates human rights crises through the stories of the men and women who experience them. Visit voiceofwitness.org for more information.

Now Available:

SURVIVING JUSTICE
America's Wrongfully Convicted and Exonerated
Edited by Lola Vollen and Dave Eggers   Foreword by Scott Turow

How does it happen? Could it happen to you? After reading these oral histories, told by people from all walks of life, you will believe that through a combination of all-too-common factors—overzealous prosecutors, inept defense lawyers, coercive interrogation tactics—anyone can be a victim of wrongful conviction.

ISBN: 978-1-934781-25-8   469 pages   Paperback

UNDERGROUND AMERICA
Narratives of Undocumented Lives
Edited by Peter Orner   Foreword by Luis Alberto Urrea

By living and working in the U.S. without legal status, millions of immigrants risk deportation and imprisonment. They are living underground, with little protection from exploitation at the hands of human smugglers, employers, or law enforcement. *Underground America* presents the remarkable oral histories of men and women struggling to carve a life for themselves in the U.S.

ISBN: 978-1-934781-15-9   379 pages   Hardback

Coming in 2008:

OUT OF EXILE
The Abducted and Displaced People of Sudan
Edited by Craig Walzer
Additional interviews and an introduction by Dave Eggers and Valentino Achak Deng

Millions of people have fled from conflicts and persecution in all parts of this Northeast African country, and many thousands more have been enslaved as human spoils of war. In this book, refugees and abductees recount their escapes from the wars in Darfur and South Sudan, from political and religious persecution, and from abduction by militias. In their own words, they recount life before their displacement and the reasons for their flight. They describe life in the major stations on the "refugee railroads": in the desert camps of Khartoum, the underground communities of Cairo, the humanitarian metropolis of Kakuma refugee camp, and the internally displaced persons camps in Darfur.